Social Work with Lawbreakers of Society

Social Work with Lawbreakers of Society

Volume 1

S. K. Bhalla

MD Publications Pvt Ltd
New Delhi

For information:

MD Publications Pvt Ltd
'MD House', 11, Darya Ganj
New Delhi - 110 002
Phone : +91-11-41563325 (Customer Service)
+91-11-41562846 (Editorial)
E-mail (orders): contact@mdppl.com
Website: www.mdppl.com

ISBN: 978-81-7533-157-0 (Set of 2 Vols.)
978-81-7533-158-7 (Vol. 1)

Published and Printed by Mrs. Rajni Gupta on behalf of **MD Publications Pvt Ltd** at Times Press, New Delhi.

CONTENTS

PREFACE

The criminal justice system has three major components: law enforcement, the courts and corrections. If these components are seen on a continuum, corrections encompasses the latter end of the continuum and deals with individuals who have been convicted of a criminal offense. Prisons and jails are the most visible correctional facilities for adults. However, probation, parole, and other alternatives to incarceration also fall under the aegis of corrections and account for more than two-third of the adult correctional population.

The social work profession's involvement in the justice system began in the area of corrections. In the late 19th and early 20th centuries, much social work activity was directed toward institutionalized adults and juveniles, as well as to individuals on probation. Prior to the 1970s, during the years when rehabilitation was a more accepted correctional philosophy than it is now, social workers were visibly employed in probation, parole and correctional facilities.

As social work has continued to evolve, however, it has largely abandoned the field of corrections. Several reasons have been offered for the profession's move away from this field. Predominant among these is the coercive nature of corrections, which is contrary to the social work profession's emphasis on client self-determination. Similarly, within direct social work practice the emphasis is on providing care and treatment to clients from a nonjudgmental stance. Within the field of adult corrections, the emphasis in one's approach to offenders is primarily on control and punishment from an authoritarian stance. These basic philosophical differences between social work and corrections have discouraged social workers from active involvement in correctional settings. Even though social work as a profession is not as active within the field of corrections as it once was, there is substantial evidence that the need for the profession's involvement is greater than ever.

The need for social work involvement is apparent in both the fields of juvenile justice and adult corrections. To this end, social work education should include content in both areas of practice, training students in multiple methods for work with juveniles or adult offenders. However, the correctional philosophies, needs, and intervention strategies within each field differ significantly.

The number of individuals under some form of correctional control continues to increase. At year end 1998, just under 3% of the U. S. adult population, or about 1 in every 34 adults, was either incarcerated, on probation or on parole. Over two-third of the individuals under correctional control, well over 4 million adults, are supervised in the community. These individuals and their family members often need the services provided by social workers in a wide variety of agency settings, as do the large number of individuals who cycle in and out of jails and prisons.

There is a great deal of overlap between offender populations and the individuals and families with whom social workers come into contact in other settings. For example, about 16% of male and 23% of female jail inmates have been identified as mentally ill. The rate of confirmed AIDS in the prison population is more than five times the rate in the general population. Almost 60% of female state prisoners report experiencing prior physical or sexual abuse. In addition, over 75% of prisoners are alcohol- or drug-involved offenders.

Racial and ethnic minorities are disproportionately represented behind bars and comprise over 65% of the prison population. The lifetime likelihood of going to prison is 29% for black men, 16% for Hispanic men, and 4% for white men. As social workers strive to address societal practices and policies that adversely impact certain groups, the disproportionately high number of nonwhite inmates in correctional populations deserves attention.

The incorporation of content on offenders and corrections into existing curricula will not, of course, provide students with the depth and breadth of information that an entire course or specialization in the topic would. Concern has been expressed that areas of specialization that require work with involuntary clients, including corrections, decreased within schools of social work from 1979 to 1989. As more students pursue career opportunities that offer the possibility of private practice and third party payments, the primary focus of social work has been moving away from working with at-risk and disenfranchised groups. This should concern the profession. Indeed, if social work hopes to make a significant impact on the field of corrections, there must be a much greater presence of relevant content in the profession's accredited academic programs. The vast majority of offenders belong to at-risk and disenfranchised groups. A beginning step to strengthen students' interest in fulfilling their professional responsibility to address the needs of at-risk groups is to ensure that the curriculum includes material about these groups.

However, as needed and beneficial as specialized courses in corrections are, many schools do not have the faculty expertise or the space in their curricula to provide them. Recently, social work educators have addressed the incorporation of diverse content areas into social work curricula, including content on violence, family reunification and legal issues. The integration of content into an existing graduate social work curriculum is a good alternative to adding a new course and provides relevant information to a majority of students when lack of resources precludes other options.

These benefits indicate the positive outcomes that could result when content on offenders and corrections is integrated into the social work curriculum. Integration of material may be useful in increasing student awareness of relevant values, concepts, and strategies underlying work with offenders and in helping students understand the complexities of a social problem. Benefits could also include expanding students' knowledge of practice with diverse populations, encouraging interest in an avenue of social welfare, and providing specific examples of practice to which students can apply their more general social work training.

Several key principles should guide the incorporation of material on adult offenders and corrections and be made explicit to students when discussing work with offenders. These guiding principles are widely accepted within the social work profession. However, because of the stigma attached to offenders, these principles bear repeating. Even within the field of social work, some clients tend to be considered more "worthy" of assistance than others, and criminals are often at the bottom of the list. The following principles are considered essential for effective work with offenders inside or outside of correctional settings. They are set forth as basic assumptions that should guide educational efforts within social work curricula.

The value and worth of all individuals must be upheld. In part this means embracing the assumption that given the right supports and services all individuals have the potential to succeed. Society might not be willing to expend the resources that are necessary for success; indeed, society might not even know what is needed many times, but the individual human potential exists. Both educators and students must be open to examining their own value systems and beliefs about the worth of all individuals, even those who commit heinous acts.

Activity on behalf of offenders, inside or outside of correctional settings, fits with the professional social work mission to "enhance human well-being and help meet the basic human needs of all people" described in the National Association of Social Workers (NASW) Code of Ethics. Indeed, "a historic and defining feature of social work is the profession's focus on individual well-being in a social context and the well-being of society". The problems experienced by offenders touch not only their lives but also the lives of their families and communities. Thus, positive results with offenders benefit society. In addition, according to the Code of Ethics, "social workers also seek to promote the responsiveness of organizations, communities, and other social institutions to individuals' needs and social problems".

I am very much grateful to Mr. Pranav Gupta, Director of MD Publications Pvt Ltd, for his kind cooperation and support for this book.

S. K. Bhalla

1

Community Programs and Social Work for Criminals

Introduction

Voluntary and public agencies and institutions have long traditions of social responsibility and humanitarian concern and do not deliberately convert themselves into seemingly irresponsible, semi-isolated enterprises. Study discloses, however, that they tend to become such as a result of a variety of forces: built-in values; the "distance" between public and private programs and between those manned by trained and untrained staffs; the frustrations arising from resource inadequacies in the community and from the difficulties inherent in dealings with very disturbed persons; the unintended side-effects of bureaucratization and specialization which come with program "bigness."

Despite instances of close coordination and, in most quarters, a degree of accommodation, basic weaknesses in services are not overcome, and we are not nearly effective enough in work with children in trouble. It is doubtful that we shall be unless we are able to think deliberately and comprehensively not of the individual agency but of a *community system of services*, of *a community's program for children*. When we begin to give due attention to a community plan in this sense, each agency will be seen not only as an entity but also in relation to ways in which its policies, operations, and relationships contribute to community strategy and how they might be further developed to play their role in an even more effective community endeavor.

All of this can be done without interfering with legitimate voluntary agency prerogatives and initiative, or with the special emphasis introduced by sectarian programs. It can certainly be accomplished without rigid central controls and authority. What is called for is a philosophy oriented to community strategy and integration of services, as well as that flexibility in practice which leads agencies to adapt themselves constantly to changing needs, knowledge, and values. A basic prerequisite is agency dedication to the best interests of the community as a whole and accountability of the individual practitioner not only for the *content* of his endeavors but also, for their *consequences*.

The first and crucial step in clarifying long-range community strategy is the decision to emphasize *functions* rather than agencies. And functions make sense only when viewed in relation to one another, as parts of an *integrated approach* to children in trouble, rather than when seen separately. For the lessons of social welfare history and of recent experience are clear: where agencies do not operate as part of a larger whole and are not acutely aware of themselves as part of such whole, they inevitably become symptom or procedure focused, rather than client focused. Before long they may see nothing but one symptom and regard a problem as solved if (for example) truancy stops temporarily, a child is not arrested again, or the father regains his job. They may see only parts of people or parts of families and thus render partial service. Or they may perfect their own procedures and ways of working with no provision for those who cannot use the help as it is offered. We have already described the consequences.

What is needed, then, is an approach which will grow out of the needs of clients, in this case the children and their families, translating such needs and what we know about the total phenomenon of children in trouble into essential functions. Only as functions are defined and their interrelationships explored is it possible to look at specific agencies and at their roles.

The charges to agencies might then be regarded as flexible and changeable, responsive to the changing quality and volume of need, as well as to the appearance of new agencies and resources. In fact, even the listing and definition of functions essential for each community, the very basis for the assignment of roles to agencies, must have similar flexibility and responsiveness to new knowledge and new concepts. In this spirit, *there is continuity in planning, but never a final plan. Moreover*, one can outline the functions all communities seem to require in their approach to children in trouble in the light of current experience, but at the same time emphasize that the exact alignment of services and assignment of roles should reflect a particular community's size, rates of deviant behavior, and the many elements in the background which determine the availability and relationship of various public and voluntary facilities and resources.

This is not to say that any one agency must have only one function in an over-all approach. On the contrary, it may often be wise to have multifunction agencies. Various combinations of case location and evaluation, of diagnostic and referral services, of varied treatment approaches, may belong under one roof. Further, none of this is meant to suggest that clients must be considered responsible for understanding the pattern and getting to the right place. On the contrary, all social welfare agencies and many other public institutions must maintain some kind of more or less elaborate "intake," "screening," "advice," or "steering" service to answer inquiries, evaluate applications, and decide whether the agency's own services are most appropriate, or to assure a good contact with the appropriate resource. The community also requires, we shall maintain, a widely known general "advice" or "steering" center for those who are not aware of resources and who are too shy to make contact in what is obviously the "wrong" place in the hope of being referred to a source of help.

While every agency may need some intake and steering functions, and while a given agency need not be limited to one function, it is important that the functions which are assured be related to a total strategy and that the sum total of assignments undertaken add up to the full range of required activities. Otherwise, clients will continue to be lost in the gaps between agencies, or clients will remain on the rolls of agencies unable to be of any real help to them.

To put all of this in other terms: It should be possible to describe the total phenomenon of children in trouble in the community and to define the total approach to such children. Then, each agency should be expected to *find its place* as offering a specialized service or a combination of services to some children. Symptom groups or circumstances of detection should play the smallest possible role in the determination of function or of agency alignment unless it can be shown (and there are some instances in which it may be shown) that they contribute to efficiency, effectiveness, or sound organization.

The emphasis must inevitably be on the agency's *finding its place* or on community assignment of function as part of a mutual give and take. For the problem is not one of legalisms or of charters which can be revised once decisions are made. The situation is not necessarily helped by technicalities. What is crucial is clarity within the agency about what the community needs it to do and what it wants to do. The clarity should encompass administration, staff, and board whether public or private.

The entire premise is, of course, that the community has assumed certain basic obligations for the welfare of its children and that these obligations extend even to those who are aggressive, antisocial, and destructive. In the broader national and state contexts there have been established certain minimum underpinnings for all people in the fields of employment security, housing, public education, public health, income maintenance, and social security. For children, all children, communities now affirm and, to varied degrees, seek to give full meaning to the right to competent health supervision from infancy to adulthood; opportunities for good education to the limits of one's potential; access to religious or moral training, as determined by parental background and wishes; adequate recreational facilities; vocational guidance and career planning with the assistance of skilled counselors. On this *foundation* and only on such foundation is it possible to talk of services which may be required by *some* children because of special problems. Among these are the "children in trouble."

Individual or Group Framework

It may seem, at first glance, that the categories of functions suggested (i.e., case finding, referral, etc.) are so completely oriented to the individual as to preclude consideration of all of the suggestions previously summarized as to the possible significance of family, peer group, and neighborhood in the delinquencies and the neglects. This is not necessarily the implication, but the hazard continues to exist that long tradition will cause overemphasis on the individual and lack of imaginative group approaches.

Our sense of justice and our legal system demand that we avoid "group justice" or "group diagnosis," which in a courtroom can become little more than an exercise in group stereotyping. The protection of all therefore argues for a system which begins with case finding and evaluation on the level of the individual and his family. Where court adjudication is at stake, the unit must always be the individual. None of this should block out adequate attention in the evaluative process to neighborhood and peer-group aspects of a problem; possible intervention through group services or neighborhood programs rather than through individual treatment; treatment of a whole family rather than the original individual "client." Interesting current experiments in group "intake" deserve watching, of course. Most ultimate and intermediate (primary) prevention must deal with neighborhood and community.

Because a large proportion of agencies currently do tend to take an atomized view of the individual, there is need for constant stress on the fact that we are dealing with delinquencies and neglects and that the *level* of intervention must be determined by causal patterns and by what promises effectiveness. Ultimately, the community system should be evaluated by whether following individualized differentiations and evaluations the community is prepared with an armamentarium for intervention and treatment which includes family approaches, group methods, and neighborhood mobilizations. We shall attempt to give these attention in proper context.

Protection

Before discussion of case location or of any of the other case oriented functions which follow, it is relevant to stress the urgency of sound organization to guarantee the necessary framework of community protection. Only a secure community can support services and activities which are designed to help and rehabilitate.

A community which fears its antisocial and deviant elements tends only to attack and to demand revenge, refusing the financing which effective services require and not offering an atmosphere in which reformed offenders may return to community life.

A city, therefore, cannot consider the addition of probation officers, clinical staffs, or remedial teachers without also ensuring the adequacy of police services. If a low percentage of committed offenses are cleared by the police through arrests, some of the "leverage" for change is missing from the work with delinquents.

Similarly and also to be elaborated subsequently community protection demands adequate access to facilities for (*a*) the shelter of dependent and neglected children who would otherwise be endangered; (*b*) the detention (pending court disposition) of delinquents or alleged delinquents who endanger themselves or the community—or who may not remain available; (*c*) the institutionalization of those who are best helped in an institution or whose continued presence in the community courts danger for themselves or for others.

Case Location—The First Level

To talk of "prevention" when the reference is to services for children already in trouble is to add to semantic confusion. We have suggested that there is an *ultimate* level of prevention, the level having to do with the kind of world, country, and city-county in which we live, and the influences they exert toward adjustment or maladjustment, toward social living or antisocial revolt. There is, too, what we have termed an *intermediate* level of prevention, the level concerned with efforts to interpose sound neighborhood, school, church, and other influences between all families and negative factors in the general social environment. (Both of these are called primary prevention in public health.) The more *immediate* prevention undertakings are the services and resources for vulnerable and disadvantaged families, families not in difficulty but known to have need for special backing if they are to achieve the standard of functioning expected of all. We have illustrated with reference to schools in the underprivileged areas or minority-group ghettos in our cities. Public health calls this secondary prevention. Both the community protection function described above and the intermediate and immediate prevention activities demand that there be concern in many quarters about circumstances, influences, lacks, and conditions which may generate serious deviance and difficulty. This may be referred to as *situation finding.* It is discussed more readily after a review of case location. We turn first to those children already showing signs of deviant patterns and in need of attention. To work with them may be to prevent more serious problems, and this is why some employ the term "prevention." Functions become somewhat clearer, however, if this is considered the first line, or first level, of case location or ease finding. We refer here to:

- the child who is not getting along in school;
- the child who is "acting up" or doing peculiar things in the settlement house program;
- the child on the public welfare caseload who seems, on home visits by the investigator, to be particularly withdrawn;
- the group of boys in the housing project who are always breaking rules or ignoring requests by the manager;
- the children whose mother has just been hospitalized as an alcoholic and who remain at home with their father, but who seem to neighbors to be out of his control;
- the "gang" of pre-teen boys who seem to follow on the fringes of a "fighting gang" of older boys and who annoy the school custodian with minor pranks.

These cases are not in the channels of agencies specifically concerned with delinquent or neglected children, although investigation might justify either label. Their problems may not be serious and may require little attention, or they may be very serious and may require psychiatric services, court concern, group programs, special school plans, or other help. The important thing is that there is already some sign of deviation, of adjustment problem, and that evaluation is needed. The community has been given some indication that these children may in some way be different and has reason to look at them and to see what the signal flares mean.

At this level, *case location is not specific* as to delinquency, neglect, mental illness, or anything else. Nothing is known to have been done by the child to require that certain channels (i.e., police) be used, and nobody has brought the case into specific service channels. The problem is one of ensuring that someone takes notice so that there will be adequate evaluation and follow-up.

Where does responsibility for case location in this sense belong? The logical answer is in terms of opportunities available. Case location is most effective if it takes place in the social institutions in which children spend much of their time, where the behavior norms and expectations are clear, where deviance is readily noted, and where there is already a relationship which may be the basis for getting child and family to the spot where fuller evaluation will be made. We shall describe the opportunities for case location in the schools, health centers, the public welfare department, voluntary family agencies, hospitals, churches, courts, settlement and recreation centers, housing authorities, and spots at which children and families in trouble are encountered. We begin with a description of the nature of such opportunities and then turn to discussion of some problems and of preparation for case finders in settings such as these.

Case location in the schools. Many studies have found that schools are in a particularly strategic case location position because of the universality of their coverage and the duration of their relationships with children and parents. In many school systems, however, the typical teacher is not well equipped or not in a position to identify a child in need of help and may even (unintentionally, as a rule) mistreat a child so identified by others. In the New York City school system, where size leads to extremes of specialization, school resources for case finding and evaluation are at present thinly spread and fragmented among a Bureau of Attendance, a Bureau of Child Guidance, and the vocational and educational counseling program. There is obviously need in all systems to make it possible for the individual classroom teacher to play her strategic case finding role and to clarify the backing she requires from special services, resources, and programs.

In this connection, we might note that the group intelligence tests and achievement tests now widely used in schools are most useful as devices for identifying possibly deviant children requiring more individual attention and study. The possible language, cultural, and social biases in various devices require that teachers use them with caution and follow up only if there is behavioral confirmation of need to do so. There does not exist any device which can do case finding in the sense of specifying that a given child *must* have attention. A child's need for attention is determined by the interplay of personality, family, environmental opportunity, and resources and there is no way for any mass device to consider all these dimensions.

Whatever the efficiency of formal devices, however, the teacher's observations of the child as he learns, plays, interacts with others, studies, eats, meets aggression, and faces environmental demands offer unique case finding opportunity. Teachers are shown to be very sensitive case finders in study after study. A recent study has demonstrated, for example, that teachers actually identify personality traits differentiating graduates from early school leavers.

The main problem is one of encouraging and freeing our teachers to perform their case finding roles; the means for achieving this require detailed examination.

Child health stations and public health nurses as case finders. The criterion of universality of opportunity and of coverage suggests the importance of the child health station, which may not, at present, be an important case finding agency in many places. Dr. David Levy has demonstrated that the appropriate training of public health nurses and pediatricians will alert them to difficulties in early mother-child relationships, many of which may be dealt with at the time. In other instances, more intensive attention may be necessary, through case referral. Coverage of child health stations varies with many factors throughout the country and the basic health promotion assignment of such stations remains primary. Their case finding potential in a large city is major, however, as we recall their city-wide coverage and note that the vast majority of children not under care of personal physicians may be brought to such stations with some regularity in the first three years of life. Corrective efforts in such circumstances would normally be directed to the entire family.

The public health nurse has similar opportunities and a good deal of tradition in this field. The better training programs emphasize case location beyond the delimited medical spheres.

Case location through public welfare. The welfare department is second only to the schools in its potential in this area. Records reveal that public welfare department representatives encounter evidence of severe child neglect, parental brutality, serious parent child conflict, the exposure of children to traumatic crises, and the beginning development of delinquent patterns. Although a public welfare department meets a smaller proportion of families than do the schools, its caseloads are made up in considerable measure of high-risk families and of the handicapped. By definition, the Aid to Needy Families with Children program is in contact with large numbers of children who are reared in broken families. It does not matter for this purpose whether categorical relief (i.e., Aid to the Blind, Old Age Assistance, etc.) and general home relief are administered by the same social investigators or whether caseloads are specialized, nor is it even important whether a department combines these responsibilities with the broader child care services (day care, foster care, adoption, homemaker services, etc.). What is important is the definition of the case finding roles of personnel in the first lines of contact with parents and children in all the programs, the preparation of these personnel for such a role, and the provision of necessary consultants and specialist backing. At present public welfare contacts are often "opportunities lost" as far as children in trouble are concerned.

Voluntary family agencies as case finders. Although the coverage of family service agencies may be relatively limited, the opportunities of such agencies are strategic. Large numbers of families in serious subsequent difficulty have been known at earlier points to sectarian family societies, to the Salvation Army Family Service, or to large nonsectarian family agencies. Moreover, these agencies affiliated with the Family Service Association of America nationally have high standards of personnel selection and practice. While at one time they may have regarded their methods as suitable only for those motivated to use help, there is an increasing tendency to understand cultural, social, and psychological factors in resistance and to "reach out" to clients, so as to make services more accessible. The family service field, in fact, has been discussing the possibility of a wider and larger "open door" than has prevailed in the past. One might even introduce the possibility of the family agency's potential as a general advice center.

Equipped as they are for competent social study and to obtain good psychiatric consultation service where needed, family agencies must certainly be listed as important case finders in this first line of community defense.

Medical resources and case location. By definition, medical facilities meet people when they face problems, at times quite serious problems. When a parent has to be hospitalized and there is need for social service help (in relation to arrangements for the family in the interim, post hospitalization planning, or patient and family reactions relating to the medical problem itself), the opportunity for becoming acquainted with the children and noting their need for special attention may be considerable. Currently, the emphasis more usually may be on the patient and the immediate problems confronting him or blocking the medical plan. All of this needs to continue, but the total community approach to children in trouble would also be strengthened by acceptance of the hospitalization crisis, which may be grave, as a possible opportunity for location of some children requiring additional attention.

There are, for example, children who respond to family medical crises by withdrawal or severe antisocial behavior. There are fathers who offer poor care in the mother's absence. Most often, it is a long-standing problem which comes to the fore under these special circumstances.

Many hospital social service departments are not adequately staffed for this kind of function as yet and little has been done to clarify the extent to which doctors and nurses might, in themselves, become in some ways involved.

Particularly troublesome is the evidence in hospital emergency rooms and medical wards that some children have been cruelly abused or seriously neglected. Yet, because the emphasis has tended to be on medical care and because the protective case finding potential of these situations is not defined, there is little clear statement of obligations or definition of suitable channels. Major new provision is needed for most parts of the country.

The out-patient clinic repeats the hospital experience in less intensive form and the crisis is generally not as great, since family separations are not under way. The clinic, however, does belong in the total case finding scheme; it is often, in fact, the center of work with families just before or just after hospitalization.

All of this applies, in even more emphatic terms, where the hospital is a mental hospital. In fact, current psychiatric research and theory suggest that much mental illness involves complex family group pathology which is not limited to the hospitalized member. Inevitably, the hospitalization or even out-patient treatment of a parent for psychiatric reasons means that the child or children in the family have probably been exposed to unusual, and perhaps destructive, experiences, which reflect themselves in all forms of personal deviation and pathology, from delinquency to psychosis. This is almost as frequently the case if the patient is a brother or sister. In these instances there is the obligation to look at all children in the family before determining that they do not require some special help despite such exposure.

Community child guidance clinics, while not attached to hospitals, would also do well to expand their case location activities. Since they are treating children referred to them because of specific difficulties, they quite naturally tend to give full attention to their child-patients and to work with or treat the parent(s) as their resources and philosophies dictate. In a minority of cases where other children in the family have also required child guidance services, clinics have taken the initiative and established a treatment contact. They have been limited in this, however, because of almost omnipresent waiting lists, as well as by their emphasis on client motivation for treatment. They have not recognized an obligation for some form of initiative where other children in the family present problems in need of evaluation, or seem to require other than child guidance services. Such initiative will be the product only of community-wide emphasis on case location, and the clarification of responsibility for recognition and the channels for evaluation and referral.

Churches and synagogues as case finders. Since churches do not list their contacts with social service exchanges and do not keep case records, there are no comprehensive statistical data as to their case finding potentials. Their broad relationships in every community and their direct service to many families in need of help make them major case finders. They may perform this service in various ways and in various degrees, of course, depending on the traditions and religious customs of a given group or sect. Their opportunity should not be underestimated, however, since like schools and settlements they are in the neighborhood, on the spot, and often able to see and feel emerging problems. Long-time relationships with individual families, sometimes over more than one generation, provide particular opportunity for balanced evaluation. They know of parents' concerns about their children and may be called upon to help when a child is arrested. Internal family crises are often called to their attention.

As with teachers, settlement workers, or police, the clergy have had to learn over the years which situations they can deal with directly themselves, offering religious counseling and other church services, and which require resources specialized in other ways. Most religious denominations have made important progress in these fields. Pastoral counseling courses and special psychiatry and social science offerings in theological schools have increased awareness of the implications of the problems children face and of the range of treatment possibilities.

Out of consideration of the problems of delinquents, a clergyman with special training writes:

> *The clergyman, through his relationships with parents, teachers, and young peoples' groups, and through his own direct relations with youngsters, can become aware very early of signs of disturbance in young people.*

He must, however, know the signs of personality disturbances and also of possible future difficulty. He must have knowledge of the conditions and relationships most likely to give rise to such difficulties. He must know and respect his own limitations and be ready to solicit help for any problems which exceed his ability.

The court's special case finding opportunities. The children in most serious trouble tend eventually to reach juvenile court as allegedly delinquent or neglected, if they are not sent to mental hospitals or placed in foster care through welfare authorities. These courts recognize their obligations for case study and disposition. What is too seldom understood, however, is that the courts which deal with adults, particularly those courts which are concerned with family problems, have special case finding opportunities. Similarly, it is not often the practice for a children's court or a youth court, dealing with one child in the family, to take notice, through its probation case study, of the needs of other children, and to initiate necessary follow-up.

All courts, in fact, have major case finding opportunity since the very contact reflects social or psychological causes of importance to all in the family. Currently, many so-called family courts and support courts are not equipped to do much about their opportunities. The criminal courts, in particular, would need special facilities if they were to examine the status of children in a family when a parent or an older child is dealt with, since in this kind of case location there are no legal sanctions.

Recognizing the implications for children, New York State is now implementing a court reorganization involving the potential for creating a case finding apparatus in all family actions in which children are in some way involved. Other jurisdictions already have such facilities, but usually where the case volume is small. Only fairly elaborate development of probation services in criminal courts and a broader view of their opportunities would lead to more adequate case finding generally.

Settlements, mass recreation, and case finding. At their best and when they are most successful, settlement houses and community centers know their neighborhood children and families quite well. Several children in a family may take part in club activities or in recreational or crafts programs. The parents may also have some part in the program. Staff members are aware of what is going on in the neighborhood and may know of the special difficulties a child has encountered or the dangers he faces. It may be clear that clubs or boys or gangs, in and out of the settlement, are tending toward delinquency or drug use, or at least are not constructively motivated.

Under such circumstances, settlement houses have been and should certainly continue to be important case locators. Some, in fact, have staffed themselves with caseworkers, casework units, or clinic units to help in case evaluation or even to offer intensive treatment where a child is not getting along in the program or a gang is moving toward antisocial patterns. Others have offered themselves as outposts for family service agencies and clinics to facilitate case location and the transition to treatment.

There are, of course, settlements and community centers which are not strictly neighborhood-based and which place more emphasis on mass activities and on special events. They do not generally get to know many children well and are probably not better equipped than the large public recreation, park, and after-school recreation programs for much case finding. Impressive efforts have, however, been made in some instances to have a small number of group workers trained in social work available as consultants and to give special attention to individuals and groups. Where this is possible, even the mass recreation program has case location potential.

Case finding in public housing. Elizabeth Wood has noted the case finding potential of tenant relocation programs and of the public housing projects. For a number of reasons not immediately relevant here there has been substantial self-selectivity in public housing. Public housing has high concentrations of racially-ethnically underprivileged groups, of relief recipients, of broken families, and of those who are in many other ways handicapped. Thus, a housing manager is in a position to do case finding in instances of open and violent marital conflict, below-standard housekeeping, and rent delinquencies, in addition to major misconduct of children or extremely questionable and hazardous parental behavior.

One should add, however, that public housing defeats its purpose, becomes further stigmatized, even more limited to those with recourse to nothing else, and thus even more abnormal as a daily living milieu if management is highly organized to pry into people's affairs and to interfere in their normal privacy and prerogatives. What is proper, however, is management alertness to the kinds of situations and circumstances to which all responsible citizens might react anywhere, as well as management's use of those opportunities which are routine in the management relationship: maintenance, rent collection, protection of premises, responding in emergencies to requests for help. Special social service units in housing developments or available to them may help to separate routine management from special individualizing functions.

Other case finders. It may be well to add, however obvious, that the logic which suggests case finding machinery in medical facilities is more than reinforced in all social welfare programs. Agencies responsible for foster care, those offering long-term or short-term care to the dependent and the neglected, family location agencies (in cases of fathers who desert), and those rendering many specialized services are already at work with families because it is known that problems exist or crises are being faced. Many now limit themselves to narrow interpretations of their functions. However, a family-oriented approach and a preventive outlook would dictate a degree of alertness to the implications of the problem for all family members and, therefore, a case finding role.

Certainly, agencies which already have children under their care in foster homes and institutions have major responsibility to contribute to their sound development and to ensure early detection and follow-up of signs of difficulty. To use such difficulty as the basis for returning the case at once to a court or to the original placement agency without efforts to cope with it as a parent might represents a reneging on primary child care obligations.

Advice centers—a new resource. The parent, friend, or neighbor is very often the very best case finder. He may refer himself, his relative, his child, or his neighbor, but he cannot be expected to know who is best equipped to evaluate the situation or to render service. Currently, the special attitudes and experiences of various ethnic groupings affect the choices of places to go for help; members of one group do not hesitate to turn to the police when they need help with their children; members of another group turn to the church; others may go to child guidance clinics or may have access to private psychiatric guidance.

None of this is in itself undesirable if channels are open and the initial steering is good. The problem is that our urban areas contain subgroups aware of no resources. Others know of facilities which they do not feel free to use. Still others turn to the unqualified-with disastrous consequences. The modern city needs a general advice center widely known, with accessible branches and with no intake criteria. Anybody should be free to enter for guidance and steering and feel that no stigma or disadvantages will result. Perhaps a special system of centers is necessary or it may be that welfare departments, health stations, settlements, or family service agencies are able to expand their functions in these directions.

The complications of such case location. Agencies involved in case finding at this first level have not been established primarily for this purpose, and therefore have the task of protecting their central functions. For example, the classroom teacher must balance her basic educational function with her case finding obligations if her central role is not to change. The settlement worker loses members if the public image of the agency is dominated by the case finding. The general physician may discover that he loses patients if he raises questions about a family's child-rearing practices.

It is no small task for those agencies whose primary responsibility is not case finding and who operate at the level before there is identification of delinquency and neglect to balance for themselves and for their publics their basic, necessary (sometimes statutory) functions against a relatively broad focus. Yet these are socially created agencies, institutions, and programs, and socially responsible professional people. Community interest requires more than discharge of narrowly conceived functions: the child welfare worker cannot ignore family problems; the family agency worker must be alert to the problems of children; the child guidance worker must "see" the other children and parents.

Much depends on the inclusion in the education and training of the people who are to work in these settings of sufficient material about normality and deviance in family life and child development so that they recognize signals of distress even where their training does not equip them to diagnose such distress. Both psychological and cultural content belongs in this kind of training. Where the primary tasks are in other realms, personnel should be prepared to ask for consultation or advice. Ways must also be found through education and community organization to create that heightened sense of social responsibility which generates a broad exercise of one's opportunities. The need for this and the methods to be used must vary from group to group.

All case locators on the first level are most in need of information as to where situations may be referred for follow-up and evaluation, as appropriate to the particular setting. The teacher should have access to guidance personnel, school social workers, psychologists, or psychiatrists, while the policeman on the beat may call on a juvenile aid specialist or a clinical intake unit. Nurses and doctors need to know about school resources, social agencies, police facilities, and protective casework units to mention a few. The family agency knows how to initiate proper referrals but is at a loss in certain situations if the community does not have a protective casework program. Members of the clergy require intimate acquaintance with all types of resources and how they may be brought into action. As already suggested, the settlement resident or club leader may have specialized personnel on the premises or may call upon other agencies—and what the housing manager does depends on whether a social service program is located within his own structure.

These are illustrative rather than all-inclusive statements. The method of first-level case location and the channels to which it should lead must be worked out specially in a manner appropriate to a given agency, social institution, or profession. In subsequent chapters we shall deal with schools, police, welfare departments, and settlements in some detail in this regard.

Case Location—Children Already in Trouble

Not all case finding occurs when the child is not yet known to be involved in serious "trouble" and is not in specified authoritative service channels. There are many instances in which the children who are identified seem to be caught up in acts or circumstances of a kind which may require police or court action. In fact, in some of these circumstances or offenses (acts which would be crimes if committed by adults, etc.) there is legal assignment of an obligation to intervene.

Parents and any of the community personnel described in the previous section may initiate these cases, but the formal processing the decision to ignore or proceed with situations is largely in the hands of police, courts, attendance bureaus, and protective casework units. All of these have special responsibility for follow through and all are ready to resort to delinquency and neglect petitions as necessary.

Before further examination of this level of case finding, however, it is necessary to comment about devices offered for the purpose of predicting delinquency and ensuring the early identification of children who will be in trouble—in advance of any overt difficulty.

Delinquency prediction. Considerable attention is currently being directed at the development and validation of devices designed to predict delinquency, chiefly as the result of the pioneer work of Sheldon and Eleanor Glueck. A popular magazine responded to the early publicity with an article entitled "Criminals in the Kindergarten?" In the enthusiasm about possible future availability of a device, there has been a tendency to lose sight of three important considerations: (*a*) whether the prediction instrument has been validated; (*b*) whether, if validated, it would be practicable; (*c*) whether it is socially desirable to use such a device in conjunction with a community's efforts on behalf of children in trouble.

The first of these questions need not concern us at any great length here. Although it has not yet been shown to exist, there is no technical reason why there should not eventually be available a prediction device with a known degree of accuracy, able to tell us how many in a given group are likely to be in trouble with the law and how many are not likely to be. The findings will be stated in terms of the "chances" of any individual in the group. All prediction is, by definition, in relation to group frequencies. Thus far, retrospective studies based on the Gluecks' device have shown that of those in difficulty most would have been properly identified had the instrument been used earlier and had there been available at that earlier time the data used in the retrospective ratings.

There are not, as yet, any completed and convincing studies which use the Glueck scale to predict forward; the most elaborate such study, that of the New York City Youth Board, is inconclusive in its interim report. No current findings clarify, as yet, the rate of probable misprediction, a most important matter if a delinquency prediction instrument is to become an administrative device. There is some reason to believe that the Glueck scale would tend to over predict delinquency in a normal school population.

The New York City Youth Board is seeking to convert the Glueek scale into a practicable instrument. Such an instrument would have to be administered by teachers or other school-based personnel. The much-publicized Youth Board experiment involves ratings and judgments by specially qualified and trained personnel on the basis of data assembled by a special staff from three sources: home interviews with parents, interviews with teachers, collateral information from social agencies.

The third question, that relating to the desirability of a delinquency prediction device, takes one directly into the realm of social policy. In developing ways of helping children before their problems are serious, should we seek devices to predict delinquency or to predict maladjustment? The Gluecks have written:

> It is to be hoped that similar devices for early "spotting" or "screening" or early "identification" or early "diagnosis" not only of delinquent but of emotionally disturbed non-delinquent children will be developed by others, notably by psychiatrists and psychologists, who have access to extensive and intensive case materials.

Concentration on a specialized delinquency prediction scale is reasonable where the purpose is to test a causal hypothesis; such experimentation with prediction is in the best of scientific tradition. A scientific "law" should enable one to predict. Where the emphasis is on community services, however, other considerations prevail.

Do we actually wish to stigmatize a kindergarten child or a first-grader with the label "will probably be a delinquent"? Have we the right to label, without due process; dare we label in the light of attitudes to delinquency? Are teachers, principals, and others able to deal completely objectively with a child said to belong to a group in which the delinquency likelihood is eighty chances out of one hundred? Do we not, in fact, run the risk of the self-fulfilling prophecy here, i.e., making the child delinquent because of the experiences we create for him through the labeling? To some degree deviance is a matter of self-definition.

It has been said that these negative consequences of a delinquency prediction instrument may be avoided by keeping the findings in the hands of such specialized personnel as social workers and psychologists.

Experimentation along these lines is certainly justified, although it is difficult to see how such personnel could use knowledge of predictions, without informing others, in the absence of circumstances or behavior which would alert teachers. Would not the requirement that the device be used by specialists make it impractical for most school systems, except perhaps during special, short-term demonstrations?

Most important, however, if the purpose is to help children and to avoid serious problems by early detection, attention had best be directed at the likelihood of deviation and adjustment problems in any areas; there is no special value to predicting delinquency per se. Those who would develop devices might invest their energies in this direction. As already indicated, the usual group tests of I.Q. and achievement are usable in this way to alert teachers and/or to supplement their observations. Glueck scale *items*, when validated, might be included in an all-purpose screening instrument.

Even the all-purpose prediction device cannot be introduced without recognition that being identified as a "risk" carries with it some potentially undesirable consequences: stigma in the eyes of some; being held up to standards more rigidly; being "typed," perhaps unjustly, in terms of expectation rather than performance. Prediction devices deal with group statistical probabilities and do not account for those who run contrary to the majority trends; some children are able to handle their handicaps or are influenced by factors not taken into account by the instruments.

In the light of these considerations it seems reasonable to suggest that the emphasis be on predicting "need for help," rather than "delinquency" (case location, on what we have called the first level), and that even such devices not be put into the hands of unqualified personnel.

In some school systems, skills and attitudes may be such that only clinical or guidance personnel should have access to the results of tests or screenings which identify individual children as needing help. In other systems, teachers may be adequately prepared for their use. Where there is no assurance of ability to control the consequences of a statistical prediction that a child is a "risk," it would be wiser policy to plan only for the identification of and attention to the child who already displays a problem or difficulty, however mild. Under any circumstances, there is no right to introduce pressure, formal or otherwise, for taking help, unless there is already a behavioral manifestation of its need. Parent or child could hardly be expected to be highly motivated as a result of actuarial information.

Predictions about the presence in a group of a considerable number of highly vulnerable children might lead to group programs, neighborhood programs, and community efforts—which need not single out any one child as a "risk." Emphasis on such predictions would be sound policy.

Major agencies for location of those in trouble. Repeated truancy is defined as "delinquency" by many children's court statutes. Further, countless studies of juvenile delinquents and adult criminals show that very large proportions were at one time truants and were thus identifiable through their truancy.

The school system's plans for coping with *unexplained* absence are thus part of the community's case location machinery for children who may already belong in the category "in trouble," in the sense of our discussion. Some truants are involved in stealing, vandalism, gang activity, running away, and sexual delinquency. Others are being severely neglected or brutally treated by parents who are inadequate, seriously mentally ill, or who are "lost" in a new and strange culture. On the other hand, unlawful absence may prove on investigation to result from school phobias or a variety of psychoneurotic problems, from situational school difficulties, or from environmental or economic pressures in the home.

Those who investigate unexplained absences are therefore major case finders, dealing with children in many kinds of difficulty and drawing on all possible community resources, including the courts. Whether a given school system requires a special attendance bureau or might integrate its attendance and general school social work and guidance services is a matter designated for more extended discussion.

The *police* are also major case finders, their volume of eases found being exceeded only by investigators of unlawful absence. This makes it necessary to define the relative assignments of all police and of juvenile aid bureau specialists. Should all youth cases be cleared with youth police, for example? The nature of the police case evaluation, the length of case contacts, the qualification of juvenile aid policemen become important questions. Answers must begin with the premise that the police *are* case finders and, therefore, must either make screening decisions or have help in making them.

Family courts and juvenile courts (depending on the court structure) are also case finders in the sense of this section, i.e., they are often the first official agency to which the ease is reported and are in a position to initiate formal proceedings, make referrals to a variety of resources, encourage family solutions without community help, discourage or encourage complainants and petitioners, give priority to delinquency or to neglect aspects of cases, and so on. The exact nature of the courts' "intake" or "screening" machinery which takes these actions is obviously affected by the total structure of community services. The extent to which the police do careful evaluation before coming to court is a major consideration. The existence of a case finding and social service program in the school conditions the court's procedures. Clearly, however, courts require some kind of structure and policies for handling situations not previously evaluated and not necessarily best served by formal processing.

Where children are being grossly neglected or mistreated the situation is often called to the attention of *protective casework* units—protective casework sections in welfare departments in many places, child welfare workers in many counties, state-wide (in Massachusetts) or local Societies for the Prevention of Cruelty to Children elsewhere.

These units are in the same relationship to neglect cases as are police to delinquency. Some situations are acute, severe, obvious, and there is little choice but to arrange for immediate temporary shelter and to introduce court action which will lead to long-term plans for the children. Other situations require study and evaluation, since it may be possible to develop plans or to institute treatment under the auspices of the protective unit, or on referral from them, on a voluntary basis, or at least somewhat voluntary since the potential court petitions remain in the background. Further, just as a good number of complaints to the police about children require only brief notice that the community is concerned, a portion of the protective cases need not result in prolonged contacts or services. In fact, all such units must sort out a group of cases which are initiated by local eccentrics and cranks.

Every community obviously requires a case finding service of some sort which is particularly concerned with neglect and abuse of children.

Community case finders. Families are, themselves, major case locators, as are friends and relatives. Depending on cultural attitudes, however, there are major variations in the extent to which members of different groups feel free to turn to the police, courts, schools, family agencies, and others to ask for help. Programs of education and interpretation may contribute to this process; helpful experiences for those who do go to the agencies are even more effective ways of advertising and opening the channels.

The special case finding unit. Community circumstances may dictate the creation of a special case finding unit or a system of such units. Thus, when the New York City Youth Board was launched and was committed to early case location and referral, a system of special Referral Units was designed as the necessary instrument in high-delinquency areas. After a period of experimentation as to the appropriate community base, these units were placed in the schools. Subsequently, they were moved out again because of administrative complications. Such units deal with the two levels of case finding we have differentiated.

Problems of case finders. Study of the case finding experience of special units and general agencies discloses that the case finder must solve many difficult problems if he is to work effectively. Some of them are problems peculiar to the service set up exclusively for case location, while others might confront any case finder.

For example, a Referral Unit worker may be making excellent progress with a family but must solve the technical problem of how far to carry a situation, once identified, before referral to the agency which will provide the long-range treatment. Even prior to this, the case finding agency must have on its staff professional personnel skilled in diagnosis and work with extremely complex case situations and with individuals resistive to community intervention on many grounds. This is no small consideration in the light of severe personnel shortages—as well as real gaps in knowledge and skill among the professionally prepared.

Particularly perplexing are the cases which are carefully studied, dynamically understood, but in which the parent wishes no help. Systematic and skilled work to overcome resistance and to offer service on an acceptable level do not always break through parental refusal to have outside intervention in family situations. Then, unless a child gets into difficulty, thereby justifying more formal legal intervention, it is necessary to accept the fact that further efforts are not possible. Where staff is not skillful, these cases are inevitably lost.

All agencies meet situations in which parents "use" agencies to control or to punish their children. The parental petition or request for intervention is, at times, a desperate bid for help and at others a defensive measure against their own involvement. Considerable skill, of course, is required if the interests of all are to be considered and a helping process inaugurated. These are cases which are usually found none too early, but the agency must make its own assessment if it is to do something constructive. In some instances, the steps taken only convince the children that nobody cares about them; in others a real beginning is made in constructive directions even if the mother's initial demand for placement of a child has to be met.

Case finding may accomplish little if some one agency does not take responsibility for major help to the family and for relating other resources in a systematic plan. Otherwise, a flurry of uncoordinated activity serves to confuse rather than to rehabilitate. Even where a case finding agency is oriented to continued responsibility, it often has no way under current patterns of assuring adequate reporting back by treatment agencies if referrals "do not take."

At their best, case finding agencies are characterized by a broad approach, systematic study, and careful planning. The possibilities are seen in a case such as the following:

The case was called to the attention of the Referral Unit by the school principal because Barney, age 11, was restless, wandered about, rarely completed his work, and had temper outbursts. Study disclosed that Barney was a member of a migrant family with many difficulties stemming from substandard living conditions, the need to adjust to a new culture and language, and the inability of the parents to cope with the needs of their seven children. During an eight-month period, the Referral Unit worker, who spoke the family's language, saw the father in weekly interviews, saw the mother occasionally (she was not well), and met with the boy. She conferred with the Department of Welfare investigator regularly until the family was helped to move to a larger apartment, obtain needed furniture, receive funds for clinic visits. At the end of the period, a referral was completed to a sectarian family service agency for continued help. Results were seen in a short time in the improved adjustment of the boy who was referred and of a sister who had also been having difficulty in school.

The right to intervene. Case location is not merely a matter of developing detection devices or of affirming the obligations inherent in those agencies which have contacts with many children under strategic circumstances. For the question remains: At what point does a community have the right to interfere on behalf of a child's future?

There are situations in which parents do not wish help and persist in their refusals despite all the efforts of caseworkers and others who use their skills to interpret a service and to overcome resistance. Where neglect or delinquency, as defined by statute, can be shown to exist, agency responsibility is clear. However, as we seek to locate cases early and to offer services to the deviant and to the vulnerable, we meet many situations in which, technically, there is no delinquency or neglect. Moreover, it would involve considerable stretching of both neglect statutes and current professional knowledge to hold that any parent who, under such circumstances, refuses to accept a referral is, by virtue of that fact, subject to court intervention.

While it is undoubtedly true that housing officials, schools, and public welfare authorities actually have access to certain sanctions, it is only proper to ask to what extent they have a right to seek to bring to bear services which are not part of their *primary* functions in the instance of the refusal of the parent to cooperate despite adequately interpreted offers of help. If these officials were to use their access to needed resources or their roles in the lives of children to bludgeon families into help which has been considered and rejected, we shall have changed the basic character of the social institutions they serve and undermined their primary functions. We also shall have seriously violated our concepts of individual rights. In the long run it would be wisest for the community to prepare to bow to the wishes of parents in these instances even if agency representatives are troubled about the consequences. Where experience shows repetitive circumstances in which this policy inevitably damages children, it may be time to consider amending the law with respect to delinquency and neglect. The *Standard Juvenile Court Act*, in fact, recommends a statement of neglect jurisdiction broad enough to include most circumstances in which there is evidence that a parental failure to offer or to accept service is truly injurious.

The large issue is not, however, one of offering services where there is no right to do so, but of professional competence and methods. Although many potential clients are initially resistive, their reactions are often found to be compounded of fear, lack of information, and cultural patterns which make it difficult to accept help. Many of the personal psychological obstacles can be overcome where the approach is skillful. Clients respond to the interest and psychological authority of teachers, welfare department representatives, doctors, ministers, and others. We need to alert personnel in many kinds of settings to the opportunities to help with developing problems, or with family situations out of which serious problems may spring. We also must equip staff to act appropriately and encourage a sense of responsibility about such matters in welfare departments, schools, hospitals, health stations, mental hospitals, courts, correctional institutions, voluntary family agencies, clinics, and other settings.

There may have to be legal clarification in some fields, and improvements in methods of service must certainly take place. These will tend to follow, however, as we advance the concept that to fail to identify those who need help early is to be responsible for their neglect and future difficulties. In the intimate, but isolated, interdependence of urban living, people cannot count on relatives and neighbors. They depend on community agencies in their need, and to miss the signs of desperation and helplessness is to fail in a major human obligation. To "find" a case is to locate an opportunity to save, to repair, or to prevent. And, since many undesirable consequences may follow from being labeled as a delinquent child or neglectful parent, to locate a case and not ensure adequate follow-through is destructive and punitive, whatever the intention or policy. A responsible citizen or a responsible community agency cannot permit the loss of what may be a child's last chance because of irresponsible service, a failure to follow up-or lack of community designation of some agency as responsible to help with a situation and to keep helping until there is either a satisfactory disposition or an irreparable and conclusive failure.

Situation Finding

When charity organization societies (now family agencies) and settlements were at the height of their social reform interest at the turn of the present century, there was considerable alertness to the close relationship between case location and situation finding. The community loses opportunity for protective work, in the sense described above, and for immediate preventive planning unless this relationship is reaffirmed and reinforced by agency action in the present era.

To illustrate briefly: The settlement house staff, in discovering a number of members addicted to drugs, may become aware of channels of distribution in the community. A public welfare investigator's experiences, as checked against the experience of others, may clarify a special type of housing need or may reveal a defect in housing legislation. Experience with families of several adolescents may suggest to a family agency that the community lacks adequate employment counseling and placement resources. Systematic attention to the pattern of complaints may alert a police officer to the fact that an empty school building is an "attractive nuisance" and encourages vandalism. Examination of delinquency data may reveal to a public official that social agency summer vacation shutdowns remove the props which keep some young people out of trouble.

In each instance, the step from case finding to situation finding is one involving generalization from case-by-case experience and is based on concern for community protection and prevention. At times, the agency's experience and knowledge of a situation are such that referral to the police or district attorney may complete the action. At other times, a given agency may be in a position to make a substantial contribution to the community through systematic study of a block of its cases or by assembling data from many of its clients then reporting to the community at large about a hazard, a need, a problem, a resources gap.

While, typically, the situation finding by the individual agency is triggered by specific experience with one or more cases leading to alertness, assembling of more data, perhaps to study and to generalization all agencies may also at times be confronted quite directly, rather than through case materials, with evidence as to gaps or hazards. Police, particularly youth police, search for hazards during their patrol duties. Settlement workers and others in the neighborhoods become intimately acquainted with housing, recreation, and health needs, and with the economic problems of families. They often learn about racketeering. Public health nurses, to mention one other group, have direct experience too.

Again, some of this situation finding should lead an agency or a practitioner to report directly to the police, district attorney, public health officer, or housing official. At other times, it may initiate the type of study and exploration mentioned above. In fact, direct experience with apparent hazards may encourage an agency to turn to its case files to see whether the gaps or hazards are directly reflected in client experience.

The work of coordinating and city-wide planning bodies should reflect the initiative which derives both from members' and agencies' experiences with the individual case and from agency confrontation of a general hazard. These coordinating organizations are in fact under special obligation, by charge, charter, and role, to respond to the situation finding initiative of alert agencies and to consider carrying through the necessary study, planning, and action. They are well located, by function, to communicate information about hazardous situations to the general community. They should also undertake routine statistical analysis and periodic special studies relative to social breakdown, agency services, and unmet need-thus serving to pinpoint neighborhood and population subgroups exposed to many risks and helping to suggest service.

When the community machinery is working well, the discovery of local community situations which are hazardous to children and youth, and which will not be remedied by enforcement actions of administrative agencies (police, public health, etc.), or by the addition of social services alone, should lead to special all-out resource mobilization and local self-help efforts. Settlements, neighborhood organizations, and community councils may be needed to provide initiating force and guidance.

Case Evaluation—The Decision about the Next Step

Case finders make major decisions all the time. The policeman on the beat who sees two groups of boys in a fight may merely "break it up" or may do something more. Except for those instances in which his instructions decree that certain serious offenses must lead automatically to arrest and to court petitions, he exercises a measure of discretion about recording the situation at all, considering arrest, or making a referral to the juvenile aid police. The juvenile aid officer, in turn, has access to a variety of dispositions: to drop the case; to drop the case after a letter, telephone warning, conversation with the parent, or interview with the child; to undertake full social study and to arrive at a plan that way; to make a referral to a social agency or some other service; to file a court petition.

Except in those cases where the particular offense automatically leads to a formal court hearing under court rules or where the petitioner demands such hearing, court intake workers may have access to a similarly wide range of possibilities. Also, the attendance officer in the home on an investigation of unexplained absence must decide about next steps as he reacts to what he is told and sees.

Brief screening decisions. These *brief screening decisions*, as they may be called, are a first level of case evaluation. They are the routine separating out in any agency assigned to deal with those already in some trouble: courts, police, attendance, protective unit, and so on. Public housing managers, clergymen, public recreation workers have similar experiences. These are essential and unavoidable decisions if programs are not to be cluttered with trivial or misdirected cases and if emergency or acute problems are not to be lost in the mass of less urgent ones. Many of those involved in what we have called case location on the first level are not called upon to go further than the brief screening decisions in their case appraisals.

At times, more systematic types of case evaluation are not undertaken where they should be, but the brief screening decisions are needed in their own right. They are inevitably made, because a client is there, in hand, and has to be sent home, sent elsewhere, or dealt with in the agency itself. There must be an exercise of some discretion at once, for better or for worse.

Far too often, the instructions under which personnel operate give them no choice but to make their screening decisions only in terms of the severity of the offense or the existence of a prior record of offenses. Where personnel are unprepared for the assignment, there is some protection for clients in this. Gradually, however, one might hope that all policemen on beats and receptionists in these agencies would have enough basic orientation to "the fundamental concepts of human behavior, including the need to consider the total person as well as any specific disorder," so as to be able to exercise a greater degree of discretion in knowledgeable fashion. Community policy might still dictate that certain circumstances or offenses would lead directly to arrest or to the courtroom, but there would be more skill in determining when other matters might be completely dropped and when referral for study or fuller processing in the case finding agency was indicated.

Clergymen, housing managers, and recreation workers are increasingly exposed to influences and training which might guide their decisions, but they have need of consultation resources as well. An agreement with a family agency or a clinic which permits informal conversation as situations develop is extremely helpful and may lead to competent handling by the case finder or to initiation of an appropriate referral for more comprehensive evaluation or for service.

Even at present, however, it is reasonable to expect that juvenile aid specialists, attendance officers, representatives of child protective services, and other child care *specialists* will be equipped for such evaluation. One of the major contributions of such personnel, in fact, is made through their brief screening decisions and their orientation of the less-prepared personnel as to the basis for decisions.

All personnel involved in brief screening need to understand that knowing when not to drop a situation and lose an opportunity is neither more nor less important than avoiding community involvement where the family is capable of handling its own problems. Awareness of when to request full social or psychiatric study within one's agency, or at another appropriate place, is as necessary as ability to make immediate decisions in some cases on the basis of available data.

Disposition evaluations. The line between the brief screening decision and what might be called *disposition evaluations* is not too sharp in some settings but is very clear in others. Thus, the juvenile aid patrolman makes some decisions merely by looking at the report filed by the officer on the beat who received a complaint about a child; he may mail out a letter or call somebody in to be "warned." He may, on the other hand, decide that the case requires fuller consideration and may undertake (or another staff member may undertake) a somewhat more comprehensive social study leading to a disposition evaluation.

The better-known illustration is, of course, that of the probation officer whose defined task (except in treatment and supervision cases) is to conduct a social study so as to prepare a disposition recommendation. The detention social service staff, or a court diagnostic clinic, is also often designated to undertake social and psychiatric case study for the guidance of the court in its disposition planning. While it usually houses, in its probation bureau, what might be called a casework treatment service, the juvenile court is, in fact, the prime example of an agency organized around the process of disposition evaluation (adjudication and probation investigations) and case disposition making. Detention and clinic contribute their evaluations as arms of the court.

At a subsequent point we shall elaborate on the nature of the court's most specialized and unique form of case evaluation, *adjudication of status*. The probation study, which should be used only following adjudication, is in many respects similar to the case evaluations in many other types of setting and is designed to help the judge choose from among case discharge, community based service, or institutionalization as dispositions alter adjudication.

Diagnostic centers and reception centers are specialized facilities for case evaluation, set up to implement the Youth Authority notion of a centralized authority which makes differential treatment assignments or to facilitate the functioning of a diversified network of services. Observed activities, tests, and individual case studies in such centers all contribute to the final evaluations. There has been considerable development of knowledge and skill in this work. Where diagnostic and reception centers exist, they are, in effect, allotted a portion of the court's disposition decision through statutory or administrative assignment.

Mention might be made of another type of disposition evaluation agency: there are places where a clinic is assigned statutory responsibility for determining whether a child of retarded mental development belongs at home, in a regular class, or in a specialized class.

The line between brief screening and the disposition evaluation ceases to be quite so sharp as one turns away from these specialized disposition agencies. There are, in fact, many gradations of evaluation a necessary consequence of the variety of relationships which community agencies have with those whose cases are "found." For example, the schools' child health stations, welfare departments, voluntary social agencies, hospitals, clinics, and settlement houses do not meet all their obligations or make their full contributions through brief screening of all cases to which they are alerted. Our studies show that agency failures, the disappearance of cases in the gaps between agencies, the "opportunities lost" are sometimes traceable to instances in which agencies in this category do not follow their case finding with adequate case appraisal—because it is not dictated by their functions, narrowly conceived.

These agencies are often staffed by highly skilled personnel (the family agencies or child guidance clinics, for example) or by personnel whom it would not be too difficult to prepare for the necessary evaluations. Their relationships with families and their access to information is generally such that they are well situated to go beyond brief screening if the first, brief appraisal is not fully reassuring. This is not a proposal for anything as elaborate as a probation case study, since the client in question comes into focus at a point when the agency has a good deal of background data about the family or another of its members. Moreover, since the objects of the case finding usually do not, at this point, regard themselves as in need of service, they are not prepared to have their family's relationship with the agency formally converted into a case study process. What is possible, however, is the study of data already in the record and the systematic addition of available observations and reports. These become the basis for a sound referral decision or a decision, in the instance of the family service agency or guidance clinic, to offer service to a member of the family who is not the original "client."

Where the majority of staff are poorly prepared, as in many public assistance programs, or where the professional time allocated by a specialist is too limited to permit much time for this role, as in the case of the pediatrician in a busy child health station, the responsibility for evaluation and follow-through might be assigned a qualified social worker within the department. Case consultants or social service staff members, whatever their titles, undertake the agency's disposition evaluation where the brief screening of the original agency observer (case finder) indicates that it is necessary. School social workers are formally assigned this function, providing more complete evaluations of cases which the classroom teacher screens out.

Since it will probably be the situation for some time to come that there will be disposition agencies without access to staff capable of providing all the essential disposition evaluations, and since some disposition evaluations require quite specialized (clinical, medical) judgments, special facilities will continue to be necessary. New York City's Family Court, for example, makes use of social and psychiatric study reports prepared at the court's request in detention, psychiatric reports from its own clinic or (at times) community clinics, medical and psychiatric reports from hospitals with observation facilities, reports from social agencies and special school services. A sound community plan should certainly always ensure availability of such centers which, at the request of an agency with disposition responsibility, provide necessary case evaluations to guide disposition. Planning, however, should seek to ensure that an agency with a substantial disposition function is equipped with staff adequate to its primary task even though it should not be expected to have all the specialized resources needed to appraise some of its cases.

As has been emphasized, recommendations appended to a case evaluation must be based on a realistic appraisal of facilities available. One might add that this imposes an obligation upon those who prepare such evaluations and recommendations, as well as on legally constituted disposition authorities like judges, to keep personally acquainted with the resources on which they draw.

Two major problems cause concern in this field. First, far too many cases are disposed of without access to adequate case evaluations. Second, current disposition recommendations deal more adequately with personality dimensions than they do with socio cultural dimensions, or even medical factors, which should affect case planning. Before it can be solved, the former problem will require staff and resource expansion as well as changes in philosophy in many agencies. It will also demand certain administrative and professional-role decisions best discussed in the context of individual programs. (For example: The comprehensiveness of a probation officer's case evaluation is affected by what the judge routinely does with such evaluations; the likelihood that a home relief investigator will be concerned with the development of children will reflect agency philosophy.) The second problem, that of the dimensions of case evaluations, will be affected by the rate at which broader concepts of social deviance are incorporated into training programs and begin to be understood in their treatment implications.

Case evaluations to guide service and treatment. Complaints are often heard from clinics or institutions which accept referral cases to the effect that the disposition evaluation sent by the referral source was not adequate and that they have had to undertake their own intake studies. Or the referring agencies have reported that the agencies accepting cases for treatment have not respected them and their social studies and have duplicated the work. Such complaints are sometimes justified, but they are frequently based on misunderstanding as to the nature of the case evaluation which guides an agency's services or treatment.

The children's institution must decide which cottage is appropriate for a committed child and must also assign him to a school or vocational program. Decisions must be made relative to possible casework or psychiatric plans and assignments as well. These are decisions which can be made only in the institution and on the basis of data assembled by institution staff acquainted with the prevailing treatment philosophy, bases for decisions, and current status of resources and workloads. Reformatories and prisons know that (depending on size) they require classification staff or classification units, to plan for maximum impact of program on inmates.

Similarly, a child guidance clinic which accepts a case on referral from the school cannot avoid some case study and evaluation as the basis for decisions which only it can make relative to case assignment, frequency of interviews, whether the parents are to be seen regularly and by the same staff member, whether group therapy is to be included in the program, and so on.

This suggests, then, that it is not only the case finding agency and the case disposition agency which must be staffed for case evaluation. Almost every service center, treatment agency, or institution must begin its work with a treatment-oriented case evaluation, incorporating the dimensions relevant to the program unless its peculiar relationships with the referral sources assure it of the required evaluation (as when a guidance clinic and residential treatment center are under one administrative auspices) or (as in the instance of Youth Authority programs) unless it is part of a system of facilities which receive their cases through one diagnostic and screening center.

Some comments on case classification. In a sense, the case evaluation process is one aimed at case classification, the assumption being that cases of a certain class are best dealt with in specified ways. While such classification may be too much to expect of some personnel at the level of the brief screening decisions, it is obviously the objective, the only reasonable objective, of disposition evaluations and of case evaluations made to guide service. Part of the difficulty in children's services today derives from the lack of an adequate case classification system, sometimes called case typology, to guide case evaluation. There has been some tendency to act as though psychiatric diagnostic categories might serve this purpose, but study reveals that (*a*) psychiatric diagnostic systems, particularly in the children's field, are terribly inconsistent and are very much in need of codification to permit reasonable communication; (*b*) psychiatric diagnostic systems do not incorporate all dimensions essential to treatment decisions; children in a given diagnostic category might require a variety of disposition plans in view of factors not taken into account in the diagnostic labeling. This is not an unexpected finding, since diagnostic systems have, traditionally, been based in theory about etiology.

Resource Location and Case Referral

In a responsible community system, case finding and case study must lead either to a decision that nothing more need be done or to the location of a resource which will intervene or offer service or treatment. Moreover, client and resource must be brought together (referral) in a fashion which ensures that something constructive may begin.

While this phase of service flows naturally after case evaluation, it requires special attention and deserves it own name because of its characteristic problems. In addition, there do exist agencies and bureaus which devote all, or substantial portions of, their resources to this effort, and they deserve notice, i.e., a children's placement division in a child welfare department or a placement unit in a probation department.

One cannot, with any conscience, end the process at the point of diagnosis or screening. Somebody (and more often than not it will be the case evaluation agency) must translate an appraisal into its service implications: Who can offer the help required? In the real world of waiting lists and shortages in all categories of facilities, the problem becomes one of locating the resource which is available at the time needed and which meets the basic conditions specified in the case appraisal. A community—and there are far too many—in which shortages and gaps are so severe as to make this a hopeless process is, of course, not equipped for effective work with its children.

The service-planning agency or unit which closes a case or uses an inappropriate service because "no treatment resources are available" must immediately list the case as a community failure. Its minimum obligation is a regular report to the community on the frequency of such occurrences. Some agencies assume the broader obligation to help fill community gaps.

In work with deprived, troubled, fearful, and disturbed people, it is never enough to identify a resource and provide child or parent with a referral card. The agency has the obligation of working with those who are being referred until they understand the objectives of the referral on whatever level is possible and are motivated to establish the new contact. The client's perception should then be conveyed to the agency itself in an appropriate summary. Such preparation, often a function of skillful social casework, is equally necessary when a child, whatever his attitudes, will be taken physically to a new facility (an institution). Our institutions are full of those who "do time" and who perceive themselves as community exiles; they have not been oriented in advance to the potentials of the program and do not understand why they have been committed. In fact, misunderstanding is often so extreme or resistance so completely neglected by referral or committing sources as to make success most unlikely.

Where resources are in short supply, competitive "shopping" as between agencies or between staff members in one agency may become a serious problem. It can be dealt with appropriately only if *community* priorities are identified, through the work of planning and coordinating bodies, and are translated into agency policy. Centralized community child placement or assignment of centralizing responsibility within each of the major placement agencies (i.e., court) would seem to be an essential part of planning.

Service planning, resource location, and case referral are functional areas in which many of the current community problems lie. Solutions must be based on responsible use of resources and responsible relationships between agencies; adequate agency reporting of gaps and difficulties to one another, as well as to coordinating groups and to the community at large; accountability of the agency and of the practitioner for the individual case, until the transition is made from case evaluation to necessary service.

Intervention, Service and Treatment

No one word encompasses the variety of action prescriptions to which situation finding and case evaluation lead. Perhaps three words may suffice to describe the range of possibilities: intervention, service, treatment. At times, only neighborhood organization or work with local youth gangs will do. At other times, a small group, a child, or a family may need to be assured of service (vocational guidance, a homemaker, etc.) or treatment (individual or group psychotherapy, etc.).

The costly activities involved in large-scale case finding, court hearings, social studies, diagnostic referrals, and the like may have secondary "social control" functions, i.e., showing community concern for and reaction to certain behavior. Apart from police protective work, however, they cannot be defended solely as such. The community's investment in these functions is not repaid unless this elaborate process, of finding problems and sorting those to be ignored from those requiring attention, is capped by adequate investment in well-used services and facilities. The skilled practitioner in these fields has no basis for satisfaction in the competence of his performance unless his diagnosis and recommendations lead somewhere. *Intervention* is a convenient generic term which suggests service, treatment, community planning, and social action.

To talk of a service and treatment armamentarium implies a degree of necessary diversification to meet a variety of relevant factors such as age, sex, degree of involvement, nature of causal factors, special resources required, family and community strengths and resources, a decision to intervene on the family, the peer-group, or the neighborhood level, and the like. Inevitably, as skill and knowledge develop, new methods are discovered and new considerations enter into the choice of form of intervention. A community pattern of diversified service and treatment resources is, therefore, an ever-changing and a never-completed pattern.

The following random illustrative list incorporates *some* of the facilities and activities now important to an urban area as it seeks to ensure, either under its own auspices, or through county and state resources as well, the range of required interventions, treatment, and service specializations:

1. family service agencies
2. child guidance clinics
3. general medical facilities and clinics
4. homemakers and home helps
5. mental hospital facilities and clinics, including so-called day hospitals and night hospitals
6. child welfare services

7. foster homes of various kinds
8. group day care and day care homes
9. institutions of several kinds, including training schools
10. residential treatment centers
11. forestry and work camps
12. youth residence clubs and hostels
13. probation and parole
14. big brother and big sister programs
15. special school programs for children with handicaps or particular needs
16. vocational guidance and placement resources
17. religious counseling
18. recreation and group work facilities, as well as the variety of resources in settlements and neighborhood centers
19. summer camps of several kinds
20. educational guidance resources
21. local self-help programs and neighborhood "mobilizations," with a variety of primary objectives

Resources such as these are required by many children, normal and maladjusted, not only those "in trouble" in the sense of this discussion. Reasons of efficiency as well as cost dictate that there not be separate systems of service in these categories (residential treatment and educational guidance, to take two very different examples). Whether policy or treatment considerations justify any segregation by categories into treatment facilities (court clinics, training schools for delinquents, institutions for the neglected) is best examined in the context of discussion of the specific programs.

Our basic attitude is that the detection channels must be alert to categories and circumstances under which need arises, but that the intervention system should be one diversified system in which need and potential impact, not label, determine assignment to a facility.

Emphasis on the community's entire range of service equipment and its adequate diversification places an obligation on the individual agency, whether public or private, to identify its unique role and to relate that role to changing needs and knowledge. An agency asking for support from individual donors or out of tax funds surely has no right to perpetuate services unless they are constantly validated, in the sense of being shown to be needed in the community pattern and to be effective. An agency is called upon to define and publicize its special treatment or service offerings, so that it may be drawn upon as clients' treatment-service prescriptions dictate.

We do not wish to imply that an agency is, alone, in a position to relate itself to total need or to find its place in the community resource pattern. Planning and integration functions are essential to the community, and these will be discussed below.

Reporting

Adequate data about clientele, their characteristics, their sources and dispositions, as well as caseload and staffing facts, should be regularly provided by individual agencies to the community and to other agencies. Some agencies have unfortunately been quite lax about this responsibility; others have sought to publish statistical reports regularly but have used outmoded systems, so that crucial questions are not answerable. Many large children's courts, for example, tabulate cases but do not tabulate the number of different children who appear before the court, do not record many kinds of data essential to analysis of clientele and operations, and use statistical methods which do not allow for analysis of interrelationships of factors which are tabulated (i.e., the relation between length of probation treatment and status at discharge).

The availability of statistical reports on a regular basis permits those concerned to keep informed of the size and characteristics of the problem faced and the resources being deployed to meet it.

Caseload data, data about overcrowding, waiting-list facts also serve to highlight some of the indications of unmet need and inadequate service. If the agency adds its own evaluation and analysis to this, the picture is enriched and the report makes significant contributions to community planning and improvement of services.

To all of this, however, must be addea a new concept: the obligation in certain situations to report at the point of case-closing. An agency that has accepted a referral or commitment and thereby has become the community's representative in dealing with a person who may harm himself or others is accountable to the community. Some central registration source, or, in the absence of such source, the referring agency, must know that the case is being closed following a period of what is judged to be satisfactory service, or that a client has "disappeared," "refused to cooperate," or simply has not shown improvement. When warranted, designated steps should then be taken to initiate a new attempt, to watch the situation, or to agree that nothing more will be done.

More specifically, if a boy is discharged by a court because he has begun voluntary treatment at a guidance clinic, the clinic has no right to close the case subsequently, as a failure, without some community provision for returning the child to the court, informing the school, alerting the police, offering help through a community center, or making some other responsible plan for community protection and individual treatment. Similarly, particularly where legally constituted "authority" has planned treatment after adjudication, the record, in justice to the individual concerned, should report successful completion of a course of treatment.

While the concept seems clear, the development of practical mechanisms for reporting of this kind and for avoidance of undue regimentation of agencies or of individuals has not, to our knowledge, been undertaken for any large urban area. It must be said here that while special central registers have demonstrated their potentials for caseload analysis and community planning, they have not yet continued long enough or broadly enough for their full exploitation as instruments of case accountability.

Measurement Evaluation

The entire discussion so far has presented the case for periodic evaluation of both the total pattern and single agency services, but brief remarks may be in order at this point. The ultimate test of the impact of a community pattern of services is the test of effectiveness. Research specialists agree that the establishment of controls and specification of all aspects of the service "exposure" pose formidable methodological problems. There are consequently few significant studies that measure the successes of a single agency or of a community plan. The problem deserves and has achieved high priority status in agencies and research centers, however, and must remain in the forefront of attention.

While unable to do this kind of research, the typical agency has ongoing responsibility for self-evaluation, with particular attention to its flexibility in relation to changing needs, its staff qualifications, its relationships with other services, and its "failures" (in the sense described above). Beyond this, every community must, officially or by agreement, establish responsibility for constant review and appraisal of the total community pattern of services and its component parts. There is precedent for initiative in this area on the part of community chests and councils, public bodies, and independent groups concerned with child welfare. Using the methods most appropriate to the situation and the relationships involved, such evaluations reveal gaps, set the sights for the future, and help prepare public opinion for the expenditures involved in rendering service.

Service Integration, Planning and Coordination

Tradition, law, chance, knowledge, and logic have in various combinations determined the individual functions of agencies. Some undertake case finding, evaluation, and treatment. Others are limited to one or another function or, at least, to emphasis on certain activities. There is little difference of opinion about the function or combination of functions of some agencies, whereas others are surrounded by confusion and controversy. A community which is concerned with its approach to children in trouble must review the roles of its major agencies periodically. For example: What are appropriate functions for a juvenile aid bureau? Should a court clinic diagnose or also treat? Should "neglect" investigations be assigned the police, the welfare department, or a Society for the Prevention of Cruelty to Children? Is there a separate "attendance" function in a school system? Even if well defined, for internal purposes, agency programs are not well interrelated unless there is community-wide understanding and unless coordinating devices are developed. What, for example, might be done to solve particularly perplexing problems in the field of child placement which result from information lacks, from poor coordination, and from undefined intake criteria? Analysis of current community experiences gives emphasis to the need for the following:

1. devices to *integrate* the services of one agency with the other so as to ensure a concert of services on the level of case operations and to eliminate gaps between agencies as they affect the individual case;
2. means to interrelate agency functions and to *coordinate* their *programs*;
3. provision for evaluation and long-range *planning*, so that agencies adapt and change their functions and functioning, and new services are created as required;
4. *reporting and accountability* arrangements.

In the chapters which follow immediately no attempt is made to deal with all aspects of the services of schools, courts, institutions, or police to cite a few. At all points, the concern is with the community system as an accountable, integrated network with defined goals. How is such a system to be conceived? What is each agency's contribution? Does the concept of system demand changes in agencies or new types of programs?

2

Social Case Treatment and Problem of Youth

Introduction

Methods of Changing Attitudes and Habits.— The most effective and lasting adjustments are achieved through a change of attitudes and habits. But these are difficult to change because they are frequently deeply rooted, have an emotional significance to the person, and have validity and reason for their existence. As Dewey points out:

Habits are arts. They involve skill of sensory and motor organs, cunning or craft, and objective materials. They assimilate objective energies and eventuate in command of environment. They require order, discipline, and manifest technique. They have a beginning, middle and end.

A bad habit suggests an inherent tendency to action and also a hold, command over us. It makes us do things we are ashamed of, things which we tell ourselves we prefer not to do. It overrides our formal resolutions, our conscious decisions. When we are honest with ourselves we acknowledge that a habit has this power because it is so intimately a part of ourselves. It has a hold upon us because we are the habit. All habits are demands for certain kinds of activity; and they constitute the self. In any intelligible sense of the word will, they are will. They form our effective desires and they furnish us with our working capacities. They rule our thoughts, determining which shall appear and be strong and which shall pass from light into obscurity.

Recently a friend remarked to me that there was one superstition current among even cultivated persons. They suppose that if one is told what to do, if the right end is pointed to them, all that is required in order to bring about the right act is will or wish on the part of the one who is to act. He used as an illustration the matter of physical posture; the assumption is that if a man is told to stand up straight, all that is further needed is wish and effort on his part, and the deed is done. He pointed out that this belief is on a par with primitive magic in its neglect of attention to the means which are involved in reaching an end.

To reach an end we must take our mind off from it and attend to the act which is next to be performed. We must make that the end. The only way of accomplishing this discovery is through a flank movement. We must stop even thinking of standing up straight. To think of it is fatal, for it commits us to the operation and established habit of standing wrong. We must find an act within our power which is disconnected from any thought about standing. We must start to do another thing which on one side inhibits our falling into the customary bad position and on the other side is the beginning of a series of acts which may lead into the correct posture. The hard drinker who keeps thinking of not drinking is doing what he can to initiate the acts which lead to drinking. He is starting with the stimulus to his habit. To succeed he must find some positive interest or line of action which will inhibit the drinking series and which by instituting another course of action will bring him to his desired end. In short, the man's true aim is to discover some course of action, having nothing to do with the habit of drink or standing erect, which will take him where he wants to go. The discovery of this other series is at once his means and his end. Until one takes intermediate acts seriously enough to treat them as ends, one wastes one's time in any effort at change of habits. Of the intermediate acts, the most important is the next one. The first or earliest means is the most important end to discover.

Change of attitudes is rarely achieved through scolding, admonition, punishment, but rather through the child's experiences and his desire for change when he is helped to understand the necessity for change. When the social situation is not defined, we resort to the crude and ineffectual method which Thomas calls "'ordering-and-forbidding' that is, meeting a crisis by an arbitrary act of will decreeing the disappearance of the undesirable or the appearance of the desirable phenomena, and using arbitrary physical action to enforce the decree. This method corresponds exactly to the magical phase of natural technique." On the subject of punishment, Healy and his associates observe that while no one can deny the value and the correct psychology of unpleasurable returns as a means of checking misbehavior, and while One can hardly advocate threats or holding "a big stick" over an offender's head; yet there can be no doubt that in exceptional cases, where the delinquent does not respond to constructive and kindly effort, a vigorous warning may be of great value.

It is of much greater importance, however, that the more constructive but often neglected principle of reward and praise could be generously used to prevent delinquency. Reward and praise represent the positive aspect of treatment stimulus, the encouragement to right-doing rather than to mere repression of wrong-doing.

Undoubtedly reward as a method in reeducation has its disadvantages, since the child may become discouraged over the remoteness of the reward and the losses suffered in relapses of behavior. Particularly dangerous is the feeling which may arise that every good deed needs to be compensated.

In Aichhorn's opinion the most valuable method of changing attitudes of wayward youth is "talking together and aiding to understand the causes and effects of maladjustments and displaying an attitude of forgiveness toward even the worst offenses. This served us [as psychoanalyst in a house for wayward youth in Austria] well because we had the confidence of the children." He cites the following case as an illustration of one method to be used in reeducation:

The Case of A.— An eighteen-year-old boy, expelled from a military school for stealing from his comrades and who had stolen at home and elsewhere. After he had been with us for several months, I put him in charge of the tobacco shop. The employees each contributed a certain amount to buy their tobacco in common. I told the cashier to keep an eye on the boy without letting him know and to report to me when any money was missing. Four weeks later, he reported that about half the sum taken in weekly was missing. This seemed to be the right moment to expose the boy to an emotional shock in order to bring about catharsis, although I had no clear idea how I was going to do this. I inquired how he was getting along and gradually we approached the topic of the tobacco shop. "How much do you take in each week?" He mentioned a certain sum. We continued to dust the books. After a pause, "Does the money always come out right?" A hesitating "Yes" of which I took no further notice.

After another pause, "When do you have the most trade?" "In the morning." Then still later, "I must look in on you some time and go over your cash drawer." The boy was getting more restless all the time but I ignored it, went on working and kept coming back to the tobacco shop. When I felt that I had intensified his uneasiness sufficiently I suddenly brought the crisis to a head. " Well, when we get through here I'll go and take a look at your cash." We had been working together for about an hour and a quarter. He stood with his back to me, took a book from the shelf, and suddenly let it fall. Then I took cognizance of his excitement. "What's the matter?" "Nothing." "What's wrong with your cash?" His face became distorted with anxiety, and he stammered out the sum. Without saying a word I gave him this amount. He looked at me with an indescribable expression on his face and was about to speak. I would not let him talk because I felt that my action must have time to take effect and so I sent him away with a friendly gesture. About ten minutes later, he came back and laid the money on the table, saying "Let them lock me up. I don't deserve your help—I'll only steal again." He was greatly excited and was sobbing bitterly. I let him sit down and I began to talk to him. I did not preach, but listened sympathetically to what he poured out, his thievery, his attitude toward his family and to life in general, and everything that troubled him. The emotion gradually receded, relieved by the weeping and talking. Finally I gave the money back to him, saying that I did not believe he would steal again; that he was worth that much to me. I said too, that it was not a present, that he could smoke less and pay it back gradually. So that no one should know about this, however, he had better put the money back in the cash drawer. I told the cashier that the amount had been returned and that he need take no notice of the affair. In the course of the next two months, the money was actually returned.

It is not improbable that the contrast in emotion from fear to relief brought about the solution. Practically the treatment was effective; in the short time he stayed with us, he conducted himself well. Later he was employed as a draughtsman in a furniture factory and acquitted himself creditably. In this case we had succeeded in arousing a strong emotion in him and in making use of it in his retraining. We must wait for further experience with this method to see in which cases it is applicable as a special technique.

The Case of Arline Watkins.—The case of Arline Watkins is a good illustration of how a well-established habit of stealing was overcome in a girl through kindness, confidence, provision of attractive clothes, sweets, wholesome amusements, and particularly those things for which the child had a secret longing; through fostering a sense of responsibility, a feeling of being a grown-up, and by building stronger personality traits through encouragement, response, and recognition. Gaining a new name with its implication of new personality was a powerful motive.

In this case a girl who was well on the road to becoming a "wild child," homeless, living from moment to moment, responding to every possible impulse, sustaining few of the tensions which social living requires, was converted into a responsive, adjusted well-balanced child amenable to the requirements of family life.

Petition filed in August of 1935 by the San Pedro Police Department— Juvenile Bureau. The child had been known to the Bureau on more than five separate occasions, after having been apprehended for burglary, stealing suitcases, and money; and on the occasion of the last theft of $60, her partner, a boy, was also filed on. The parents have been inefficient and disinterested; although repeatedly warned against it, they have allowed the child to roam the streets at all hours; and she had been selling newspapers. She has been described by the San Pedro Police as a "regular bandit." The neighbors have made numerous complaints to the police, who feel that nothing further can be done by their department, as the child needs supervision which cannot be given in that home. She was brought to the attention of the police several times when her uncle reported her missing. The first time she was found at midnight by the soldiers at Fort McArthur, sleeping in a truck. Later, in the company of a boy, she took a suitcase and other articles valued at $31; on the occasion of the $60 theft, she and the boy had seen a ring on a dresser through a bedroom window. He helped her open the screen, and she went in, found a wallet in the top drawer of the dresser, and took it, but did not take the ring. The boy took the wallet from her, and went to his own home. He later spent part of the money, but Arline spent none of it.

Report of Juvenile Hall Clinic

Physical Examination.— General physical appearance good. Small denuded area on lower lip, probably a herpes (cold sore). Throat slightly inflamed. Temperature 100 degrees at 11 A.M. Hymen edges inflamed, but no evidences of gonorrhea. Hymen not ruptured. Wassermann negative. Smears U—negative.

Psychological Examination.— Stanford-Binet. Physical age 10:6; mental age 8:4. I.Q. 79. Border-line or dull normal. Reads fairly well, but too slowly to pass the ten-year test. Very poor memory. Unable to give the day, month, or year correctly. Fails ninth-year arithmetic problems badly. Poor comprehension, necessary to repeat most questions; follows directions poorly.

Behavior Report (from Juvenile Hall Hospital).— The patient is apparently an untrained child who has grown up without constructive influences, or any environmental advantages. She seems crude and somewhat sophisticated. Has an independent manner, and has no doubt been much "on her own" without supervision. From the child's manner and statements it is inferred that she runs about as she pleases, without supervision or plans for her leisure time. Has been associated with various stealing episodes, but has ready alibis or excuses which show her incidental connection with these escapades. She has in all probability felt much deprivation in the home, has lacked satisfactions, and has reacted to this by unconsciously seeking other compensations, which have proved socially unacceptable.

Social History and Home Conditions (mother's statement).— Arline and her oldest brother, Fred, are the woman's children by a former marriage. Their father died after an operation when Arline was two months old. Woman married not long afterwards, and there are three children by the second marriage. Mother's statement and Arline's agree on the stepfather's behavior. He is continuously drinking, and very often brings drunken men into the home; demands food at all hours for himself and his drunken friends; is very ugly toward woman and children; curses a great deal; is untidy about his person and about the house; is so rough and unreasonable with the children that they dread being at home when he is there. Woman's relatives come only when they do not expect him to be there. He is suspicious of woman and often accuses her of being immoral with other men, and threatening to take the children from her, though she cannot understand why he would want them, when he is so abusive toward them. Woman has several times left her husband, but comes back on promises of good behavior, which are never kept. She has had him before the San Pedro City Prosecutor on charges of nonsupport, but his contributions to the family's support have always been very irregular, despite his regular $75 per month income from work in the lumber yards. Spends much money on liquor, and some on other women. Mother feels helpless to cope with Arline's stealing and other bad habits.

In September, 1934, Arline was placed on probation in the home of her maternal grandmother in San Pedro, with her mother's home only a short distance away. In December, 1934, she, in company with a seven-year-old boy, entered the Richfield Warehouse, and took from the open safe $35, much of which was recovered. Further contact with all relatives showed none able to assume the responsibility. As the stepfather and mother were again living together, the child was returned to them after the hearing. In July, 1935, Arline was brought to court on a new petition. She had remained away from home the greater part of the night, in the company of three boys, aged twelve and thirteen years. The children had broken into a garage, stolen a rifle valued at $5; the same day they had broken into a store, and took canned goods valued at $5; they then went to a garage at the rear of a court, where they slept all night. However, no physical injury seems to have ever befallen the child at the hands of the boys with whom she played. She herself was more like a boy than a girl in mannerisms and behavior. When asked once if she wasn't afraid one of the boys would hurt her sometime, she replied that they wouldn't dare so much as lay a hand on her.

At the hearing that followed the last escapades, boarding home placement was recommended and she was placed with Mrs. Florence Jones of Long Beach. She is still there, and making a very remarkable adjustment.

She is happy, and shows signs of improvement in many ways. The school reports that the child is doing as well as she is mentally capable of. The only outstanding trouble has been bed-wetting and soiling clothes, which is gradually being corrected. There has been backsliding at times, but on the whole continuous progress. She still tells some stories, and is a bit careless about her person, but there is a marked improvement. Arline has adopted the name of her foster mother, and calls herself "Arline Jones," and arranged for the school records to be changed accordingly on the approval of Mrs. Jones and the probation officer. Her mother is a little hurt by this change of name, but it seems to have had an excellent effect on Arline. She thinks of herself now as a different person, and occasionally says, "Well, when I was Arline I could do that, but since I am Arline Jones, I can't."

Interviewed Mrs. Jones, boarding mother; also Arline. Mrs. Jones states that she has had Arline with her since August, 1935, and has noticed improvement all along the line. At present, Mrs. Jones has only two girls with her, both aged thirteen years. During the past year, she has had also two older girls, but they were there only for a short time.

Only once since her arrival has Arline been known to take anything that did not belong to her. Shortly after her arrival, the girl was visiting Mrs. Jones's married daughter, who lives near by. On this occasion, the daughter was making a quilt of some very pretty material. A few days later, a square of the material was found among Arline's personal belongings in the bedroom. When questioned, she repeatedly denied knowing anything about the material, where it came from, and how it had got into the girls' bedroom. After the foster mother had failed to get any response but denials, Mr. Jones talked with her long and earnestly, telling her how much they were trying to help her, and the trouble that comes of stealing. She seemed to be touched by his kindly manner, and cried, but still did not admit the theft. Then Mrs. Jones said, "Now, Arline, we aren't going to say anything more about this mistake that you have made. Just take the cloth and go back to the place where you got it, and lay it down where you found it. You needn't say anything at all to the lady, and she will understand." The daughter reported to her mother that little Arline entered the house and laid the material on the sewing machine, where it had been on the day of the child's visit. The incident was never again mentioned to Arline.

The little girl has been several times taken into stores by Mr. and Mrs. Jones, turned loose and told to look around at things, but to keep her hands in her pockets, if necessary, to keep from picking up things. If she saw something that she felt she had to have, and couldn't get along without, to come to them and tell them about it. If they could possibly afford to get it for her, they would; if not, they would get her as good a substitute as they could afford. On several occasions, they have had to buy for her attractive clothes that had caught her eye in stores, but the urge to steal seems to have been conquered. Temptation is removed in many ways. Fruit and the wholesome candies and sweets are kept in the house at all times, and given in moderation to the children; ice cream is frequently bought. Other things that they desire may be had as rewards of good behavior and something to work for. The children go to shows once a week, but just recently have they been allowed to go alone in the afternoon. This they consider a great honor, and quite grown-up.

The girls' bedroom opens into the hall, and until a short time ago, it was always kept open. Now the door may be closed at night on good behavior. If they have misbehaved, it is a sign that they are still just children, and must be watched over at night, so the door is left open. They both feel the disgrace now if the door is left open some night because of what they have done that day. Washing dishes is a special privilege.

The most persistent habit of Arline's has been bed-wetting over the entire period of her stay. Although it has decreased considerably, it has not been stopped, despite the fact that almost everything imaginable has been tried. Her physical examination shows no particular weakness that would account for it, and when she is promised some very special privilege for not wetting the bed for an entire week, she seldom does. Mrs. Jones has tried to shame her, deprived her of privileges, and talked with her about the extra work that she made her boarding mother, who was already very busy. About two weeks before the visit, Mrs. Jones, wearied and discouraged, told Arline that she was tired of continually having to wash out clothing after a thirteen- year-old girl, and that hereafter all clothing soiled by Arline would have to be washed out by Arline, and that the girl would have to take money from her savings to buy her own soap. This was a bitter ordeal, and probably hurt the boarding mother more even than the girl, who cried long and loudly while washing the clothing. But this drastic measure seemed to make her realize the amount of work that bed-wetting did cause, and the soiling of clothing has since been almost nil.

Both children go by the name of "Jones" providing that they live up to the good name of that family. They are told that the Jones family is well known and respected in the community and the children that are known as theirs must be a credit to them. They are very proud of their new name.

Children who have stolen because of an acquisitive impulse not too seriously complicated with other factors should not be deprived of their pocket money, as is frequently done, since the deprivation often gives them an added incentive to steal. It may seem paradoxical to advocate that their allowance be increased. Burt observes that "the readiest way to cure the robber is to use him with unexpected generosity; give him, not only pennies to spend, but sixpences to save and a cash box of his own to lock them in. Ownership is the best school of responsibility and faithfulness."

Older boys and girls may be given opportunities at home to earn more and more as their needs increase. If they work outside the home and earn, definite but reasonable arrangements should be made to their satisfaction as to how much should be saved, how much should be contributed to the family exchequer, and how much retained for pocket money.

Sweets, toys, clothes, amusements, special coveted articles, should be provided by adults, as far as possible, in large enough amounts to overcome any impulse to acquire them illegitimately. Where financial circumstances do not allow purchases of articles not absolutely necessary for maintenance they can be made at home. Though crude in form they may have more meaning, when properly interpreted and made with the assistance of the young, than many ready-made articles.

When a child has made a genuine attempt to conquer his habit of stealing he should be generously rewarded for it. The reward is more than a material gain; it also means heightening his status and self-respect.

Methods of Dealing with Lies.— The act of lying is not the chief concern of the case worker. His real concern should be "Why did the person lie?" It is often a healthy thing to ask oneself: "What have I done to cause the offender to lie to me or to be afraid of me?" It seems almost too trite to repeat that the basis for lying, as for other unadjustments, can be traced to other more fundamental and deeper underlying causal factors. Few people lie simply for the sake of lying. At times, no lie is intended. The person may possess only partial knowledge of facts; he may have a tendency to generalize too broadly. His memory might have tricked him or he may have made the wrong mental associations.

If the worker is concerned chiefly with personalities, the products of psychological metabolism, he will be interested in the inconsistency of the account only in so far as it indicates that the offender has or has not fully revealed his attitudes. Professor Lindeman remarks:

> *Even if the answers are false, they may serve to define the ultimate conclusions. In fact, the psychiatrist who makes inquiries of his subject does not anticipate true replies, but he nevertheless makes use of such responses as he receives. What is in a person's "mind" may or may not be true but it is the sum total of his rationalizations upon which his life has proceeded. If he acts upon the basis of these rationalizations, they are in so far significant in explaining his behavior.*

The interviewer must distinguish between (1) lies as defense mechanisms; (2) pathoformic lies; (3) conventional lies or so-called white lies; (4) lies due to mental conflict; (5) seeming lies which arise in differences in point of view regarding matters; (6) accidental lies, due to tricks of memory, illusions; (7) lies due to a desire to control the situation. Professor Cooley says:

Even telling the truth does not result so much from a need of mental accuracy, though this is strong in some minds, as from a sense of the unfairness of deceiving people of our own sort, and of the shame of being detected in so doing. Consequently the maxim, "Truth for friends and lies for enemies," is very generally followed, not only by savages and children, but, more or less openly, by civilized people. Most persons feel reluctant to tell a lie in so many words, but few have any compunctions in deceiving by manner, and the like, persons toward whom they feel no obligation. "Conscience is born of love" in this as in many matters. A thoughtful observer will easily see that injustice and not untruth is the essence of lying, as popularly conceived.

Aichhorn states that no child is absolutely trustworthy, so we must weigh his statements carefully:

> *We do not yet know whether he told the truth. The statements of delinquents should always be checked. However, when we catch a child in a lie, we should not shame him. Expressions such as "You lie," "You must tell the truth," should always be avoided. It is much more efficacious to act as if the child had made a mistake. We can say, for example, "Are you sure you meant what you said?", "Now think a minute," or "Take your time; tell me again," etc.*

Cyril Burt has given a very comprehensive discussion of the analysis of children's lies and their prevention:

> *The telling of untruths is a frequent reproach, not only against habitual delinquents, but also against children not otherwise unprincipled. "One of my pupils is an incorrigible story-teller. What am I to do with him?" The appeal is a common one, and the first reply is another question: "What kind of stories does he tell?" Children's falsehoods are of many forms, and the treatment differs with the type. ... Here it is not with moral but with psychological distinctions that we have to do. Classed by their underlying causes, we may recognize at least six or seven varieties, all broadly distinguishable, yet running imperceptibly the one into the other.*

1. There is, first, what may be named the playful lie. Tiny children are full of make-believe: "Let's pretend" is their favorite game, and much of their amusement owes its charm to a passing or a partial self-deception.

2. There is, secondly, the lie of confusion. Children are exceedingly suggestible. They see little disparity between a fact that is real and a fancy that is vivid. What they have genuinely witnessed gets easily jumbled in their minds with what they have simply imagined or what they have merely been told. All such misstatements are to be dealt with for what they really are accidental errors or illusions and not downright untruths....

3. "The lie of vanity." Lies designed to attract self-notice. Such lies may range all the way from the empty but straightforward boasting of the braggart boy, to the subtler and more highly colored romances of the self-centered semi-neurotic, sensation-mongering girl; they merge, at an older stage still, into the baseless complaints of persecution or illness made by the truly hysterical. They express wishes, not perceptions, and are frequently the impulsive utterance of fancies that have long been dwelt upon in daydreams. The most morbid form consists in false self-accusations, in the bogus confession of imaginary misdeeds that have been neither performed nor intended.

4. Graver still lies where the object is not to extol or magnify one-self, but to belittle, annoy, or even endanger another the lie of malevolence and revenge. Where a serious charge is falsely laid, the outcome may be tragical. Sometimes the persons so traduced are the very ones who have been nearest and dearest to the child. Sometimes, too, the statement—not infrequently an accusation of a sexual assault seems so foreign to the thoughts of a healthy child and the childish denouncer herself seems so guileless, plausible, and innocent, that credence is given at once without inquiry. As a rule, after careful exploration, some analogous experience in the past, hidden or half forgotten, can generally be brought to light, and may be shown to have provided a basis for the calumny, though the doings or sayings recollected have been fastened, for private and malignant motives, upon a person entirely guiltless.

5. In most of the foregoing examples, harmless and heinous alike, the child is often self-deceived as well as

deceiving. In the excusive or exculpatory lie, the child is acutely conscious of deception. The purpose is usually plain.

There is something done or something left undone for which the dissembler is anticipating blame. Such lies, in the main, are not constructive fictions but negative disavowals or denials. Most thieves lie to cover up their wrongdoings, and nearly every offender will perjure himself over the offenses which with him are most habitual or for which he has been constantly condemned. But even among the honest and obedient, there are few who have not upon occasion proffered a false explanation for being late, for forgetting an errand, or for breaking a cherished vase.

6. In the more hardened and unprincipled, the positive line is exploited no longer as a fear-stricken excuse, but as an audacious pretext—no longer to shirk punishment, for what is past, but to gain profit or pleasure in the near future. Cheating at games and at lessons is the commonest and perhaps the least objectionable form of what may be termed the selfish lie. Where the lie is deliberately manufactured as an instrument to some further offense, the practice becomes more reprehensible. "Mother says will you please lend her a penny for the gas meter," is a favorite ruse for fraudulently obtaining a coin. The begging tales of the young delinquent are, as we have noted, at times most elaborately woven, and the wiles of the juvenile swindler are often miracles of ingenuity. One curious feature, making it harder than ever to detect the lie and to visit justice upon the liar, is to be found in a result well recognized, namely, that the habitual imposter may lose all sense that he is simulating and grow to believe implicitly in the truth of his inventions. Frequently he is himself his own most perfect dupe.

7. Lies of loyalty and convention are not uncommon among older children. In the elementary school the spirit of a sportsman like comradeship which prevents one child betraying another to an elder is not so general as in the public school, and everywhere it seems rarer among girls than among boys and older youths. To keep up a joint or completed lie is much easier for male conspirators than for

female. To girlish lips it is the lie courteous rather than the lie of allegiance that comes with greatest readiness.

Conventions differ greatly in different social classes, and just as the poorer classes are sometimes shocked by what seem to them the shams and hypocrisies of their betters, so the so-called better classes regard as indefensible untruths and shameless falsehoods what are no more than traditional tactics tactics quite justifiable in the eyes of the humble diplomats themselves, when they feel themselves confronted by an inquisitive stranger from an alien social sphere.

Lying, then, takes countless shapes and has a thousand different motives. It may be employed to compensate for almost any form of intellectual weakness. It may be inspired by almost any emotion by fear more than any other, but also by greed, anger, self-display, submissiveness, and even by mistaken loyalty and affection.

1. Differential Treatment.— In dealing with a particular lie uttered by a particular child, the first step is to ascertain whether that lie is a single isolated lapse or one of a numerous series; if the latter, it becomes important to inquire what type of lies he generally tells and what may be their animating motive. One lie does not make a liar. All children tell occasional untruths, and many have fits and periods of dissembling. The sense of systematic truthfulness comes late.

Different forms of falsehood call for very different remedies. As a rule, what has to be attacked is not the lying, but some deeper trouble in the background, and this may vary from child to child. To treat the lie as a simple, self-subsistent mode of perversity, to scold and castigate the liar each time he is found out, will seldom purge him of his tricks; it will only teach him a sharper cunning for the future. Accordingly, the basis of every lie must be explored before the lie itself is dealt with.

2. Avoid Provocative Occasions.— Both the incipient and the habitual liar must be protected from situations setting too great a tax on their intelligence and candor. A regular

thief who has been as regularly punished for his thefts should never be questioned as the sole source of information and thus presented with a gratuitous chance to tell yet another untruth. So far as possible, all lies must be immediately detected; the first exculpatory falsehood that a child happens to palm off with success is often the starting point of a long series of deceptions, each cooler and more calculated than the last. Never let the child see you are uncertain whether he is speaking the truth or not. Rather throw the uncertainty to him; let the blusterer feel puzzled whether you may not be laughing at him in your heart for a bluff so silly and transparent. Equip yourself beforehand with conclusive evidence; never challenge him on the strength of pure suspicion, trusting, from a downcast head, a stammer or a blush, a shifting eye, or a brazen stare, to detect his consciousness of guilt. Should you, indeed, be doubtful allow him the doubt's benefit, accepting what he says with punctilious civility, just as you would accept the statements of an equal. Treat the deceiver just as though he were trustworthy and you may shame him out of his deceit. Grant him, therefore, the fullest credit for every particle of fact his fabrications may contain, with the dictum of the practiced charlatan always in mind.

3. Confession.— No punishment should follow a confession. To extort an admission publicly, in the face of the whole class or in front of the injured party, is to make that admission insuperably hard and a shuffle irresistibly easy. As a means of eliciting facts, the practice of urging a clean breast of things should be abandoned.

It is amazing how almost every teacher and parent expect the most hardened little sinners still to tell the truth about their sins—as if a lie were the last and worst offense the child could fall to instead of the easiest and the first. Should a child be bad enough to steal, he is almost certain to be bad enough to equivocate about his theft, when taxed with it outright. And once he has begun to delude you, a barrier is set up and any free and friendly discussion about his general situation becomes all but impossible. In the rare case of a frank or voluntary avowal, the outlook is most hopeful. With the remainder, it should be almost an unbroken rule never to begin with a direct interrogation—"Did you or did you not take that sixpence?" For thus asking the child to own to his undisclosed misdeeds, there is but one justification; it might be put to the culprit in such terms as these, though it is better expressed by an attitude than by an argument; "You and I have been friends hitherto. We can remain friends no longer if you are conscious of misleading me and I am conscious of mistrusting you. Let us each be unreserved and open, so that we may start afresh on the same happy basis as before. I am asking you to tell the truth, not because I am too lazy or too stupid to get decisive proof myself, much less I am asking you to bear witness against yourself that I may then reproach and punish you. My only motive is that I may understand you better. Friends have no secrets from each other not even shameful ones. And if everybody lied to everybody else, society would be impossible and all intimacy poisoned." At times in seeking a confidence it is wise to disarm a possible dread beforehand by saying, plainly and explicitly: "You need not answer if you do not wish ..."

The utmost discretion must be used as to when to expect an acknowledgement of guilt. Demand it too soon, and the agitated conscience, all eager to disown the misdeed even to itself, may be hustled into a lie it never for one moment meant to tell. Defer it too long, and the child may feel that, after all, the blame has not been brought home to him, and in reply to some more hasty questioner, he may have committed himself to a denial already and may not think it too late to retract.

4. The Encouragement of Confidence.— With young children truthfulness is at first no more than loyalty to persons, a return of gratitude to those who are sympathetic and kind to their mothers, to their favorite teachers, to their closest companions and friends. Children, like savages, feel that frankness and candor are precious gifts, pledges of affection, to be bestowed upon near and understanding comrades, and that a stranger, or an elder, or a representative of authority, is a sort of impersonal or potential enemy, an

alien and a spy, with no title to the free exchange of confidence, an inquisitor whose entrapping questions are rightly countered with an equal craft.

Should any form of rebuke or punishment seem necessary the best measure is not to stigmatize the child to his face as a liar, nor yet to thrash him there and then, much less to expatiate on how lie has pained you: it is rather to cur or cold-shoulder him (as you might any adult acquaintance whom you found dishonorable) until of his own accord he resolves to prove himself worthier of your trust and credence.

5. Literary Instruction.— ... With the young fabulist who is telling himself or others extravagant romances because his own life is so limited and dull, the best course is to enlarge and enrich his range of actual experiences. Let him learn that truth may be more thrilling and more entrancing, as well as stranger, than fiction. Travel, school journeys, visits to places of interest, will give him authentic matter to relate. With older children the over-active imagination may be given its needful grist through good fiction, good poetry and good romance.

6. Scientific Instruction.— Crude homilies on the sinfulness of lying are of small avail, and to cite the fate of Ananias may create more harm than holiness. The child should be led to understand what a baffling thing it is to formulate the precise and literal truth. The task of the truth teller is two-fold, first to know, and then to express. Each is a science in itself.

To the youthful mind, an ounce of scientific instruction and of linguistic practice is far more helpful and wholesome than any quantity of high-flown narrative or of trite and tedious moralizing.

7. The Avoidance of Pious Figments.— Finally, if you wish the child to tell no lies to you, have a scrupulous care to tell no fables to the child. Myths about Father Christmas, the all-seeing Eye, the origin of babies, and the riddle of the sex, should never be offered as facts to the young and sensitive inquirer. The strongest shock may ensue when

the child finds out that those whom he thought impeccable have told him tales about the most solemn of mysteries, and it is no more than a natural reaction should he start fabricating lies and legends of his own.

Pathological Lying.— Both Healy and Burt maintain that pathological liars are rare. Pathological lying, says Healy, is falsification entirely disproportionate to any discernible end in view, engaged in by a person who, at the time of observation, cannot definitely be declared insane, feeble-minded, or epileptic. Such lying rarely, if ever, centers about a single event; although exhibited in very occasional cases for a short time, it manifests itself most frequently by far over a period of years, or even a life time. It represents a trait rather than an episode.

At times workers will spend considerable time in checking and verifying information, or in attempts to change a person's attitude, in having him follow a particular course of action only to discover that they have been deceived at each step. While persistent and pathological liars are comparatively rare, they present perplexing problems, which, if undetected, will cause much concern and loss of time.

There is little that the general worker can do with pathological liars. They are subjects for psychiatrists and psychologists. However, he must be able to recognize the pathological liar and not waste time nor delay getting the patient into competent medical hands.

Redefinition of the Social Situation.— The cases of Milton M. and Dora J. are illustrations of successful treatment through rather striking redefinition of the social situation and vision of the workers handling the cases.

Case Study of Milton M.— Petition filed in behalf of Milton, fourteen years of age, arrested in company with another boy his own age. They admitted they had pulled a fire-alarm box at a given address on a certain date. These boys also admitted breaking the glass in three other fire boxes in that vicinity recently. The petition stated also that the Fire Department reported numerous false alarms coming in from that particular locality. The filing was made under

Sub-division 13, of the Juvenile Court Law of California and charged specifically Malicious Mischief. The boys were held in custody in Juvenile Hall.

Probation Officer's first call on Milton at Juvenile Hall found him readily admitting participation in this mischievous habit, telling of such activities covering a large area over a long period of time in the section of the city in which he lived. He even boasted of being the leader of a gang that specialized in false alarms.

Family Cooperation.— Milton is an American-born Italian boy; his parents had been born in Italy. A call on them found them ready and willing to cooperate in any manner of probation. The parents believed that it was more than a year previous when their younger children had first come to them with the story of Milton's breaking the glass in a fire box. They stated they had questioned him from time to time but the boy had always denied any wrongdoing.

The Juvenile Hall Clinic next reported that a physical examination showed the boy well developed, nutrition poor, twelve pounds underweight, jerking movements of muscles, tonsils large, especially left, pus in posterior nasopharynx, adhesions of foreskin to gland, puberty pro, marked course tremor of finger; Wasserman negative. The psychological examination showed physical age of 14:6, mental age of 11:6, giving an I.Q. of 79, dull normal or borderline; just misses twelve-year vocabulary (Italian spoken at home); poor in linguistic (verbal) type of test; successful in arithmetic induction and reasoning (fourteen-year level); quiet, rather indifferent effort, gives up quickly with a shrug of shoulders. The recommendation from the Clinic was for a tonsillectomy and intensive feeding.

School Report.— Showed the boy to have a good attendance and by an Otis primary intelligence test given a year previous, the boy had received an I.Q. of 77; his marks for all twelve subjects he was studying at school were all twos and threes with the exception of spelling, in which he received a four; his behavior was reported as quick-tempered, sulky, inclined to "pass the buck"; was frequently reported for quarreling, impertinence, and failure to do his work; gives up easily when task is rather difficult. The school reported the parents as being cooperative.

Process of Treatment.— Milton was released from Juvenile Hall and taken home to await the hearing in court. At this time the father stated the boy practiced masturbation and that probably this was the cause for his trouble, and the mother added that Milton was a bed-wetter and she thought this might be the cause of his trouble. Just as probation officer was leaving the house a policeman came to the door to ask if he might come in and talk to Milton. There had been reports of two more false fire alarms having been turned in on the night previous in that district but Milton had been in Juvenile Hall.

In court Milton's story was heard, and the boy was duly admonished. He was declared a ward of the court and was instructed as to just what would be expected of him in the future. It was further ordered that arrangements be made for an operation for tonsillectomy and circumcision. Those physical adjustments were made in due time but on account of the boy's great fear of doctors the final winning of Milton over to having the operations performed would make a story in itself.

Now started the period of supervision. In nine days Milton had pulled another box. He denied his guilt to the police but later admitted to the probation officer that it had been he. This particular box had been pulled at 10:30 P.M., the streets had been slippery from a rainy afternoon although the night was clear and I remembered having read a newspaper account of how a serious accident had been narrowly averted between a fire truck and a privately owned machine. It took three days to get the boy to admit his guilt, so on the evening of the third day Milton and myself were at the fire station for a confidential chat with the captain. Almost an hour was spent in telling the boy of the hazards of sending the fire department on "wild goose chases," of the many dangers to the traveling public when the big machines rolled out on a rainy night; the cost to the city for these extra runs; the wear and tear on the nervous systems of the firemen, getting up and dressing two and three times and sometimes more, a night, for no good reason at all. The boy had been very favorably impressed with this friendly chat. Two days later he had written in school what he remembered about the talk He seemed to have remembered all the high points of the visit. One week later, however, Milton was caught by an alert policeman pulling another box while three of his companions looked on.

Again Milton was told what persistent antisocial conduct could lead to. Then it was proposed to him to become a fireman himself. Milton seemed to be interested in becoming a fireman, but was wondering how he was to become one, and when. Part of the next day was spent in telling the plan to the parents and getting their full cooperation. It was decided that the boy actually thought enough of his home so that the contemplated action would not cause him to run away. So, with everything ready, three nights later the cure began. The probation officer called at the home at 11:00 P.M. The father went with him to the boy's bed; he looked very comfortable and snug and in two minutes time he was out of bed and being hurried to a greater speed at dressing. Once outside he at last came to life and asked where we were going. "To a fire," was the casual answer, but when we got there it appeared the alarm had been false.

This period lasted for five and one-half weeks; an average of two calls a week were made. On four occasions two calls were made in one evening; on one particular good night we got in three calls. When more than one call was made in an evening, just enough time was given the boy to get nicely snuggled back under the warm covers between the first and second call. It might be said that extreme caution was always used not to expose the boy to any dangerous draft or otherwise harm his health. The boy never had to be forced out of the house after he was once up and dressed.

At the end of two weeks it was hoped that Milton might ask for a truce. However, he lasted the five and one-half weeks; the last night of the probation officer's call, Milton had established his sleeping quarters under the bed rather than upon the top under the covers. When he was under the bed he came out on his knees and with considerable emotion fervently begged to be discharged from the fire department; he would never molest another fire-alarm box, and he added that he would see to it personally that none of his gang ever did either. He further promised he would study at school; that he would obey at home and stay in nights.

These promises were all voluntary on Milton's part. It was then he announced with thanks and offered to me as an inducement to cease the treatment the fact that the many trips up at night had caused him to overcome the habit of bed-wetting.

Milton was taken at his word and evidently he meant what he said. At the end of the year his case was dismissed. He made good in much less than that time. He had likewise helped several others to make good. There has never been any further trouble with false fire alarms in that neighborhood.

A probation officer must have not only considerable imagination and power to win the parents' cooperation, but he must also be deeply in love with his job to undertake a series of nocturnal visitations to the home of a boy and wild-goose chases to reputed fires.

The Case of Dora J. , eighteen years of age, senior in high school, has run away from home, secured work as mother's helper in a near-by town, enrolled in the local high school and refuses not only to see her mother and to return home, but to have her mother visit her.

Dora was legally adopted as a small child by Mrs. J., once a well-to-do woman. Dora knows of her adoption but says that she "has no feelings on the matter," but "is violently opposed to her mother because she would not let the girl out of her sight, insisted on sleeping with the girl in the same bed, interfered with all of her interests and activities." The girl accuses the mother of "cruelty to one husband who was driven away from home, and to another who was driven to his grave"; of making a "mess of her business affairs," and of ruining "her life as well as Dora's." She repeated that her mother was cruel, unethical, un-Christian.

The tensions and conflicts between the daughter, who had little opportunity to participate in normal situations, and an overanxious mother are intense and of long standing. Even in her new environment the girl was "unable to forget the treatment at the hands of that neurotic, un-Christian like woman," and continued to be moody, hard to deal with, and at times even desperate when her mother tried to communicate with her. An interview with the mother substantiated all of the statements Dora made regarding her and convinced of the impossibility of any rapid or drastic changes in her.

Dora's health broke down, unable to stand the strain of the conflict and unaccustomed housework. It was necessary to remove her to a rest home, but she applied for relief rather than to accept any help from her mother. Relief was given pending investigation, and considerable attention was given to the medical aspects of the case.

The girl was hard to manage at the rest home because of her morbidity, threats to commit suicide, irregularity of eating. She changed rest homes every few weeks, which created additional irritations and seriously undermined her morale.

It is obvious that in order to work out any permanent plan for Dora a great deal more information must be secured regarding the adoptive parents, the real parents, Dora herself, her health, her relations with other people, and a host of other things. However, the immediate problem facing us calls for some immediate treatment to prevent complete demoralization and physical breakdown.

Dora found life too hard; her antagonism to the mother was at least partially justified, but the girl could not divorce herself from her past and could not create a different social environment even though she was separated from her mother. It was obvious that little could be expected of the older woman which the younger one would recognize as love for her own sake. It is necessary then to arouse, if not genuine affection, tolerance and Christian charity in the girl. A picture was painted of the mother's state of mind and emotions and of what was expected of an ideal daughter under such difficult circumstances.

Since Dora had rather well-formed conceptions of ethics and Christian principles, repeated appeals were made to her to aid her mother, who was unfortunate enough to be left all alone and unable to change her ways because of advancing age and undermined health. Dora's tendencies to self-pity were turned into constructive outgoing energy toward another human being, and the attention on self was converted into a relationship demanding sacrifice and charity. It was not planned for Dora to return home but in order to remove the mental conflict the girl had to acquire a different definition of the whole situation.

3

Social Case Treatment of the Family Group

Introduction

The following summary of an interview during a home visit with Mrs. Jordan is an illustration of what the agency on the case called "an unfortunate approach."

Father.— Norman Jordan, thirty-four years, born and reared in California, one of two children. Came from a broken home and shifted for himself a good deal after the age of seven years. Father's mother was erratic, periodically deserted. Mr. J. completed the eighth grade at fourteen years, herded sheep, worked in a garage, joined the navy at eighteen; married at twenty; secured work as for interurban railway at about $130 a month, and has continued to work there. Main interest is his work; also he has always wanted to buy a home.

Mother.— Lillian, thirty-seven, one of a family of eight, born on a farm in the Middle West, reared in California after her fourth year. Completed high school, worked in an office for a short time, then remained at home, where she was indulged because of a heart condition (this later cleared up entirely) until her marriage at the age of twenty-three. Was secretary of a small club of employees where she was employed, enjoyed music, dancing, and sewing. Marriage was successful until the death of Mrs. J.'s mother several years ago, and Mrs. J. was put entirely on her own responsibility. The situation recently reached a crisis, due to Mrs. J.'s pregnancy.

Children—Marie, eleven; Norma, seven; each had a slight attack of infantile paralysis a year ago, which resulted in shortening and lack of growth in one leg in each child.

2-13-34. A visit was made on Mrs. Jordan in response to a call from her stating she cannot bear her situation any longer. She feels badly due to her pregnancy; both children are sick in bed; Mr. Jordan leaves her alone evenings and is cruel and abusive when he is at home.

The house itself is in good condition, has a large sunny location, no near neighbors, plenty of air space, and is large enough for sufficient privacy for individual members of the family. The atmosphere inside is wretched, however. There is practically no furniture, no rugs, and no curtains. Everything is in great disorder and does not appear to have been cleaned for days. Marie (eleven years) has been sick with bronchitis but is now well enough to call her mother every few minutes and Mrs. Jordan went to her every time the child called, although she wanted nothing after her mother arrived. When Mrs. Jordan did not go, Marie started to scream. Worker finally dosed the door, leaving Marie by herself. At this she cried all the harder out of sheer anger. Norma (seven years) also had bronchitis, according to Mrs. Jordan, and should be in bed but is so restless and stubborn that Mrs. Jordan has been unable to keep her there. Norma is a very spoiled child who is constantly trying to get attention, and when her behavior does not bring the desired result, she gets pouty and defiant, starts slamming doors and kicking the furniture. Mrs. Jordan was in a complaining frame of mind and several times started to cry, saying that after the years of unhappiness she has given up all hope and is utterly discouraged. She resents having to stay home all the time while Mr. Jordan can leave every evening.

Mrs. Jordan is approached regarding the children and it is suggested that they should have some responsibility in the home instead of being waited on all day. Although Mrs. Jordan does not mind it now in a few years the children's behavior will no longer be "cute" and by that time Mrs. Jordan will have difficulty in controlling them. Mrs. Jordan realizes this but she has nothing to do all day but spoil the children; also they are the only thing she has to cling to in her wretchedness; she is not willing to give up this last consolation. She is told that the children will not be much consolation to her if they are not better trained, as they will not respect her. This will mean that they will be inconsiderate of her just as her husband is and she realizes how unhappy she is over the latter. Also, the children will not be able to get along either in their studies or with other children at school unless they have been taught fair play, habits of obedience, and attentiveness. Since Mrs. Jordan loves her children so much and more than anything else wishes to prevent unhappiness for them, she must not lose further time. Mrs. J. had not thought of the matter from this angle before and now feels worried about it. Worker promised to introduce her to a parent-education class at the school to help her work out habit charts, etc. Mrs. Jordan accepted the idea happily as it will give her a new interest.

The problem of clinic care for Mrs. Jordan was discussed. At first she refused to go, saying she can neither take the children nor leave them alone.

She is told to go on the day the girls go to the hospital for their treatments. Her next objection is that she has no clothes to wear. Worker suggests working out a family budget so that the family can be better clothed, and offered to give Mrs. Jordan some clothes to bridge the gap until the budget can be made to function. Mrs. Jordan then said that she had a fear of doctors and hospitals; that her mother had the same fear. Mrs. Jordan was reminded of how pleased she has been with the care and service recently given her children at the Children's Hospital. She stated that they are being treated for a definite disease while she is merely going to have a baby and cannot see the need for medical care. The worker reminded Mrs. Jordan that she had been complaining ever since Norma was born that she was not feeling well and another birth without medical attention may make her condition worse. She gets exasperated at all her husband's complaints and she is putting herself in the same position, if she will not try to remedy her situation. It is explained that she has always been very conscious of her bad teeth; that unless she takes care of herself now, her teeth may get worse and in addition the coming baby will have a poor start. Mrs. Jordan thinks it would be embarrassing to have a medical examination. She was told she will gain self-confidence by being one of so many expectant mothers at the clinic. If her health is improved, she will have more vitality and consequently be able to meet her present problems better; also, she will be more attractive in looks and personality and can start to win back her husband's affection. Only recently in speaking of their early married happiness Mr. Jordan spoke of how vivacious and sweet-looking his wife had been. If Mrs. Jordan will compare herself now with six years ago, she can see that perhaps all her unhappiness has not been her husband's fault, as she has neither cared for herself nor her house. It follows that Mr. Jordan has nothing pleasant to stay home for in the evenings. In addition to the physical appearance of herself and the house, and the children's lack of training, Mrs. Jordan is in an unhappy frame of mind and goads her husband into ill-temper. Mrs. Jordan can "get farther" with honey than with vinegar. This platitude appeals to Mrs. Jordan immensely, and as she is anxious to make peace with her husband, she agrees to go to the clinic on February 16 and says she would like to make a better home but has nothing to work with. The household equipment is gone over and it is found that Mrs. Jordan is much in need of equipment of every kind. She becomes enthusiastic during this inspection and enthusiastic about the budget idea, on the basis that there is sufficient income in the family if it were properly managed. Mrs. Jordan will have a chance to prove herself, should her husband accuse her of wasting all the money (the chief family trouble), and worker is certain Mr. Jordan will agree to this and he can readily understand how impossible it would be for him to do his own work without tools.

Mrs. Jordan will spend the next week figuring out the family "bills" so that we can have definite data for working out the budget at the next call, and worker will explain the matter to Mr. Jordan in the meantime.

We shall discuss only some of the more obvious transgressions of good case work procedure and rules of common courtesy and proper social relations. (No attempt is made here to discuss the shortcomings in the social study of the case, chiefly because it is only a summary.) The worker did not act as a visitor in the home when she "closed the door and left Marie alone by herself." This act was a reflection on the mother's discipline and an unwise procedure in the presence of the child. Such acts create subtle or open conflict between worker and client and result frequently in the necessity of "closing the case because the client did not cooperate." The client's failure to cooperate is often a reflection upon the worker's inability to secure cooperation.

"Mrs. Jordan is told ..." It is difficult to project oneself into the thinking and past activities of a worker who perhaps does himself injustice by summary recording of a case, but the reader has only the written account by which to judge. Perhaps also the very force of the worker's dignified personality and proper tone of voice eliminate much of the sting of being told by an agency representative what one should or should not do (even though what the worker does tell is constructive). We need not elaborate on this point here since it is dealt with in another connection. We may only raise the question regarding the relative effectiveness of being told as against being led to believe as accomplished through a discussion of the problems involved and questions raised which would oblige the mother to think the situation through for herself. (For example: Mrs. Jordan was asked what the probable effect of her waiting on the children will be on them as they grow older.) The worker through her behavior succeeded in angering the child and worrying Mrs. Jordan. It is evident that little rapport was established since the client was not free to discuss her problems with the worker and gave one alibi after another, avoiding the main issue. The worker may also have laid too much responsibility on Mrs. Jordan for the rift in the home, without taking into consideration the possible contributory factors by Mr. Jordan's behavior. While it is necessary to talk to Mr. Jordan in order to understand the total situation, the worker should avoid "explaining matters" which the wife can or should be able to explain to her own husband. Many women nurse an undercurrent of resentment at the intimation that another woman can manage her man better than she. On the other hand, a client, inclined to self-pity and complaint was brought out of her mood. It should be observed that the worker not only recognized the major issues contributing to Mrs. Jordan's unhappiness, but in many instances effectively interpreted them to the client. The worker also attempted to utilize some available community resources which would provide instruction for child training, prenatal care, and dental service. Some form of recreation should have been suggested for the family.

Case of Harold Crane

In the record of Harold Crane, which follows, both the family and the boy presented serious problems but the probation officer failed to deal with either. He worked under difficult conditions, which explain in considerable measure the character of the treatment administered—probation as surveillance.

The Boy.— Harold Crane. Born in Montana, Dec. 23, 1916. He is in the seventh grade, attending Crescent Special School. Is reported to be in good physical condition and of normal mentality. He has never been a behavior problem in his home. Is not interested in school. Has few associates. Attends Sunday school regularly.

The Complaint.2-26-32.— Police Officer P. E. Jones arrested Harold Crane and James Emerson, Edward Stone, and Earl Andrews for stealing a Chrysler sedan of Howard Smith's and abandoning it after driving it to V. and back.

Boy's Statement. 3-16-32.— Boy at home. "The gang and I was coming out Sixteenth Street; saw a car parked over across the street and James said, 'Let's get in it' so we went in there and got it. We drove around until about 9:00 A.M. and parked the car on Twentieth Street and left it there. On our way to the beach, some boys asked us for a ride and we gave them a ride to the beach. From there we went to V. and later returned, intending to park the car where we found it."

The Mother.— Born in C., Texas, 1892; has high-school education. Works as a trained nurse. Married Arthur Crane in C., Texas; divorced in 1922. She married Willie O., 8-22-24; divorced after twenty-one months. Assumed her maiden name of Williams. "Harold is always good and never gives us any trouble." Mother belongs to Eastern Star.

The Father.— Arthur C., born 1888 in C., Texas. Eighth-grade education. Cook employed by himself. Remarried; belongs to Masons.

Brother.— John, twenty-three, musician, married.

Sister.— Mary E., twenty-one, married.

Home Conditions.— Family lives in an eight-room frame house at C. Street. Household consists of the boy's mother, his brother, his brother's wife, his sister, her husband, another sister, and her daughter. All are employed and contribute to the support of the home. It is orderly, well kept, and well furnished. It is, however, in the midst of a deteriorated neighborhood and not far away from two families whose boys have appeared before the court on several occasions.

Finances.— The earnings of the children, $125; mother $60. Family owns car, piano, and phonograph.

School.— Harold attends Crescent Special School regularly and seems to be getting along fairly well.

Community Activities.— Harold belongs to no special organizations; attends the Baptist Sunday school.

Remarks.— There is a crowded condition in the home and a laxity of supervision. The boy states he did not know the seriousness of his offense other than that it was wrong. Promises never to steal again.

Recommendation.— Since this is the boy's first offense it is respectfully recommended that the boy be released to his mother in the custody of the probation officer. It is further recommended that the boy be reprimanded and admonished, forbidden to ride or drive any car without the permission of his mother; he is to return immediately to school; to keep away from his associates who exert an evil influence upon him; and to remain under strict supervision by the probation officer.

History

3-18-32. Boy interviewed; attending school regularly; in early; good conduct.

3-24-32. Not at home.

3-25-32. Interviewed mother at home; good report.

3-31-32. Interviewed boy at home; getting along nicely.

4-15-32. Boy and mother at home; doing well in school and living up to terms of his probation.

4-25-32. Not at home.

5-17-32. Interviewed boy and mother at home; boy had participated in a track meet at school and had won first place in the fifty-yard dash, first in relay, and second in seventy-five yard dash; good report.

5-25-32. Boy interviewed on Twenty-second Street Playground, which he attends; good report.

6-9-32. Mother in office; states boy has a sore throat; good report.

6-30-32. Boy at home; doing well and living up to his obligations.

7-21-32. Interviewed mother at home; states boy stays at home, helps, and is congenial and no complaint.

9-26-32. Interviewed mother; she is trying to arrange for a transfer to regular school; she has gone to the Board of Education and made quite a fuss.

10-24-32. Talked to mother and Board of Education regarding transfer of boy to regular school. It was agreed that the boy should be transferred at the end of the semester, if he makes good.

11-22-32. Interviewed mother at home; states boy is now sixteen years old, has auto license; drives mother's car; good report.

1-27-33. Mother at home; boy attends Crescent Special School regularly; states he believes the teachers discriminate against him. The boy was asked to come to the office on 1-28-33 for explanation by probation officer.

2-11-33. Boy was promoted to B-8; transferred to Jordan Junior High School; appears to have a changed attitude toward school; prospects look good for the coming year; good report.

3-21-33. Mother at home; states boy seems to have better attitude since being transferred; attends school regularly and goes to show once a week.

4-4-33. Interviewed mother at home; boy does not seem to be progressing as fast as he should; attends school regularly; congenial at home; good report.

5-6-33. Probation officer called; family moved; left no address.

5-9-33. Interviewed Principal of Crescent Special School, who states "Jordan had kicked him out." This boy does not seem to adjust in school.

5-23-33. Interviewed Principal of Jordan School, "The great trouble with this boy is his attitude toward school; does not like to be told things." No behavior problem; absent.

5-29-33. Interviewed R. W. Forrest of Newton Police Station; states Harold Crane and Kenneth F. stole a jack from a truck on Central Avenue.

5-31-33. Interviewed boy in jail; admits charge; admits being out of school and that mother did not know he was out of school; spent his lunch money to go to shows (see report).

5-31-33. Later: Mother at home; family moved to 0035 East Twenty first Street; mother thought boy was attending school; there had been no trouble at home. Mother ill of heart trouble; states she told boy to notify probation officer of new address.

6-6-33. Boy in jail; states he is tired of jail; we believe he will profit by his experience; "another boy kicked him in the eye and he thinks differently about himself."

6-8-33. [The case brought into court. Probation officer's report summarized the case to date and made the following analysis and suggestions for treatment.]

Diagnosis and Present Problem.— (1) Poor association; (2) poor school adjustment; (3) lack of religious affiliation; (4) lack of interest, obstinacy, and heedlessness.

Plan of Adjustment.— (1) More careful supervision by parents; (2) return directly home from school; (3) choose better associates; (4) read more good books and magazines; (5) join the Y. M. C. A.

Recommendation.— It is, therefore, respectfully recommended due to the fact that the property was returned to the owner in this case and that the boy has had a chance to learn by experience of confinement in this matter the duty he owes to the law, that he has promised to follow any course of instruction mapped out for him and that we will never have an occasion to bring him into court again, it is our opinion that it is worth while to give this boy a chance to exercise his diligence in carrying out these promises made. Therefore, we recommend that this boy be released to the custody of the probation officer to return to his home and enter school, and that a rigid plan of supervision be made; that the case be continued two weeks for submission of plan.

6-9-33. Interviewed boy and mother at home; boy attending Crescent Special; he is docile since being in jail; mother's attitude toward probation is changing.

6-14-33. Boy and mother at home; attending Crescent Special School regularly; plan of supervision talked over with mother and boy.

6-16-33. Interviewed boy; attending Crescent Special School and expects to go to Lake Elsinore with the mother on vacation; good report.

7-24-33. Interviewed boy and mother at home; boy seems to be living up to the terms of his probation; home influences do not appear conducive to the highest moral good.

8-12-33. Letter requesting boy to come to office 8-18-33.

8-18-33. Boy in office; states he stays at home most of the time; plays on the piano; does not care for athletics; worried; non communicative.

Later: Mrs. B., police officer, brought Mrs. Crane, Mrs. Jones, and May Jones—neighbors—to office to report that May is pregnant and to file a petition in behalf of May. Harold admits responsibility; both mothers are willing for children to be married.

8-26-33. Home call; boy not at home; several men were in the room, one appeared to be intoxicated. Mother asked to be excused to talk to probation officer. The home has an atmosphere of immorality. Mother not convinced that the boy should marry.

8-30-33. [Case again in court. The probation officer's report reviewed the case. He added the following recommendations.]

Although the parents of the girl are anxious for the girl to be married to Harold, so that the coming child might have a name, and further that the boy's mother might be induced to give her consent, the probation officer feels that such a step would not serve the best interest of the boy, girl, nor their obligation to society. The girl is the product of parents of retarded mentality and of a home in which there have been behavior problems, in that her sister was once a ward of the court as an unwed mother, and at the present time, her younger brother, John, is a ward of the court, all of which would indicate poor supervision of the children in that home. On the other hand, Harold, the boy in the case, has not been amenable to discipline, nor to the social forces which would develop good citizenship in him. He has been tried on probation and has violated his trust, and by his most recent acts shows that he is devoid of supervision in his home. It is respectfully recommended that this ward be detained in Juvenile Hall Clinic for medical and psychiatric examination, that the case be continued two weeks for further report and recommendation.

8-31-33. Boy sent to clinic; later talked with aunt, Mrs. C., and grandmother, also Mrs. C., at East 13th Street; both believe they should be married.

9-6-33. [Case again in court. The probation officer now recommends as follows.]

It appears from further investigation made by the probation officer into the possible financial affairs of both families, that the boy's mother is probably in a better position than the Jones Family to assist the young couple. The records show that once before, an older daughter of Mr. Jones was an unwed mother, and at that time he agreed to take her into his home and to provide for her. Later, he applied to the court for aid for his daughter and became indignant because he was refused.

Several conversations with the boy since the last hearing brought out the fact that Harold and May had been sweethearts since childhood days in Montana and have been practically reared together. They seem to be deeply in love with each other and both are very anxious to be married. By their own statement, they plan to continue school, Harold going to part time and she going to full-time school after her baby is old enough to be left with someone for the day.

It is respectfully recommended that in view of the attitude of both families toward the young couple, their love and devotion for the children, and their apparently sincere promise of protection and financial aid, that the boy be permitted to marry May Jones. It is further recommended that Harold be instructed by the court to avail himself of such program of training and attendance at classes as will instruct him in the duties of a father and a husband and to carry out such program as the probation officer might outline for him from time to time; that the case be continued two weeks for presentation of plan.

9-8-33. Telephoned Harold and May; asked them to come to office; accompanied them to license bureau for marriage license; both extremely jubilant; Mrs. Jones present to give consent.

9-15-33. Called at home; boy married 9-12-33 by Rev. Robinson in old courthouse; he seems very happy over solution to his problem; wife and sister sewing on baby clothes; the family was disappointed by Mr. Jones's insistence on the immediate performance of the marriage; they wanted the ceremony at home with friends and flowers; boy is frank and communicative; wants to transfer to part-time school and look for work. Mother plans to make arrangements for May's confinement at hospital next week. Boy does not drive car; family does not possess one now.

9-25-33. Checked marriage with County Recorder, Vital Statistics, Book 1173, Page 7, Marriage Records.

9-29-33. Mr. Olson of Crescent Special states boy came to school one week, stated he was going to be married and left school; he was not properly checked out.

10-5-33. Message from Children's Protective Association that they will continue work with May.

10-9-33. Called at request of mother, who states that boy is unruly, refuses to go to school since married; saw another drunk at the house; boy promised to reenter school immediately.

10-11-33. Phoned Mr. Olson; states boy returned to school.

10-21-33. May had a Caesarean operation; baby well; mother fair; Harold excited; out of school all week.

10-23-33. Mother phoned; Harold's wife died at the hospital at 3 A.M. today; boy is stricken with grief.

10-24-33. Mr. Jones shopped among undertakers for a cheap funeral; called at 4 P.M. to claim the body. Infant was named Barbara.

Later: Home visit; boy went for a walk with his father-in-law; arrangements for the funeral had been made for the following day. Mother states May was taken to the hospital very ill. Father refused operation at first until the following afternoon. Harold and others gave blood; Mr. Jones gave only a little; there were five transfusions; she died at 3 A.M. next morning.

10-26-33. Home visit; boy playing jazz on the piano; boy has transferred his interest to the baby; May was buried in Paradise Memorial Cemetery.

10-28-33. This home with its loud, electric, slot-machine phonograph and loud voices, and secrecy is still a puzzle. Mother asked aid for infant.

10-30-33. Mrs. White of C. Welfare Department on phone states that mother of boy applied for aid for child of son and she believes she is trying to get aid for all of the family; the attitude is that the child is a public responsibility.

11-2-33. Mrs. White on phone states mother will keep child without aid. A case will be opened.

11-10-33. A headline article regarding the police breaking in and beating the mother and her eldest daughter without cause or warrant, appeared in the East Side Star. A suit has been filed against the officers and the city. An attorney has taken the case.

11-30-33. Boy at home; it is his birthday; he has been out of school for two weeks and seems indifferent to it and wishes to go to work and support the baby.

1-19-34. Called at home; boy away; mother and sister cleaning house; phonograph has been removed; boy not attending school; thinks he will go to Montana and visit father for a while; baby had pneumonia at Christmas, had to be taken to the hospital but is improved.

2-1-34. Boy in office; promises to return to school; plans to apply for enrollment in CCC; mother no longer has lodgers; plans to move to a smaller house; older sister convalescing from operation for tumor; baby is doing well; boy is anxious to buy a car.

2-7-34. Principal reports boy out of school fifty days; asks cooperation.

2-13-34. Letter asking boy to report.

2-20-34. Boy not in school.

3-13-34. Principal reports boy out of school again; he refuses to work when he does attend.

Later: Called at home; boy expressed a dislike for Crescent Special; family not in sympathy with his refusal to attend school; mother and two sisters living at home; aided by Welfare Department as mother has no income; boy stays around home most of the time; goes to show once or twice a week; at times is disobedient.

3-14-34. Principal of Crescent School is considering filing a petition for nonattendance.

3-21-34. Supervision of Attendance of City Schools on phone; boy is to be expelled for nonattendance.

3-24-34. Home call; boy away; mother and sister at home; believe family sells whisky; not much to work with in this family.

4-20-34. Boy is not living up to court order; recommend change of plan.

5-7-34. Called at home; boy and mother sign new plan; boy likes it; boy promises to get work in a week or two.

5-14-34. Boy and mother at home; Harold lives a happy, carefree existence; boy wants to perfect his piano technique; family no longer has a piano; infant happy and well cared for.

5-24-34. Called at home; Harold does not seem to take life seriously; has made little effort to secure employment to support child; family in poor financial circumstances.

6-2-34. Boy in office; his plans for immediate future are indefinite; has only one ambition, that is, dismissal from probation.

6-15-34. Family seems to enjoy enforced leisure; Harold plans another attempt to enroll in CCC; baby well; boy carrying out all instruction, except going to school.

7-12-34. Call; boy at home; not making much headway at employment; wants driver's license to secure job as chauffeur; but it is believed that he just wants to drive for pleasure.

8-6-34. Boy takes life easily; does not care about present obligations or future security.

8-14-34. Harold on playground; not working and not going to school.

10-11-34. Call at home; boy's only desire is to be free from supervision.

1-6-35. Boy seen in car.

Later: Call at home; states the car belonged to a relative and he had permission from his mother.

The work carried on in the case of Harold Crane is typical of the work of the overburdened and untrained probation officer. He is responsible not only for the high rate of recidivism and rapid increase of the case load but also of the continued demoralization of the offenders, who tend to implicate others in the mire.

The probation officer was aware that Harold lived "in the midst of a deteriorated neighborhood and not far away from families whose boys were before the court on several occasions," and that these boys "exert an evil influence upon him." Assuming that this evaluation is correct, it might have been a good plan to induce the family to move from the district. A change of residence and removal from demoralizing associates, a change of school, properly chosen, is frequently desirable.

"To reprimand, to admonish, to forbid" and "to order" to keep away from evil associates means adoption of a negative course and leaving the boy with nothing constructive to fall back on, or, as Cyril Burt points out:

To lecture the misguided weakling and then do no more, to appeal to him to "give up those who do him no good" without removing him from their dominance, or simply to shut him up indoors during out-of-school hours and so deprive him of all recreation, good as well as harmful such a course, though often the sole refuge is usually unavailing and frequently unfair. The child himself has his own loyalty to his comrades; they in turn, with jeers and solicitations, will make it hard for him to throw them over; and any curtailment of his liberty by prohibition or confinement is likely to provoke deceit, resentment, and even forcible flight. The only effective step, therefore, may be to take the child where his old confederates can neither expect nor oblige him to renew their perilous acquaintance.

The probation officer's chief concern seemed to be the boy's regular attendance at Crescent Special School. What did this school offer the boy from an educational standpoint and from the standpoint of the satisfaction of his wishes? No medical, psychological, nor psychiatric examinations were made. There was no plan of treatment followed. The boy was interviewed at very irregular intervals from one to nine weeks apart.

One wonders what is meant by "good report," "getting along nicely," "doing well and living up to his obligations," and so on, when in the midst of these reports the boy becomes implicated in more and more serious offenses.

It is known to the writer that this probation officer carried a case load of 150 cases, an administrative difficulty over which an individual probation officer has little control. Under such circumstances there can be little more than a monthly visit and a history of the type which is described in this record. Note, however, that the delinquencies of this boy continued over a period of nearly three years, from February 27, 1932, to January 6, 1935. What is the financial cost of supervision, court hearings, of arrests, and further supervision over a period of three years? What is the financial cost to the community of several petty and grand thefts? What is the social and human cost to Harold, to his mother, to May, his wife, to their orphaned infant, to May's parents, and to the community? Obviously these questions imply that had the boy received adequate supervision and social therapy, in accordance with a well-ordered, systematic plan, the financial, social, and human costs would have been greatly minimized. One can expect nothing else, if he is to retain his faith and confidence in a system of probation. If probation is to be maintained at all it should be well ordered and systematic. "A child who is amenable for evil is often equally amenable for good; and it may prove as easy for a sensible friend to guide him right as for a corrupt acquaintance to lead him astray."

On the basis of the meager information contained in the record it is difficult to suggest a plan of treatment. It is, however, evident that the probation officer might have at least appealed to the Eastern Star or Masons to contribute their financial and moral support to this family. A Big Brother might have been secured for the boy under the supervision of the worker. A contact might have been made with a trade school and the boy's interests enlisted. The personal services of a family welfare agency and those of other community resources might have been secured.

Judging from the description of the home circumstances, of the mother's associates, and of the guidance afforded the boy, he should have been removed from his home. The officer recognized the fact that the home was unfit but he made no attempt to remove the boy from it nor to reconstruct it. There was no attempt made to orient the mother to the source of the boy's problems. The social problems multiplied as the boy continued his probationary period.

We need, of course, to remember that Harold lived in a home and community which supplied very little, if any, moral support for an adequate probation plan. Failure is "normal," perhaps, under these conditions even with the best of case work. While it is true that organized persons can and do live in disorderly homes and communities the chances are so heavily weighted against it that had Harold been energetic, wholesome, efficient, orderly, it would have been very difficult to explain that situation. In no case, however, could we expect a radical reform, such as occurred in the case of James R. , even though intimate relations had developed between officer and boy. It seems highly probable, moreover, that the family itself is not prepared to swim against the social currents in which their lives are being lived. This was a case for foster home placement for the boy, change of residence for the family, and a consistent and enduring guidance for the family during Harold's absence from the home and after his return into it. Perhaps this form of concentrated service might have prevented the initiation of disorganizing forces into the third generation, which will undoubtedly continue to exact a heavy social and financial cost.

Edwin J. Cooley, formerly Chief Probation Officer, Catholic Charities Probation Bureau in the Court of General Sessions, New York County, gives us the benefit of his study of almost fifty thousand home visits made by probation officers in the homes of their probationers:

Home Visit

During the period of its supervisory work, the Bureau constantly endeavored to keep in mind that the family and not the individual must be the unit of treatment. Little social improvement could be expected of the delinquent unless his father, mother, brothers and sisters, and other relatives could be persuaded to forget their resentments and disappointments regarding the offender who had brought disgrace to their good name. Inharmonious relationships and undesirable conditions had to be removed as a first step in this process. The methods and services of the modern family welfare organizations in the adjustment of family relations was made an integral part of the case work of the Bureau.

The greater proportion of the probationers lived with their families one of the most frequent problems was: How could the parents exercise effective supervision and control over the children? With the assistance of the officer, many such problems of discipline were successfully solved. Health problems, involving tuberculosis, undernourishment, or mental defect, which required diagnosis, treatment, or possibly institutional care of the afflicted members of the family, were frequently met with and attended to by the officer.

In adjusting important problems involving the mistress of the home, such as excessive burden of work, necessity for managing on an insufficient income, the efficient and economic purchase of good food and clothing, proper diet and cleanliness, the assistance of home educators of cooperating social agencies was enlisted.

Family plans for home ownership, purchasing new furniture, establishing the father and son in business, and securing safe financial investments were worked out in collaboration with the probation officer. Each member of the family was also encouraged to contribute his quota to the maintenance and to the upbuilding of the household.

Job analysis and vocational guidance were not limited solely to the probationer, but included the whole family, especially the younger members, who were aided in obtaining positions which afforded congenial employment, and possessed possibilities for advancement and adequate remuneration.

The brothers and sisters of school age were encouraged to complete their education in elementary or high school or, when employment seemed more advisable, to pursue courses in night and continuation schools. The parents, wherever necessary, were persuaded to attend Americanization schools.

Recreation outlets for the family were studied, and the resources of the community were ascertained. Such outlets included club and library membership, affiliation with neighborhood activities, and the attendance at lectures and public meetings. The main objective was that of developing and exercising the play spirit of the family as a group, rather than as separate individuals.

The establishment and the maintenance of a spirit of friendliness and harmony in the home involved the solution of a great number of problems of human relationship. To reduce the friction and resentment between the reputable family and the delinquent member, to solve the problem of the over-stern or over-indulgent parents, or to eliminate the nagging of brothers and sisters, the assistance of the psychiatrist and the psychologist was sometimes required.

Where it was not possible nor desirable to keep the family together, the question of child-placing or of finding a home for older members of the family sometimes arose. Where the breaking up of the family was of a temporary nature due to the illness of the mother and the presence of young children in the home, the counsel and the sympathetic oversight of the officers of the Bureau were valuable and often resulted in such arrangements for the care of the members of the household as were calculated to facilitate the family reunion as expeditiously as possible.

In this work of adjusting the family within itself and within the community, the various social agencies and community resources were utilized, particularly the Church, the school, neighborhood forces, and the employer. To increase the sense of family solidarity, to regenerate and build up its spiritual life, and to strengthen and augment the wholesomeness of the influence of the home constituted the aims of the Bureau. That the family might not remain in a static condition of negative non-delinquency, constantly balancing itself precariously on the border line of disreputability and dependence, but that it might constructively direct its efforts towards social and economic stability, which would be maintained without assistance after the conclusion of the probationary period, was the objective kept in mind by the probation officer.

How Do We Rate as Parents?— The Los Angeles County Probation Department has found very useful the following extract from Goodwin Watson's "Scale for Rating Home Contribution to Personality Development of Children," in discussing the type of home which destroys character and the one which builds character.

How Do We Rate as Parents?

What do our children think of us? Apply this scale to your home.

Compare each item in First Column with Same Number in Second Column

THIS TYPE OF HOME DESTROYS CHARACTER	THIS TYPE OF HOME BUILDS CHARACTER
1. Child feels that both parents hate him, he is a nuisance, a "nut," an expense, one of the world's worst liabilities.	1. Child feels that both parents wholeheartedly want him, love him, appreciate him.
2. Parents constantly quarreling, threats of separation, each tries to prejudice the child against the other.	2. Parents wholeheartedly love each other, and all happy together, considerate of each other, trusting each other completely.
3. Jealousies and favoritisms in family. Intimacy and tenderness between child and parent of opposite sex, antagonisms to other. Emotionally unweaned.	3. Wholesome enjoyment by each person of understanding relationships with each other in the family.
4. Child's every whim must be satisfied. No sacrifice too great, anywhere, by anyone, if the child wishes it. At the slightest sign of reluctance, the child fusses, and is given his way at once.	4. Child is expected to consider others as they consider him. Many things good for adults are not good for children. Many disappointments can't be helped. Make the best of things. Co-operate in best solution.
5. Parent's every whim must be satisfied. Any resistance on the part of the child met with extreme severity, or with whining protests of ingratitude, pleas for sympathy.	5. Child is treated with intimate courtesy. Parents ready to make adjustments and sacrifices, where helpful, without pretense, or demand for appreciation.
6. Variable discipline, conduct laughed at today, is met with blows tomorrow if parent is more irritable. upon, it is pursued steadily until consciously, thoughtfully modified.	6. Consistent attitudes. Once a working solution has been decided
7. Complete dependence. Child unable to decide anything by himself. Unable to meet new situations; or, anxious, worried, with sense of world on his shoulders.	7. Growing independence of child. Increasing opportunity to make choices and enjoy or suffer consequences. Developing technique for deciding.
8. Discipline all negative. Blows, nagging, sarcasm, mean remarks, contempt.	8. Comments on child's behavior largely praise, appreciation. Any criticism points in matter of fact fashion to more helpful response. Emphasis on consequences.

9. Child ignored in family planning. Expected merely to submit. Seen and not heard. Domination by one member of family.	9. Democratic family. Wishes of each taken into account. Plans for choice of apartments, room decorations, meals, budget, vacations, time schedules, use of equipment, made co-operatively.
10. Obedience to an arbitrary person. "Do as you are told."	10. Understanding recognition of unchangeable features of situations, and co-operation in group agreements.

Dr. Van Waters lays down certain maxims for parents, which in reality must become the responsibility of the worker to interpret and to teach, wherever necessary. A brief summary of the major points made by Dr. Van Waters and a few references to recent literature added by the present author, which will help to orient parents (with an inclination to read books) to some of the wider implications of the serious business of being a parent would include the following:

1. Parents must learn to evaluate social resources to be tapped for the development of their children.
2. Parents must thread their way through a maze of scientific theories and religious dogma.
3. Learn from their experience that behavior can be modified and that parental patterns are the explanation of many traits which children exhibit.
4. Parents must know the world in which the child lives.
5. Parents need to realize that children must have security, steady love, and the unshaken faith of stable parents, and an assurance that nothing is too much trouble for their development.
6. Parents must know that children should learn the meaning of sex in early childhood.
7. Parents should learn that children must pursue their own spontaneous interests and be initiated into the delights of sustained activity.
8. Parents must learn that children should have cooperative living and shared responsibility as well as an opportunity for being alone.

It is not to be assumed that reading of books will solve the difficulties of the parents or their children. But they provide facts and may create an inquiring attitude of mind; they may orient the reader to the existing problems and provide a basis for discussion with an intelligent counselor. It must be remembered that at best families will have difficulty in concentrating on any program of child welfare as long as the home continues to suffer from financial straits, unemployment, neighborhood and community demoralization, urbanization, mobility, and a host of other problems besetting the family in the modern city.

4

Role of the Police in Social Work with Criminals

Introduction

Brief History of the Crime Prevention Movement.— Los Angeles and Seattle were among the first cities to establish special juvenile bureaus to deal with minors who had been placed under arrest by any police officer or against whom reports were received from parents, schools, neighbors, or other citizens, whether as offenders or victims.

The following notes, from the office of Justin Miller, Chairman of the Attorney General's Advisory Committee on Crime, prepared by Miss Helen Fuller, indicate the recent work of certain crime prevention bureaus in this country:

> *Police Departments in most cities engage in some type of preventive work, ranging from one officer assigned to juvenile duty to a well organized Crime Prevention Bureau. One of the most popular types of programs has been an athletic team or a boys' club, under sponsorship of the police officers. Crime Prevention Bureaus have a wide range of activities including inspection and supervision of commercial amusements, case work with individual delinquents, building constructive forces into the life of the community, sponsoring Coordinating Councils and recreation projects, and*

developing friendly attitudes on the part of youth and the community toward the law and law enforcement agencies.

There are two distinct ideas which have been attached to the meaning of the term crime prevention in regard to police work; first, preventing criminals from operating, and second, removing temptations and situations provocative of crime and guarding the young against criminal influences and tendencies. This first phase of crime prevention has received greater attention than the second, and action arising from this concept has generally proved manageable through the existing administrative set-up. The second phase, in many cases, requires the more specialized handling of a division or bureau especially designed for such work. Since research has shown that a large percentage of criminals begin their careers as juvenile delinquents, most of these special divisions center their work on the prevention of such delinquency. Departments which are engaging in this work have found it necessary not only to secure properly trained personnel for the prevention division, but also to reeducate the whole force in their attitudes toward young offenders and toward the prime importance of crime prevention.

We have obtained reports from the following cities that are doing special work in the field of crime prevention.

Berkeley, California—Crime Prevention Division.— This division was organized under the leadership of August Vollmer in 1925. One of the features of its work is the close cooperation between it and other community organizations. The policewoman in charge is a member of the Berkeley Coordinating Council, and through the Council often obtains follow-up contacts of school counseling, guidance clinic and health center attention for the child who has been under police surveillance. Many juvenile cases are disposed of in an unofficial manner, adopting something like a clinic procedure. The results of psychiatric and other investigations are made available to probation officers and the Detention Home.

San Francisco, California-Crime Prevention Bureau and Big Brother Bureau.— Police officers of the San Francisco

Police Department were detailed to a special study of forty problem boys of the juvenile court, and out of their activities grew a Big Brother Movement. Chief Quinn is visualizing his policemen as future boy workers with personal contacts forming the basis of a crime prevention program.

Denver, Colorado—Crime Prevention Bureau (Founded 1931).— An outstanding feature of the work of this division is the emphasis which it places on the importance of cooperation with existing crime prevention agencies. Through its part in the Denver Coordinating Council, the Police Department has established close working relations with the Probation Department, private social agencies, the School Attendance Department, and the Bureau of Public Welfare, helping them to remove investigation of particular localities as has been described in relation to other large cities. In addition, this Bureau has assumed an important function in attempting to seek out the problem child prior to his becoming officially delinquent and offer constructive outlets to him as a means of crime prevention. This work is done with the cooperation of the schools and courts in providing the "trouble list" for the attention of the police officers. A third phase of the work in New York is concerned with creating recreational facilities and leisure-time activities through stimulating other agencies to act, or conducting programs by their own officers. Several hundred WPA workers supervise dozens of street and play center projects throughout the city, and many new community centers are to be provided during the winter. Activities of the Police Athletic League are also being expanded. Organization of 150 out of a contemplated 300 neighborhood Councils has been completed for the purpose of examining and improving community conditions detrimental to the proper development of youth.

Cincinnati, Ohio—Juvenile Registry and Friendly Service Bureau, Department of Safety.— Through the Juvenile Registry of this department, the delinquent child whose case does not warrant an arrest is handled by a social case work procedure. The Department of Safety is also cooperating in the establishing of Community Councils to consider the problems surrounding this delinquency. The Friendly Service Bureau deals with the problem of Negro crime in Cincinnati. The job of the Negroes employed in this division is to ferret out potential crime breeders in the Negro districts before crime develops, and to coordinate all the social and religious forces in this district with a view toward better citizenship. Another form of prevention undertaken by the department is the enlisting of public cooperation for care in the protection of property in order to prevent criminals from operating.

Columbus, Ohio— Friendly Service Bureau (Founded in 1925). The purpose of the Bureau is to assist the migrant and maladjusted to become adjusted to city life. During the lifetime of this division the number of arrests among Negroes in Columbus has decreased 60 per cent. The basis upon which the work proceeds is that of acquaintance and friendship between the families and groups in the problem areas and the social workers and the volunteers connected with the Bureau. Community surveys determine neighborhood conditions, and organizations, social agencies, and industries are called upon to assist in remedying them. The Big Brothers Council with fifty members copes with the problem of delinquency among these unadjusted families.

Philadelphia, Pennsylvania—Crime Prevention Division and Civilian Crime Prevention Unit.— The work of this division is with the "older boy" group between the ages of 16 and 21, and its aim is to get the boy off the street, on the job, and teach a useful trade and wholesome play. Officers work with parents, employers, and school and recreation authorities to effect these ends. Several thousand boys have been enrolled in supervised clubs, many of them organized by the police, and arrests among this group have steadily decreased since the beginning of the program. Lately, WPA and other relief agencies have provided a large group of workers known as the Civilian Crime Prevention Unit which has materially broadened the scope of the work. The division has a section devoted to social case work with the individuals and another devoted to contacts with the public in relation to community development.

Los Angeles, California—Juvenile Police Bureau.—Since the Los Angeles Juvenile Police Bureau is one of the most prominent we cite it as an illustration of this type of organization. Lieutenant E. W. Lester, the Director of Boys' Work in the Crime Prevention Division of the Los Angeles Police Department, writes:

> *The Crime Prevention Division of the Los Angeles Police Department had its beginning in 1909 when one officer was assigned to handle all children's cases originating in the Police Department. In 1910 the first policewoman in the United States was appointed to serve with the Los Angeles Police Department. This distinction was accorded Alice Stebbins Wells who is still a member of this Division.*

In 1913 the staff was increased and the name Juvenile Bureau first applied. As the volume of work increased and the duties became more complex, personnel was added until 1924 when a reorganization of the work was effected. At this time the Juvenile Bureau, the City Mother's Bureau, the Men's and Women's Municipal Probation Offices were united under one head and the name Crime Prevention Division applied. The next noteworthy development was a specialization of the work effected by the establishment of separate units to handle case work. These units consisted of the Boys' Detail, the Girls' Detail, the Detective Detail and the Missing Persons Bureau. In 1930 a decentralization plan was developed whereby juvenile officers, both men and women, were placed in outlying police divisions. This made juvenile work much more effective, since the officers became well acquainted with neighborhood conditions and with the problem children of the district. Other units have been added from time to time as the work of the Division expanded.

In 1929 the Dancehall Detail was created, in 1930 the Juvenile Traffic Bureau was established, and in 1934 the Bicycle Registration Bureau was added. The latest unit to be created was the Special Juvenile Night Patrol which was established in December, 1935. This was the most outstanding step yet undertaken by any police department in the field of crime prevention. Thirty-two officers, under the supervision of a police lieutenant, have been assigned to this new detail. Two of these officers work in each police division at night, wearing civilian clothes and cruising the district in a radio car. Their ... work is to discover children who are in danger of becoming delinquent, and to find and eliminate all moral hazards affecting the youth of the community. They will be especially persistent in their efforts to eliminate the sale of liquor to minors.

Children arrested by officers of the new unit are handled in the customary manner by the juvenile officers of the division of arrest. It is to be expected that juvenile arrests will increase materially with the adoption of this plan. With thirty-two additional officers fresh from an inspirational, short course in their new duties intent upon reaching the very source of crime, it would be surprising indeed, if much delinquency was not disclosed delinquency that might otherwise have remained undiscovered.

A confidential file, which does not constitute a police record, is one of the most vital factors in the new set-up. Sufficient information is taken to clear with the Social Service Exchange and a history of police contacts, voluntary recreational programs, if any, and progress reports are entered briefly on the 5 by 8 card.

The work of the Crime Prevention Division is predicated on the idea that prevention of crime is just as essential as prevention of physical disease and that waiting until a crime had been attempted or committed means shortsightedness which is very costly to the taxpayers. Regarding the underlying philosophy of the Juvenile Police Bureau, its unique functions, and methods of work, Lieutenant Lester writes:

The Underlying Philosophy of Juvenile Police Work.—Juvenile Police work is based on the premise that a special police technique is required in the proper handling of children's cases. The Police Department is usually the first agency that comes in contact with the juvenile delinquent. Many times this first experience is a deciding factor in the child's future conduct. First impressions under the stress attendant to arrest are likely to form indelible concepts in the plastic minds of youngsters. Therefore, it is extremely important to have such cases handled by an expert who is conscious of the part he may be playing in the lives of these children and through them, the lives of others who may be influenced by social contacts.

Juvenile police work is concerned with the social adjustment of the child and contemplates correction but is in no way punitive. On the other hand, social justice for adults is based on the theory that the person who violates the law should be punished. One theory being the exact antithesis of the other, it is readily understood that the police officers who become adept in applying the one theory might find it difficult to apply the other fairly and justly. Because of this underlying principle it is even more essential that juvenile work be more specialized than other phases of police work. Unique Functions of the Juvenile Police Bureau.— The Crime Prevention Division of the Los Angeles Police Department renders the following community services:

1. Twenty-four-hour emergency service in all matters of crime and dependency affecting children.
2. Complete investigation of all criminal phases of cases involving children.
3. Investigation and prosecution of all adults who have committed crimes against children.
4. Discovery and elimination of the causes of delinquency through investigation of individual cases and community conditions.
5. Detection of children in danger and the minimizing of these dangers by suggested supervised recreational and character-building activities.
6. Counseling with parents in matters of supervision of pre-delinquent and delinquent children.
7. Complete cooperation with the Detective Service in clearing crime reports and making application of modus operandi.

Specific Methods Used by Juvenile Police Bureau.— The Juvenile Police are required to make prompt and thorough investigations of all cases where crime has been committed by or against juveniles, followed immediately by a proper presentation of all facts to the Juvenile Court. In the conduct of such an investigation it is necessary to:

1. Secure all details from the offender and the victim and go over these matters carefully with the suspect in an effort to determine two things: Has an offense by or a crime against a juvenile been committed? Did the suspect commit the offense or the crime?
2. Weigh all evidence and determine the advisability of detention or release. (Less than 50 per cent of the boys and girls arrested by the Los Angeles Police Department are detained even as long as overnight.)
3. Go into full details with the parents or guardians and learn the answers to the following questions:
   a. Has the child been a problem in the home? If so, how?
   b. What standards are used by the parents in reaching their conclusions?
   c. Observe the parents and their attitudes—are they dependable? Do they alibi and offer excuses? Are they reasonable? Do they blame the school, associates—the police?
   d. Are the parents in any way responsible for the offense? If they are incapable of controlling their child, can they be helped to overcome their weaknesses?
   e. Are the parents capable of making an adjustment? Do they need help? Who can best give this help?

If it is necessary or advisable to take the child before the court, all facts brought out by the investigation must be presented. If the juvenile officer's work is properly done, he is in a position to offer helpful suggestions in the matter of the court's disposition of the case.

The juvenile officer must know the objectives and facilities of all social agencies in the field of child welfare and in the conduct of his investigations must ask himself these questions: (1) Can any of these agencies be helpful? (2) Will they accept the case? (3) How can the greatest assistance be given to the agency that undertakes the follow-up work?

If the parents request voluntary supervision by the juvenile police officer, a supervised program should be arranged when it would occasion no conflict with the officer's duties as an investigator. The officer must determine the objectives of such a program and how they can best be realized. Will the child cooperate voluntarily or through compulsion? Can the program be rearranged in the event of failure? When is supervision to be relaxed or withdrawn? What constitutes a satisfactory adjustment?

The juvenile officer must analyze many factors in the conduct of his investigations and must determine the answers to the following questions:

> *(1) What other facts has the investigation brought out? (2) Were other juveniles involved in the commission of the offense? If so, were they found and were their cases thoroughly investigated and proper dispositions made? (3) Were adults involved? If so, was evidence preserved and were apprehensions and prosecutions successful? (4) Were other crimes committed? (5) Was modus operandi carefully applied? (6) Was all property recovered and returned to the victims? (7) Were moral hazards affecting children in the community disclosed by the investigation? If so, were they successfully removed? If not, were all community facilities brought into play in an attempt to remove them?*

In the determination of a proper disposition of a case a number of factors are important. Many times the offense is less important than such factors as previous record, school reputation, community reputation, social history, intelligence, physical condition and environment.

Since police work concerns itself primarily with investigation, the duties of police officers assigned to the juvenile branch differ little from those of the rest of the service. This is true even of the work of police units whose efforts are basically crime preventive. Here, however, the emphasis shifts from the individual and his conduct to the community and the moral hazards that endanger youth.

It is the responsibility of the police to protect life and property and to preserve the peace. The fact that a juvenile is a suspected perpetrator of an offense does not lessen in any way the responsibility of the police. It is just as important to recover and return stolen property to the victim of the offense as in any other case.

The methods employed by juvenile police officers investigating the criminal aspects of a case are of vital importance to the ultimate adjustment of the delinquent child. Juvenile officers in Los Angeles long ago realized that efforts to obtain truthful statements by inhuman treatment are seldom effective and never justified. The ineffectiveness of so called "third-degree" methods is overshadowed only by the brutalizing effect upon both the accused and the person resorting to such measures. Mental torture is as much to be deplored as physical violence, and resort to either is an indictment to the intelligence, experience, and initiative of the officer who employs it. Brutality, long abhorred in relation to juvenile cases, is just as intolerable when applied to adults.

To be effective the police approach must be gentle but firm must be with a sympathetic understanding but without condonement. The child's confidence must be gained but never violated. The wise and experienced officer does not bargain for the truth. His technique is such that the child finds it easy to make a complete, truthful statement. As a case in point I recall a fifteen year old boy who was charged with grand theft of an automobile, burglary, kidnapping and robbery. The detectives of two cities and special agents from a large public utilities corporation investigated the case for several days and although the boy was positively identified by two of the victims, he stoutly maintained his innocence. The importance of securing a truthful statement from this lad lay in the fact that he had said to each of his victims, " If I'm ever nabbed by the cops and you dare to identify me, it will be the last thing you ever do, because I'm a member of a gang and everyone of us has sworn to kill any person who puts the finger on any member of our mob." This boy was finally surrendered to us by a sister city and brought to our

Bureau where, after hours of friendly, earnest conversation with a juvenile officer, he made a full statement of the facts and confessed more offenses than he was known to have committed. When asked why he had been so stubborn and uncooperative, he said, "Well, I thought I was a big shot and it would look like weakness if I helped the cops any," but he admitted that the talk with the juvenile officer had changed his point of view and ... he was no longer proud of the crimes he had committed and was ashamed of the tough attitude he had assumed throughout the investigation.

The success of interviews with a boy or girl suspected of an offense cannot be measured alone by the truthfulness of the statements made but is likewise dependent upon the mental attitude assumed by the child regarding his or her confession. The child should never feel that he has been trapped into making admissions. His self-respect should be heightened, not lowered, since it is the misconduct, not the admission, that should bring remorse.

The various factors contributing to the cause of the individual delinquency are of greatest importance to the juvenile officer. By a careful study of the cause a better understanding may be reached with the child and a ready solution sometimes offers itself. At the same time invaluable information thus obtained makes possible a more comprehensive plan for crime prevention. It is generally agreed by students of social problems that a complete knowledge of underlying causes of crime is essential with individual delinquents for the success of any preventive program. Any deep sympathetic understanding is logically based on a thorough knowledge of the underlying causal factors of delinquency.

When the juvenile officer has the authority to decide what action should be proposed, it is important in cases that may be handled out of court, that the background as a whole be scrutinized and the disposition made in view of all the facts. The attitude of parent and child, the previous record and social history, are often far more important than the offense in the consideration of proper disposition of the case.

It is not essential that the juvenile officer investigate extraneous phases of the conduct of a child, such as the school record and home relationships in those cases where the very seriousness of the offense demands court action. This work must be done by the probation officer and duplication and overlapping of work should be avoided whenever possible. This is particularly applicable to that percentage of cases involving definite criminal tendencies to which the Juvenile Court must give proper recognition through clinical diagnosis and careful application of scientific methods, lest Dillingers and Hickmans unwittingly may be allowed to develop in our respective neighborhoods.

Possibly the greatest advantage in having juvenile police lies in the value of coordination of community effort to effect two things—a whole some district in which to live and rear children, and the satisfactory adjustment of the unfortunate youngsters who find themselves in conflict with society. Complete cooperation is always dependent upon a full understanding and appreciation of the other fellow's viewpoint. Before the attitude of an agency can be understood, it is necessary to have an intimate knowledge, not only of its objectives but also its facilities. A close relationship between the juvenile officer and other agencies interested in the welfare of children makes it possible to formulate a program that encompasses the whole field of crime prevention.

From reports received from various parts of the country it is evident that the police work in behalf of juveniles as developed in California has much to offer to other communities. In many communities most of the work is done by policewomen. Henrietta Additon has done much toward the development of the Crime Prevention Bureau of the New York City Police Department, but this work has been greatly curtailed at present.

As Professor Sutherland maintains, "at the time when strenuous efforts are being made in several departments to build up the respect for the police and the morale of the police, it is rather ungracious" to hurl any criticism against it, particularly since the police officers in the juvenile bureaus are more discriminately chosen and undoubtedly possess far higher qualifications than those in the regular police department. But in order to understand the situation with reference to crime prevention it is necessary to state some of the objections raised to this form of police work. There is the general criticism in the mind of the average citizen of inefficiency, lawlessness, brutality, lack of education of the average police officer. It may also be added that the officers in police juvenile bureaus rarely have the educational background and training to carry on social investigations in the field of juvenile delinquency and to engage in social treatment of offenders and their families. The above criticisms have been directed rather indiscriminately to the patrolmen on the beat, local precinct officers, and those in specialized bureaus dealing with children's problems. The more faithful and efficient officers and departments are rightly "smarting under this criticism."

Vollmer and others have done much to indicate the responsibility of the public in the work of the police and have shown under what serious handicaps the police must work. The White House Conference on Child Health and Protection adds:

Much of the criticism heaped upon the police for their failure to enforce the laws and preserve the peace successfully should be directed to other law enforcing agencies. The public often forgets that the police, daily, display a high degree of intelligence, bravery and devotion to duty. Not only would a more just attitude toward them raise the esprit de corps of the entire police personnel, but children also would respond to the same attitude, coming to look upon the policeman as a friend and protector.

Sutherland maintains that the concept of preventive police work has not been clearly defined:

> *It seems to include a great variety of methods, including "hounding the hoodlums," attacks on criminal hangouts, frequent patrolling, warning residents and business concerns to keep doors and windows locked, friendly acquaintance with the residents on the beat, friendly relations with boys' gangs, organization of recreational activities in areas where delinquency rates are high, concentrated and cooperative efforts to influence boys who*

are getting into trouble, and social service work with families or individuals in distress.

On the other hand, much of the preventive work of the police must be done by the regular male policemen, and must become a part of the regular police program. This preventive work by the regular staff has been well developed in Rochester, New York, and in Berkeley. Efforts are made to build up friendly relations with the schools, and in case conferences with the various social agencies which are interested in programs for individuals who are inclined toward delinquency.

Jonah J. Goldstein maintains, however, that a rather regrettable attitude prevails on the part of the Children's Court toward the Bureau of Crime Prevention in New York:

The records of the Children's Court are a closed book to the Bureau of Crime Prevention. Not only have there been no conferences with the Bureau but its activities are resented.

The Children's Court judges have, in conferences with street railway officials, sought to prevent the turning over of youngsters who hitched on trolley cars to the Bureau of Crime Prevention and requested that they be brought to the Children's Court instead. Since when is hitching on a trolley car or a taxi-cab evidence of juvenile delinquency? What normal boy did not at some time or other steal a ride? For his own safety, stealing rides should be stopped, and can be stopped much more effectively in cooperation with the Bureau of Crime Prevention than by arrest, arraignment and adjudication as a juvenile delinquent in the Children's Court.

Instead of seeking an increase of business for the Children's Court through conferences with the railroad companies, such conferences should be held with the Bureau of Crime Prevention. A social check up on the intake would prevent this ridiculous spectacle.

Methods of Cooperation with Other Agencies.— Albert J. Sargent, Chief probation officer, Municipal Court of Boston, points out how to secure police cooperation by the probation department and how each can be of service to the other in their close contacts which they make daily in their work. His observations regarding the possible resentment by the probationer against the scrutiny by both a police and a probation officer are of interest. Although the following statements are written chiefly from the point of view of the adult probationer, they apply with equal validity to the juvenile probationer.

The inevitable meeting of police and probation work at various points brings at the very outset of a case an opportunity for immediate mutual help between the police and probation systems. The arresting officers come to court in many instances possessed of information of valuable, preliminary interest. Arrests in certain types of crime do not occur until after close and continued observation by the police officer during which he has acquired a knowledge of the defendant which embraces the local activities or even more remote facts of marked significance to the probation officer, whose job it is to gather the essential social history if he can.

Intelligent police officers, experienced in their work and the performance of their duties, who are under proper supervision, are as a rule observant and logical. Frequently they see beyond the crime, and pursue their inquiries to the point where information is gathered which is of direct value to the probation officer. Their investigations in connection with the acquisition of evidence preparatory to prosecution of a case often bring them in touch with factors in general social history, which though in many cases inadmissible at trial, are of pointed interest in the disposition of the case and, therefore, of special interest to the officer in court. This information should not be lost through silence or apathy on the part of either the police officer or the probation officer. When brought to light at the earliest possible moment it may be developed to its full value through efficient investigation. The very details of the offense upon which the officer bases his complaint are occasionally illuminating and serve as a guide to the trained court worker.

The probation officer in court should not pass over with indifference or judge too lightly the impressions of the arresting officer when honestly given in an effort to be helpful. These opinions on the part of the police officer usually spring from observation and thought, and if in some particulars their value may be later disproved by investigation they are often an aid to a well-rounded study of the case under consideration. Not the least of the advantages derived from early conference with the police officer is the correction of false information given by defendants to the probation officer or the detection of evasiveness. A check-up by the probation officer with the police frequently reveals conflicting statements by the defendant and results in a more definite persuasion of the latter to a reasonable and truthful viewpoint, thus avoiding misdirected efforts in the early stages of investigation.

The police officer's contact with the case in its initial stages generally makes him a source of helpfulness to the probation officer. The fullest cooperation between the two cannot fail to produce beneficial results. The police can render most acceptable service to the supervisor in the field, as they are generally more aware of what is happening in the community than probation officers. Their personal knowledge of the activities of probationers living within their district and coming under their supervision should therefore be of considerable help to the supervisor.

An objection might be raised that a probationer would be stirred to resentment or repelled from full cooperation if he felt that he was the object of scrutiny by both police and the probation department and that therefore the real purpose of persuading him to a better mode of life might be seriously endangered. The assumption by the police officer of the clear-cut duties and responsibilities of the supervisor is not what is contemplated in the situation just described; it relates instead to the confidential, timely observation and notice made by the police officer which may enable the supervisor to exert prompt and effective guidance of the probationer. The average probation officer has a heavy load to carry, he is charged usually with the care of a large number of cases and is unable to meet all the demands upon his time and attention. It is in these circumstances especially that the police officer's help may prove opportune in stemming developments which might seriously affect the success of supervision.

James K. Watkins, recently Commissioner of Police, Detroit, is inclined to take a middle road in the preventive work among young people. He says:

Insofar as police departments are concerned, there are those who take the position that the police should leave the problem almost entirely alone and should not attempt protective work with young people. The exponents of this theory assert that the police are trained for their main job and that to use them in the protective and preventive field will necessarily result in poor work. They say that this work should be done entirely by other agencies probation officers, child-caring agencies, boy scout organizations and the like. On the other hand, there are those who advocate the development in a police department of a bureau working among the youth of both sexes, and developing a protective and preventive organization of broad scope even involving treatment work with the individual. My own view is that the proper function of the police lies between these two extremes. I think that they can properly go some distance beyond the older and narrower conception, but that there is a line which cannot, it is true, always be clearly defined, beyond which the police should not go. The development of crime preventive programs in police departments has been necessarily slow and is still largely in the experimental stages.

The great question is just how far they should go in their work and I believe that the limits can be fairly well outlined. Let us assume that we have the organization suggested above, with a detail assigned to each precinct. The regular officer walking his beat should be competent to recognize that a problem exists, for example, in connection with a gang of boys making trouble in a neighborhood, but he is probably not trained either to diagnose the difficulty or to administer the treatment. If the proper spirit of cooperation within the department is developed, he will report the condition to his superior officer, who can then direct the juvenile detail to investigate the situation. A member of the detail can then make a careful investigation, and, if he is properly trained, can determine in a general way the causes of the trouble and the proper agency to deal with it. It may be that the whole trouble is due to the influence of one dominating leader among the group. It would be within the scope of the officer's duties to get full information regarding this individual. It might then be the proper thing for him to see that a complaint is made against the boy and that he is brought before the juvenile court. On the other hand, this might be entirely wrong and the officer should perhaps see that an agency dealing with boys is brought into contact with this individual and, through him, with the group.

This, it seems to me, is as far as the police should go. I do not believe that the officer should himself attempt treatment. In a very short time the case load would be altogether too great. Again, the officer on the beat should be qualified to judge whether the conditions surrounding a poolroom or a dancehall are good, or bad, but he will not ordinarily be in a position to do very much toward remedying them, if he feels that there is need for improvement. He should report the condition to his superior officer and the matter should be assigned to the juvenile division, and if it is a dancehall, both the juvenile and the women's detail. They, working in cooperation, can perhaps themselves remedy the situation. If there are individual cases, however, which need attention, then they should be referred to other agencies. The women's detail in a precinct may learn, either through their own investigation or through the report from a citizen or another officer, of a case of neglected children. The work of the detail should be to make a thorough investigation of the situation and determine the proper steps for correcting it. But, in general, it will not be possible for the detail itself to bring about the improvement. Again, the case load would become altogether too heavy. Our woman's division last year, for example, had personal contact with some nine thousand girls and young women. With thirty three officers in the division it is obviously out of the question to expect detailed attention to the individual case. All they can do is to take such immediate action as may be essential and then see that the matter is brought to the attention of the proper agency, public or private, for individual treatment.

Looking at the matter purely from a selfish police viewpoint, there are definite advantages to be gained from a juvenile division. Some of the boys with whom the officers come in contact are bound to go wrong and it will unquestionably be of help to the department to have the information gathered by the juvenile detail when, at a later date, the detective division is forced to handle a problem involving the individual or the gang. I feel quite certain that as time passes the detective bureau will receive invaluable assistance from reports of the juvenile detail, particularly in connection with the activities of certain gangs.

Should Police Officers Carry on Social Case Treatment?—It is apparent from the foregoing excerpts that the juvenile police officer is concerned with more than "the immediate needs of the child and of the general public security and the enforcement of particular laws," functions ascribed to him by the White House Conference on Child Health and Protection. Some of the juvenile police officers are also concerned with serious conditions of family maladjustment, conflict with the law and social norms.

The police officer—the patrolman, or the officer at the local precinct, or the specialized juvenile officer—as stated before, is generally the first representative of the law with whom a delinquent child or "a child in trouble" comes into personal contact. He is in the most strategic position of all. His conduct, his approach, his attitudes toward "law-breaking and law-breakers" are of utmost importance in the tense and emotional situations in which these children find themselves. He needs a comprehensive knowledge of child psychology, of human nature, and of the adolescent world in order to do justice by them. Furthermore, "the people" depend upon the police officer "to determine the fact of conflict between children and organized society and to exercise discretion as to whether it is sufficiently serious to merit arrest or court action." Thus he is called upon again to make decisions which involve a knowledge of the prevailing social norms and legal precedent in relation to child welfare. Therefore, even though the officer should concern himself with nothing more than the immediate needs of the child and the safety of the community he needs training in the various fields applying to human nature and the social order. There is no more reason to believe that—with the above demands put upon a police officer he should be exempt from training and from a knowledge of, at least, the fundamentals of social work, any more than the probation officer making a social investigation relative to the various petitions filed in the matter of child delinquency should be exempt.

But should the juvenile police officer concern himself with "serious problems of maladjustment and home visits" beyond the initial contact? The White House Conference on Child Health and Protection is very emphatic in its statement that "the police should not undertake intensive and continuous direction or responsibility for a child." Such responsibility should rest with the child guidance clinics, probation departments, and other child welfare agencies—according to the nature of the problem which have been organized to deal with the intricate processes of therapy. It has been proved by such authorities as Healy, Burt, Lenroot, Shaw, Burgess, Thomas, and others previously referred to be far more expedient to have the problematic child referred to competent specialists in social therapeutics at the earliest possible moment and without any missteps.

The average juvenile police officer is not equipped to approach child welfare problems from the specialist's standpoint, and even if he were in a position to do so he would be duplicating the work of other agencies specifically organized to perform these functions.

With the establishment of children's courts, the view has been widely accepted that only these courts, through their probation officers, should deal with children's problems, and that the police, by virtue of the nature of their work in suppressing crime and their past failures in dealing with social problems, are disqualified or unsuited to assist in the solution of children's problems. If we accept the present conventional police methods as something that cannot be changed, then we must agree that this therapy is correct. It is believed, however, that most police departments gladly will cooperate in any reasonable plan pointed out to them, for the welfare of children and the prevention of delinquency and crime. That this belief is well founded is indicated by the attitude and practice of many individual police officers.

Justice is a single operation, working through a number of agencies. While the police start the process, it is left to ... courts and other agencies to complete it.

William I. Thomas and Dorothy S. Thomas are also of the opinion that all problems of retraining of the child should be referred to regular child welfare agencies:

> *There is no question that the police should be associated with social work, that women should be a part of the police and that the entrance of women into the activities of the police will facilitate the socialization of police work. The main problem relates to the division of function between the police and the other agencies doing social work. The visiting teacher work, the social aspects of the child clinics and child guidance institutes, the study and management of cases under investigation and on probation, are now largely in the hands of women. The case workers themselves are dependent on the psychologists, psychiatrists and sociologists, and their work is becoming progressively a study of behavior in connection with the treatment of the case. Bad behavior trends are often set up in infancy, mental deviations, disabilities and conflicts are involved, the case worker has always a problem of retraining, and under the best handling and during long years the result is frequently disappointing. The participation of the police will be a benefit to the whole situation and what the limitations of their functions are will be determined by experience, but "prevention and protection" as used in their programs is not a simple matter. It involves cooperation and integration of work between persons specialized in different ways.*

In addition to the juvenile police officers, patrolmen on the beat and the safety patrol as well as neighborhood precinct officers come in numerous contacts with juveniles. "Not infrequently individual policemen show by their work that they have a fine perception and appreciation of social values, and for this reason are qualified by temperament, if not by training to work with children." Talks by police officers at schools regarding safety precautions in traffic have helped in making "the cop" a friend.

It is of utmost importance that the attitude of the policeman on the beat be friendly and sympathetic toward the children. Fortunately one hears only occasionally of such police attitudes as expressed in the following quotation by Caroline Ware.

My opinion of the people on this street is that from five years up to sixty they are all thieves. They are all born criminals; I wouldn't trust any of them over three years old. You try and do something for them! It's no use; you might as well work on that sewer over there. You see the tin water drains on the church there? Well, they were all copper once, but the kids stole them all, and when the priest tried to chase them, they threw stones and broke the church windows. In ten years they'll all be gunmen and gangsters. If I had it to say, I'd send them all to Sing Sing. I wouldn't build no playgrounds for them; that won't do any good. I've been on this beat for twenty years and I ain't seen no change yet!

Such attitudes promote constant hostility and aggravate an already aggravated situation. Such officers tend to use "third degree" methods in their dealings with minors, a situation which has aroused considerable public condemnation. On the other hand:

> *Friendly advice and admonition will usually be accepted by the child in the spirit in which it is given, but threats of punishment (in terms of the criminal law), are both ineffectual and foolish, as the child usually knows when the officer is bluffing and if he does not, is likely to take a chance in order to find out. Nothing will produce confidence in and respect for an individual more than the knowledge that he is honest and sincere, that he keeps his word when given, and that he will not threaten to do something impossible.*

Police Field Work Cases.— Eleanor L. Hutzel, Deputy Commissioner of the Detroit Police Department, and Madeline L. Macgregor, Chief of Social Service of the Grand Rapids Child Guidance Clinic, cite a number of interesting "field work cases," showing procedure and facts obtained by questioning, during patrol contacts. However, no case treatment is attempted. Three of the twenty-four cases cited are reproduced here for purposes of illustrating a possible approach to girls by police officers, police procedure in difficult circumstances, the data obtained in a short interview, and the referral of cases:

Patrol Contact.— Policewomen observed young girl on street corner in downtown district at 3 A. M. At that hour in the morning policewomen on patrol question any unaccompanied young girl whom they observe on the street.

PROCEDURE	FACTS OBTAINED BY QUESTIONING
Police-women approached the girl. Identified themselves as police officials. Explained that because she was alone on the street at that hour they wished to be sure that she was properly protected.	Age—given as 17 years.
	Present address—recognized as that of a cheap hotel where young girls were admitted without question.
	Previous address—also recognized as questionable.
	Parents living in another state. Said she could show letters that they were satisfied to have her here.
	Unable to find letters from parents.
Accompanied girl to her room in hotel in order that she might show letters from her parents. Interview in hotel room.	Articles of masculine clothing observed in room which girl explained belonged to her husband.
At this point man entered from an adjoining room.	Girl noticeably disturbed, introduced man, named him, and hurriedly added facts about the date and place of marriage.
One policewoman asked man to step into hall where she questioned him.	Policewoman noted that the girl's introduction of man gave him facts which he would have known if they had been married.
The other policewoman continued questioning girl.	What was wife's maiden name? No answer. Where had they lived since marriage? No answer. Where did wife's parents live? No answer.
	Girl admitted that she was not married to man; that her home was in Detroit. Gave her correct name and address of parents—correct age as sixteen years.

Man and girl taken to office of Woman's Bureau.	
List of missing girls showed that girl had been reported as missing by the Juvenile Court.	
Man charged with contributing to the delinquency of a female minor. Held at First Precinct Station.	
Parents of girl notified that she was located.	
Girl held at Juvenile Detention Home as police witness and for Juvenile Court.	
Special report written and left for Supervisor.	

CASE OF PEARL 13-W

Patrol Contact.— Girl observed loitering along the street in the downtown business section at 11 P. M. Policewomen followed girl for several blocks. She made no attempt to attract men but her aimless sauntering and her youth influenced the policewomen to speak to her.

PROCEDURE	FACTS OBTAINED BY QUESTIONING
Policewomen approached the girl, identified themselves, and explained that they would like to ask her a few questions.	Where are you going? Am waiting for my girl friend. How old are you? Sixteen years. Where do you live? 1801 B Street. (Fair residential district.) What is your friend doing downtown at 11 P. M.? She works in a restaurant. Where is restaurant? Do not know.
Policewomen then explained to the girl that in order to protect her, they would remain until her friend arrived. It was evident that the girl did not want this but the policewomen continued friendly conversation which was so casual that girl did not realize she was giving information about herself.	

In a short time the policewomen learned that the girl was not waiting for anyone. They then offered to take her home. Her reaction to this offer was such that the policewomen appreciated that there was something wrong. Further questioning resulted in information that the girl was thirteen years old and had run away from home.	
Girl taken to office of Woman's Bureau. No telephone at her home. Precinct asked to notify parents that girl was located. Mother refused to come for daughter.	
Girl taken to Juvenile Detention Home. Special report written and left for Supervisor.	Precinct later reported that girl left home early in afternoon after a quarrel with mother.

CASE OF MARTHA 14-W AND VERA 15-W

Patrol Contact.— Policewomen observed girls coming from an all-night restaurant at 2 A. M. Girls looked young and were dressed and "made- up" in a way that attracted attention.

PROCEDURE	FACTS OBTAINED BY QUESTIONING
Usual approach. Followed customary procedure of questioning girls separately.	Ages—eighteen and nineteen years respectively ... Living? In nearby apartment house. No relation. No friends. How long at apartment? Five weeks. Employment? None; living on money from home. Other questions about their recent living, their families, etc.
Girls were then told that police-women would take them home in their automobile. As soon as girls were in car, officers compared facts which they had obtained. There was enough disagreement to arouse suspicion, and the police-women, explaining this to the girls, asked permission to verify statements by inspecting apartment.	

Took girls to their apartment in a building which was known to officers as one where management was lax. Upon entering apartment found two men there. Girls became frightened when the men were found in the apartment.	One man said that he was the husband of Vera, calling her "R," and that he could show their marriage certificate. Said other man was his friend who visited him occasionally. He was asked routine questions and contradicted statements made by the girls.
Girls taken to bedroom by one policewoman; the other remained to question the men.	Girls gave their correct ages as fourteen and fifteen years; admitted they had come from Canada; Vera denied marriage.
Sent for manager of apartment. Explained situation.	
Telephoned for policemen to take men prisoners to office of Woman's Bureau.	
Girls taken to Woman's Bureau in policewomen's car.	
Woman's Bureau card index checked. Both girls known to department.	
Office interview with girls, after explaining that parents had reported them missing.	
Girls held at Juvenile Detention Home as police witnesses and for medical examinations.	
Men charged with pandering. Held at First Precinct Station.	
Parents notified that girls were located.	Records showed both girls were Canadian, reported missing for two months.
Special report written and left for Supervisor. Policewomen, in report, called attention to the fact that the girls should be further questioned in regard to any criminal responsibility of apartment house manager.	Girls stated they came to Detroit immediately after they ran away. Met one of the men found in apartment soon after coming to city. He arranged to rent apartment and brought the other man. Girls had prostituted with customers brought to the apartment by these men. Men did not live there but were in and out with customers.

The police officer in referring cases needs to familiarize himself or herself with the existing native institutions and key people as well as with the major social agencies serving the particular community, the "character-building agencies," the schools, the child caring agencies, the private protective agencies, the welfare agencies, health clinics, guidance clinics, and, needless to add, the probation department and the juvenile court. The newspaper reporter may at times prove an important asset, if he is cooperative in "printing items to which the Police Department desires to give publicity, but which have no particular news value." The Police Officer and Neighborhood Conditions.— Smith Bruce points out that police schools still relatively few in this country "usually emphasize such necessary elements as marksmanship but give little attention to methods dealing with juvenile problems or maintaining clean community conditions."

The maintenance of clean community conditions is one of the most valuable contributions that the police can make, and if effectively performed, under able leadership, will not alone insure physical and moral safety for children but in the end will result in a material reduction of crime. This service should include street patrol, inspection of parks, playgrounds, theaters, dance halls and similar services. Unattended children found in public at night should be taken to their homes and their parents warned that if such conduct recurs they will be prosecuted for contributing to the delinquency or neglect of their children.

Both the juvenile police officers and the regular officers in many communities concern themselves also in addition to the services cited above with the discovery of adults "polluting the morals of minors," with children at street trades, particularly at night, with sale of liquor and of salacious literature to minors, with "undercover operations," and other similar situations.

Hutzel and Macgregor in their Policewoman's Handbook add the following services which already are performed in some localities or should be performed by policewomen: looking out for discouraged unemployed women or girls who may be led into sexual promiscuity; secluded automobiles "under suspicious circumstances," or "cruising cars" occupied by men attempting to pick up young girls, or cars driven recklessly by hilarious young people; gambling devices and places; terminal stations; suspicious rooming houses and hotels, motion picture "palaces," over crowded and unsanitary housing conditions, and others. J. P. Trought's description of the Children's Police in Amsterdam gives interesting additional functions which might be assumed:

> *Day and night officers supervise minors in the streets, railway stations, markets, cinemas, dancing saloons, public-houses, etc., for the prevention of mendicity, truancy, vagrancy, and for maintenance of those prohibitive regulations especially established in the interests of the child. Their work is preventive, corrective and, where necessary, repressive; their prime object is to be counsellor, helper and protector to the minor brought before the court of first instance. General police who come into touch with a juvenile offender give notice to the children's police.*

The headquarters of this service is as unlike a police-station as it is possible to make it. Here the harassed mother brings her obstreperous son for guidance as to his management. Here the pre-trial investigations are prepared for the children's judge, and the arrangement for placing in an institution or under other guardianship carried out. The collection of data for research work is filed together with information concerning offenders.

Recommendations by the White House Conference.—The White House Conference on Child Health and Protection offers the following recommendations in dealing with juvenile delinquents by police officers:

> *In most instances it is unnecessary to arrest child offenders. Only in exceptional circumstances, or for the purpose of identification, should a child be placed in detention. When the child's identity has been determined and his correct address ascertained, he should be returned to the care and custody of his parents, preferably at his home, and the parents informed of the nature of his misconduct and of the probable action of the police. Under no circumstances should a child be arrested in his own home, except on warrant issued by the court.*

When a child is apprehended committing an offense that will necessitate his being brought to the attention of the court, the case should be referred to the children's bureau or detail for preliminary investigation and disposition.

Whenever possible, children should be interviewed in their homes, and not in police stations.

In case it is necessary to send a child to a place of detention, the patrol wagon should not be used. Most departments are provided with passenger cars which have no markings to distinguish them from privately owned automobiles and this type of car should be used. Under no circumstances should handcuffs be used. The procedure followed must depend upon the facts and circumstances in each case. No set rules can be adopted that will fit even two cases, let alone many. There is no reason why there should be a difference between day and night procedure in dealing with children's cases.

If it possibly can be avoided, children should not be taken to police stations, and when brought in should be sent immediately to their own homes or to the house of detention. It is inexcusable to place children in cells with adults. The period of time between the arrest and hearing should be reduced to a minimum. As indicated before, it is only in exceptional cases that it is necessary to detain the child pending hearing. It is unwise to book a child on the regular police blotter because of the publicity, but a modern card system should be installed for use in children's cases and a record made of every contact or observation by the department. Where a social service exchange is available, all cases should be registered with it. By this method the police will be brought into more intimate touch and cooperation with other agencies. When it is necessary to interview a child in a police station it should be done in private. Where a children's detail is maintained, all interviews should be conducted by members of this detail. Third degree methods never should be used. A girl should always be interviewed by a woman. In case a child is placed in detention the parents and the juvenile court should be notified immediately. There should be the highest degree of cooperation between the children's bureau or detail and the juvenile court and probation department. It is a distinct advantage to have these departments housed in the same building.

Special effort should be made to secure the cooperation and coordination of police service with other agencies in the community, particularly the schools; education, health and welfare departments; boys' and girls' clubs; and all other agencies dealing with social problems affecting children. Berkeley, California, under the leadership of Police Chief August Vollmer, has established a coordinating council, composed of the executive heads of the several departments and meeting at frequent intervals for the discussion of common problems.

There can be no question but that the police have a definite place in dealing with children's problems which they cannot avoid entirely, even if they would, and which affords a real opportunity to make a liberal contribution to the care and protection of children, and the general improvement of social conditions surrounding them. It is not the province of the police to undertake social case work but rather to act as official observer and report to the agency, either public or private, best qualified to handle the particular problems. Neither should the police undertake intensive character rehabilitation as provided in the probation program. They must, of necessity, make contact with children and it is, therefore, highly important that the result of the contact be an asset and not a liability.

Situations often arise when it is not possible or advisable for a police officer to interview a child in his own home, particularly when neighbors become curious or other children listen in. It would also be unwise to take him to school or a social agency for an interview, since such procedure would violate the privacy with which the police like to handle the case, particularly before it is ascertained that the child is implicated in a delinquency.

5

Coordination and Planning in Social Work

Introduction

Other "soft spots" in the system may be eliminated through the development of *accountability machinery* of the kind already described. However, the problems of an era of specialization, large-scale organization, social instability, and professional innovation also require something more: *adequate coordination and planning on several levels.*

While this volume addresses itself to the specific requirements of an urban area, the present chapter must turn initially to statewide planning and coordination structures. It may then focus on the problem of planning and coordination at the city level.

First, however, some additional concepts require specification. *Planning*, as the word is employed here, is the process concerned with evaluating alternatives, developing proposals and timetables for the *future*, and indicating the methods and stages for implementing proposals. It involves formulation of criteria or goals relevant to choices to be made. It requires research and fact finding as well as decisions about goals, values, pace, and priorities.

Coordination, on the other hand, deals with the meshing of agencies, programs, services, and activities in order to accomplish basic objectives. Each agency or unit requires information about the activities, areas of responsibility, and policies of the others so that actions and plans may be appropriately dovetailed. Adequate coordination is based on communication, interpretation, and interchange as well as provision for negotiation, settling differences, and arriving at agreements relating to policy or procedures. At times, where differences of opinion exist about objectives or methods, and where the differences involve mutually contradictory courses, coordination may demand devices (hearings, policy decisions by those in authority, agreements for test periods, etc.) to ensure that some common course is adopted by all concerned.

For present purposes, it is helpful to differentiate between coordination relating to *agency programs*, policies, objectives, scope, and plans, on the one hand, and coordination of work *on the level of the individual case*, on the other. The latter phenomenon has already been referred to as *service integration*.

When a great many planning activities are carried on by different groups, there is need for *coordination of planning* to minimize inconsistencies, contradictions, and costly duplication, as well as to define roles and responsibility. A major objective in adequate coordination of long-range planning is the formulation of acceptable, coherent over-all goals, which become the point of departure, in the particular field, for those undertaking major responsibility in specific subareas.

State-Wide Structures

The field of services to delinquents and other children in trouble has become increasingly concerned in the past decade with the need for adequate state-wide coordination machinery. Less attention has been given to long-range planning. The urgency of adequate provision was highlighted by the U.S. Senate delinquency subcommittee and by the 1960 White House Conference on Children. Each legislative year brings changes in some states, so that no published work can be complete and up to date. Trends may be noted and alternatives posed, however.

The state welfare department. While a considerable proportion of the professional literature urges that a state's department of public welfare take on the major coordination role in relation to delinquency, three major public patterns are actually discernible in practice: (1) state coordination and planning in the hands of a public welfare department (approximately 13-15 states); (2) coordination and planning assigned to special youth commissions or committees, created by legislative enactment and/or gubernatorial appointment (7-8 states, totals depending on definitions); (3) coordination and planning by a youth authority or one of its derivations (7 states). Impressive, if piecemeal, contributions to planning and some limited coordination have also been effected by voluntary state-wide citizen machinery—initially, the groups established to follow up the 1950 White House Conference on Children and more recently, in several states, the Citizen Action programs. In many states the leadership-coordination task is divided—or not assigned.

The American Public Welfare Association states very clearly the claim of a state public welfare department:

> *State government should place responsibility in a single state agency which it can hold responsible for planning, for facilitating coordination, and for seeing that needed services are made available either under its own or other auspices. The state welfare department is most advantageously situated to accept this responsibility. In carrying out this assignment, it is essential that the department work cooperatively with other organizations and agencies having appropriate functions in the field and that it contribute in every possible way to the strengthening of their programs. This is especially true in relation to juvenile courts which have a major and essential responsibility in the treatment of juvenile delinquents.*

The case for this policy proposal is quite clear. Delinquency is considered to be symptomatic of deprivations and disturbances affecting an individual's total life-situation.

Prevention and treatment require a broad range of services "which in most respects are concerned with the same problems that are dealt with by public welfare agencies in all of their areas of responsibility. These include economic dependency, family breakdown, desertion and abandonment, domestic discord, parental neglect and abuse, behavior problems and emotional disturbances." Moreover, a state public welfare agency has an existing structure in every locality of a state, is already in touch with large segments of the most vulnerable part of the population, and is always "deeply involved in community organization for developing needed services for families and children."

Of some interest is the fact that this point of view envisages that the state public welfare department will have both operating responsibilities (which in turn may include direct administration of services, standard setting, supervision, licensing, consultation) and planning-coordination responsibilities. The department will also encourage, and perhaps provide staff services for, creation of a "statewide structure for broad citizen involvement in planning, decision-making and coordination of programs." Citizen social action will be welcomed.

This general perspective has considerable support and is implemented in a number of states in varying degrees depending on state standards for services to children and the salience of the delinquency problem. Various professional groups and individuals on the national and state scenes, too, have resisted organization of services for delinquents apart from their broader child welfare or public welfare context.

The influence of the approach may be illustrated with reference to Pennsylvania. Within the State Public Welfare Department an Office for Children and Youth operates certain institutions and facilities directly, reimburses localities and voluntary agencies for institutional and child welfare services, and carries on a program of standard setting and licensing. Responsibility for prevention and treatment of delinquency is in a Bureau of Youth Services located within this department. The bureau operates the state institutions, supervises the other institutions, seeks to build up services for prevention and control (work with gangs), and subsidizes training of probation and police staff. Its consultation, research, and planning activities are modest but are expected to expand.

Many similar functions are assigned to the Youth Rehabilitation Section of Idaho's Division of Mental Health, Maryland's Bureau of Child Welfare under the Department of Public Welfare, and Washington's Division of Children and Youth Services in a Department of Institutions. In addition to statistics systems, research, consultation, training, administration of institutions and forestry camps, and responsibility for aftercare activities which tend to characterize these agencies, they also have community services bureaus. The latter offer consultation to localities and may also, in some instances, become actively involved in upgrading individual agencies, supporting citizen action programs, or operating local community services.

Why, then, specialized coordinating agencies to deal with services to delinquents and young offenders? The answers are as often historical, political, and pragmatic as they are principled and substantive. (1) It is frequently possible to rally citizen and legislative interest around one problem, particularly an alarming, urgent, and unpleasant problem, where an ongoing program which has many facets cannot command attention or funds. (2) It is sometimes necessary to create a new structure for planning and coordination in order to ensure an energetic and creative staff and citizen board, where an ongoing department is bogged down in its traditions and long-accumulated limitations and roadblocks. (3) Sometimes the problem is so large and so urgent as to demand the creation of a body which will give it substantial and concentrated attention. (4) Even a public welfare department does not encompass all facets of a program for delinquents. Education, health, and mental health agencies in a state also conduct crucial programs. A case may therefore be made for a structure independent of any of these departments.

Thus, despite the strength of the public welfare position, one should not question alternative structures merely on the grounds that they are not state public welfare departments. The real issue is whether these alternative structures have adequate relationships to the welfare department and to other departments and whether they ensure implementation of the crucial functions. The American Public Welfare Association, in fact, recognizes this alternative in its statement:

> *Specifically in states where specialized correction or youth-serving agencies or authorities have already been created and are dealing effectively with parts of the total program, the public welfare department should not duplicate such services but should work with them in full cooperation.*

A youth authority. The Youth Authority Plan is frequently mentioned as an alternate coordination structure, concentrating on juvenile delinquency and youth crime. Its history, implications, and strengths are reviewed in a number of readily available sources.

What has become known as the youth authority movement arose as a reaction to an exposé of New York City practices in dealing with offenders in the 16-21 age group. The American Law Institute drafted a model statute after considering a report and recommendations from New York's Community Service Society. As the result of a variety of local circumstances and a decade of crusading by John R. Ellingston of the American Law Institute, a number of states adopted youth authority plans and others were influenced in various aspects of their programming and administration of services. California led the way with its Youth Authority in 1941. Other plans (many since revised) were adopted by Minnesota (1947), Wisconsin (1947), Massachusetts (1948), Texas (1949), Arizona (1951), Kentucky (1952), Illinois (1953), the federal government (1956).

The states listed deviated considerably from the model act and developed wide variations in the programs implemented. For the most part, for example, youth authorities affect juvenile delinquents rather than youthful offenders, who were the original objects of interest. The "typical" authority, if there is one, accepts courtordered commitments (usually juvenile court) for terms which are indeterminate after court adjudication and court decision as to whether probation or another community-based decision is desirable. Committed children and youths are then sent to a receptiondiagnostic-classification facility which makes a treatment plan. The authority has, or should have, access to a diversified group of treatment institutions. Authorities have pioneered in the use of conservation camps, following the California lead. In addition, most of the authorities have functioned in what is usually called the "prevention" area, although the specific programs show considerable variation. Several have undertaken training responsibilities, administrative research, and long-range planning.

Beck has acknowledged the extent to which youth authority programs have improved services to delinquents, but he has also asked whether all states need such a plan. The separate elements —commitment to one agency; central diagnosis and screening; indeterminate sentences; operation of new treatment facilities do not require a new agency as such. In fact, Bloch and Flynn, as well as Beck, cite instances in which all of these have developed without an authority: Virginia has committed to a state department rather than one institution since 1922; New York and New Jersey have diagnostic centers; many states have forestry camps. While granting the advances a new agency may make because of enthusiasm, support, and publicity, they ask whether one should pay the price of separating out services to delinquents from the general field of child welfare when there is general conviction as to the need for a full range of child welfare services for effective prevention and treatment.

The California Youth Authority, the oldest and most widely known of the authorities, has a program of diagnosis and treatment (reception centers, camps, institutions), administration, research, field services (probation, parole), prevention, education, and some coordination. It is a major agency of state government, responsible for more than a dozen institutions camps reception centers and ten branch offices. Over 15,000 children are in its care in institutions and on parole, and an experimental community treatment program is being launched. The board itself is responsible for acceptance and rejection of cases; initial classification and assignment to institutions; release on parole; suspension, revocation, and restoration of parole; and final discharge of wards. The authority director is board chairman; in his capacity as director he administers the facilities and "prevention" work. Included in the latter is consultation to localities on probation services, juvenile detention, and county camps (there is a generous state-aid program). In addition, a field staff assists localities which wish to initiate broader prevention services. The authority has carried out many kinds of training courses and institutes for probation officers and law enforcement personnel. It has an outstanding research program.

Recent California legislation has joined the Youth Authority with the Corrections Department in a new, larger unit. California also has an active and effective Governor's Advisory Committee on Children and Youth, which brings citizen opinion to bear on planning, provides informal interdepartmental coordination, and also deals with child welfare and mental health issues beyond the range of the authority.

The Massachusetts Youth Services Board was created in 1948 in order to place responsibility for custody, diagnosis, care, and treatment of juvenile delinquents in a single specialized agency. The board consists of three members appointed by the governor. Its chairman is also director of a Division of Youth Services which has been placed in the State Department of Education since 1052 but is "not subject to its control." As new facilities have been developed, they have been assigned to this division, which now administers a state-wide parole service, detention and reception centers, and state training schools (called "industrial schools"). Juvenile courts commit adjudicated delinquents to the board, which then selects specific facilities. The court continues to decide between community-based dispositions and adjudication.

Since 1953 a Bureau of Delinquency Prevention and Research, under the Division of Youth Services, has been developing a variety of consultation, survey, and training services. As is generally the case with such programs in many states, efforts are made to encourage local initiative and planning. State consultants make broader knowledge and experience available. The creation of local youth commissions and coordinating bodies is encouraged. A small staff of professionally qualified "detached workers" is available for "loan" to localities to cope with special problems and to conduct demonstrations. The board is also the channel to localities for a state-aid program involving the creation of school guidance and counseling programs.

The overburdened board has great difficulty in meeting its case disposition responsibilities, and it requires expansion. The history of the program would seem to provide no special evidence as to the validity of joining this role to that of providing leadership to local prevention efforts and stimulating state-wide planning and coordination. Since the delinquency program "umbrella" is inevitably limited and since this official state program, apparently, does not rally sufficient voluntary initiative, there is also an active statewide Massachusetts Committee on Children and Youth, now in its third year. Within the state administration there is an Interdepartmental Committee on Children and Youth.

The modified structures which have been developed in Wisconsin and Kentucky also offer interesting ways of achieving some of the youth authority advantages while ensuring the sound relationship of the youth authority program to the public welfare structure. As the result of a series of events related to special conditions in the state, the Wisconsin statute was revised at an early date, leaving the youth authority functions divided between the Division of Children and Youth and the Division of Correction both of which are parts of the State Department of Social Welfare. Related functions are placed under the Division of Mental Hygiene. In Kentucky, the Youth Authority as such became a Welfare Department division. The Bloch-Flynn evaluation is convincing: "The Wisconsin plan, which provides integrated services for delinquents within the framework of an omnibus department of welfare, seems most suitable *when the reorganization of state services for those of juvenile court age is required*".

The Wisconsin community organization program is deserving of special mention because of its substantial development. It began in 1949, taking its cue from the Social Security Act provision for subsidy to states "for developing state services for the encouragement and assistance of adequate methods of community child welfare organization in areas predominantly rural and other areas of special need." The state statute stresses coordination of planning in education, recreation, health, welfare; development and strengthening of preventive programs; establishment of councils and a variety of other local coordination structures. Professionally qualified community organizers have been provided, and the well-led Division of Children and Youth has deployed them in district areas (each covering fifteen counties) and as specialist consultants in a central office. As have other states, Wisconsin has developed through this agency improved statistical reports, consultation and training for law enforcement officials, a degree of improved case finding in the schools, youth participation, extension of recreation facilities, and more public information activity.

For purposes of the present discussion, special note is made of the field assistance to local communities and its emphasis on planning and coordination. White House Conference recommendations have been followed up. Another unique feature is the program of local community surveys supported by Division of Children and Youth staff services and the cooperation of other state agencies, if the community meets conditions relative to an official request from a county board or a city council, broad community participation and involvement, distribution of the report, and acceptance of responsibility for follow-up. The program has proven to be an excellent, yet economical, way of ensuring citizen involvement in programs and a planning-coordination instrument which is quite effective in most communities in which it has been employed.

In the past several years the Minnesota program has evolved in a unique direction. Its youth authority, the Youth Conservation Commission, had carried out a program of case assignment, training school and camp administration, and limited work in probation and prevention. In 1960 a unified Corrections Department joined the youth program with the previous adult institution program and the independent adult probation and parole agency. The new department is responsible for all these plus jail inspection and consultation. State subsidy permits probation and parole expansion to all counties through state aid or state operations in localities. Plans are under way to expand community organization and training activities. The department is organized in three divisions, Adult Corrections, Youth Conservation, and Administrative Services—but there is considerable across-the-board policy making and planning. The Youth Conservation Commission continues to sit on institution assignment and release.

These brief reviews of several youth authority programs point to a program in transition. On the one hand, authorities have become arms of state government, administering training schools, camps, staff training, research, and community prevention services. On the other, they continue as "boards" which accept cases on court commitment and are responsible for the choice of specific facilities, for release on parole, and so on. Each of these functions requires examination.

To the extent that youth authorities are operational agencies, the authority concept per se is not relevant or functional. It may be a device for initial rallying of support and funds, but there is no special value to the authority per se. Indeed, as in the instances of California and Massachusetts, the authority chairman becomes an administrative officer of a state agency. There is then every reason to unify the program with broader governmental units. California and Minnesota have now chosen the corrections "axis" for such unification, while Wisconsin places delinquency services in public welfare. Massachusetts uses education as the administrative "home" for its authority but true unification has not yet taken place.

Similarly, the "board" role of authorities may be in transition. It is certainly a major step forward when courts give up the attempt to decide from among the elements of an institution network and relegate the task to a board whose members visit the institutions frequently and are informed as to their facilities. Further progress has been made when authorities create diagnostic centers and rely heavily on their case analyses and proposals. Is it not reasonable to predict that the next and logical step may be to define the choice of facility and the decision to release as a purely technical task, assigned to diagnostic center staffs? It may be some time before this final step is taken both because states lack adequate diagnostic resources and because there is a desire to have nontechnical involvement in decision making. The process is nonetheless under way. In several of the states board members are now either too burdened to review and challenge most records or have high respect for technical recommendations; boards change only a small proportion of actions proposed by the staff.

Should authorities eventually transfer their disposition responsibilities to technical staffs, there will remain the need for a "public presence" which will periodically review disposition patterns in the light of public objectives. This, however, would be an advisory body, comparable to advisory welfare committees or institution visiting committees. There would be no reason for it also to assume administrative responsibility for institutions, probation, and so on. In fact, as youth authority administrative operations take the form of a typical state department, one public advisory group could fulfill several functions.

There is need for additional study of the so-called prevention activities of several youth authorities. Although not proposed in the initial statute, most of the authorities have developed programs which encompass surveys and self-surveys; community organization to increase local participation in surveys and in the implementation of recommendations for new facilities or for new ways of working; creation of local councils and coordinating bodies; consultation to the localities; educational programs of a variety of kinds. There may be modest grant-in-aid funds too. These efforts sometimes concentrate on the improvement of services for delinquents, but are more often based on the philosophy that delinquency is best prevented by "the betterment of all facilities for all children."

As authorities and state governments look ahead, they will want to consider whether the delinquency problem is the best point of departure for their efforts at encouraging local initiative, planning, and coordination in health, education, welfare, corrections, and recreation. To some extent the answer will depend on where the authority is placed in state government. Under the Wisconsin plan, for example, the community services program has a broad public welfare basis. To some extent, too, the evaluation will depend on what other provision there is in the state for broadening the perspective. As noted, several youth authority states also have statewide citizens' committees on children and youth. Many other states also count on such committees to relate government action to citizen priorities and concerns.

Commission on children and youth. The assignment of major coordination responsibility to a public welfare department would seem to be the most advantageous way to obtain optimum integration of a substantial number of services vital to effective treatment. Assignment to a youth authority provides for the possibility of intensive and concentrated, but perhaps separate, institutional treatment facilities for delinquents. Each may undertake planning within its defined scope. However, the attainment of coordination and planning on even a broader front, plus the stimulation and support of citizen involvement and action, is perhaps more effectively handled by a state-wide committee or commission with official or semiofficial status, free of service responsibilities, and with some form of relationship to or the participation of key state commissioners.

Such nonoperating agencies or boards received particular stimulation through the nationally promoted follow-up effort after the 1950 White House Conference on Children. There was further encouragement through the 1960 Conference. Many of the programs obtained official or semiofficial status. One might illustrate with reference to such statutory bodies as the Tennessee Commission on Youth Guidance, the Florida Children's Commission, the Louisiana Youth Commission, the Mississippi Children's Code Commission, the New Mexico Council on Children and Youth. Each of these has its own special history and characteristics, but such functions as the following are found in a number of the programs: study, planning, advice, evaluation, consultation, coordination, legislative drafting, organization of citizen action in the localities. The concern is generally broader than juvenile delinquency. Unlike youth authorities and state agencies, the commissions or councils do not operate training schools or other diagnostic and treatment facilities.

The Louisiana State Youth Commission, which may be taken as an illustration, has statutory status, having been created by legislation in 1950 as the successor of an earlier Juvenile Court commission which found its charge too narrow and its resources too limited. The commission consists of nine members appointed by the governor. It has an executive secretary and a very small office staff. It is defined as "advisory, investigatory, consultative" but not as administrative. It is authorized to collect facts and make studies of conditions affecting children and youth, to keep abreast of developments, to provide for a mutual exchange of ideas and information, to conduct hearings, to make recommendations, and to coordinate the services of state agencies serving children.

Since the Louisiana commission is not an administrative body, it must emphasize advisory, investigatory, and consultative operations. Its coordination must be severely limited although it may encourage exchange of information and cooperative activities. To some degree it is able to initiate concerns in operating departments; it sits in at interdepartmental committee meetings but does not convene them.

Local governmental bodies and citizen groups and state-wide voluntary groups may ask for consultation from the commission or may follow through vis-à-vis legislative or local bodies to obtain implementation of its legislation. Unlike many other state bodies, it is not itself staffed to initiate citizen action or to organize any largescale citizen study of youth and child welfare problems.

Maryland's program, by contrast, is a nonstatutory one and does ensure far more citizen involvement. The related statutory agency is a Child Welfare Bureau in the Department of Public Welfare, organized into a Division of Training Schools (for consultation, not administration) and a Division of Consultant and Prevention Services. Consultation is technical, emphasizing probation, police, court services. The nonstatutory Maryland Commission for the Prevention and Treatment of Juvenile Delinquency (now Commission for Children and Youth) was appointed by the governor in May, 1956, after a state-wide governor's conference and is composed of forty-four citizens from a wide variety of backgrounds, as well as directors of state departments directly concerned with children and chairmen of affiliated local commissions. The chairman of the Youth Participation Committee, sponsored by the commission, is a member. Approximately half of the commission is lay, half professional. Staff services are provided by the State Department of Public Welfare through the Division of Consultant and Prevention Services.

The Maryland commission sees itself as a vehicle for citizen planning and action and seeks to "make more possible the coordinated efforts of agencies and individuals concerned with children and their families." The approach is broad:

> *The Commission was established with the conviction that if the community makes it possible for children all children to grow up with greater psychological and physical security than many of them are now privileged to enjoy, juvenile delinquency will be substantially reduced; as will the tragedies which come in the wake of it. This conviction has become even more firm as the Commission moved forward. Therefore, the approach taken is a broad one concerning itself not only with specific measures*

pertaining to delinquency treatment, but also with most of the crucial areas which touch and affect the lives of Maryland's children.

A group of thirteen program committees has served as the source of action proposals and has given detailed attention to the recommendations of the well-attended annual governor's conferences, which include considerable youth participation. The committees are assigned such subjects as community organization, family life, health, education, employment, police, juvenile courts, aftercare, etc. Six action committees are part of the permanent structure and are concerned with the formulation of annual recommendations for action by the executive committee and the commission, and with implementation.

Increasingly, the commission has stressed broad citizen participation in the governor's conferences, the establishment of local commissions (half the state is covered at this writing), and the sponsorship of local conferences. It is felt that this approach ensures widespread interest, the pinpointing of the most vital problems, and the necessary support for legislation growing out of the commission's program.

Consideration of this kind of program would suggest that its educational and social action potentials are perhaps its greatest strength. More systematic fact finding and long-range planning requires a research staff and formal relationship to administrative agencies. Coordination, on a level beyond that of interchange and the important informal accomplishments which derive through joint participation in meetings and conferences for formulation of program recommendations, must develop in a coordination structure of administrative personnel who address specific problems.

California has developed its Governor's Committee on Children and Youth as an effective device for tapping citizen opinion and achieving informal interdepartmental coordination. It tends to function in an area broader than the Youth Authority. This citizen group is composed of prominant members of several professions and active lay leaders. It is called upon by the governor from time to time to provide advice relative to special or continuing problems of children and youth in the state. It often coopts members to special subcommittees for basic study of major problems. The over-all committee and its subcommittees frequently obtain special foundation grants for basic research. State-wide and local conferences may be called to tap public opinion and proposals as many as eighteen in a year. Studies of youth services in given localities may be encouraged. In addition, the committee makes recommendations on pending legislation.

The vitality of this advisory committee is noted in its scope and achievements. A random list would include reference to its systematic state-wide surveys of services to children and youth in preparation for the last White House Conference on Children, its studies—with foundation assistance of major child welfare problems such as adoption and detention, its comprehensive delinquency prevention program prepared at the governor's request in 1960, its continuous community-wide interpretation, the excellent participation of representative citizens in many local meetings, and its effect on pending legislation.

Since interdepartmental coordination of services to children and youth is an important concern in any state, it is interesting to note the extent to which the operational pattern of the governor's advisory committee makes a contribution in this realm. The total budget of the advisory committee is spent for travel allowances for citizen members, and staffing is the responsibility of cooperating departments. Each department assigns a senior staff person to a Staff Committee and the chairmanship rotates annually. The Staff Committee meets in advance to prepare the agenda for the citizen group and assembles again after each meeting to follow through on decisions. Responsibility is assigned to the departments as appropriate, and they commit whatever staff resources are required. If necessary, interdepartmental *ad hoc* subcommittees are created for study, policy clarification, and action. The directors of the various departments are themselves ex officio members of the governor's advisory committee and each senior staff representative develops a reporting practice appropriate to his department. Since departments and governor both receive committee recommendations and considerable interpretation at several staff levels and through citizen leadership it is not surprising to note the high degree of success in effecting executive action and the drafting of legislation by the administration.

The New Jersey Youth Study Commission, which recently completed its task, lacked many of the elements in the above programs but illustrates a unique fact-finding and research structure. The Jersey body was created in 1954 as a Juvenile Delinquency Study Commission and was renamed Youth Study Commission in 1957 to take account of the range of interests which inevitably developed through conscientious pursuit of its charge to conduct studies, recommend legislation, and publish reports relative to juvenile delinquency and ("as . . . related thereto") health, recreation, and education. It was composed of two members from the New Jersey State Senate, two from the Assembly, eight citizens at large, and the Commissioner of Education, ex officio. Appointments were made by the governor and the presiding officers of both legislative houses.

In the tradition of English legislative commissions, a tradition well over one hundred years old, the Jersey Youth Study Commission conducted hearings continuously in various parts of the state, drawing upon the experience of lay citizens and professionals and sometimes calling upon outside experts as well. With the aid of a small but outstanding research staff, which helped to define the focus of the hearings and to locate appropriate witnesses, it published comprehensive and sophisticated annual reports, based on the hearings, its own deliberations, and relevant research literature. It made specific action recommendations to the legislature each year. In addition, its reports represented outstanding planning documents, suggesting policy direction and priorities. In completing its assignment, it recommended a broader and more permanent coordinating structure.

Utah, which has a Committee on Children and Youth, created early in 1961 a unique new agency, the State

Council on Criminal Justice Administration, "to observe the criminal law in action" and to report its findings and recommendations. Existing agencies may not be relieved of statutory duties by this new body, which is specifically limited to consideration of basic principles and administrative processes.

The plan grew out of concern in the state with prison disturbances, the inadequacies in the juvenile court system, poor coordination between law enforcement and other services, and the general need to strengthen prevention and control programs. It was devised by an *ad hoc* legislative committee after careful study.

Evaluation of this device is, of course, not possible at this stage but it would seem to have the potential of the New Jersey Youth Study Commission and the advantage of a stronger charge and permanency. Ex officio members represent key public and private groups (supreme court, attorney general, legislative council, public welfare commission, board of corrections, state bar, state medical association, state social welfare conference, peace officers' association). In addition, the governor appoints six members. The council is both informed and in a position to channel its findings. Staffing, of course, is important.

NCCD Citizen Action Program. The NCCD Citizen Action Program, financed originally by the Ford Foundation for the period 1955-59 and recently renewed, began with the recognition that most communities do not have adequate juvenile courts; many delinquents are detained in jails rather than detention facilities; youths are often committed to inadequate training schools where probation would be the more appropriate disposition but is not available; most courts lack adequate diagnostic clinics; prisons are often obsolete and parole policy outdated. Modern knowledge and skill too often are not being applied to delinquency and crime, personnel are not provided, and funds are not voted. Legislation is often out of date and a handicap.

Our progress depends on public understanding, public leadership, and public action. Without public support, professional workers will remain severely limited in their efforts to control delinquency, family breakup, and crime.

In the past, wherever appreciable progress was achieved in correctional services, it was responsible citizen action that was the spark plug. Citizen action was largely responsible for developing the idea of probation, for promoting the juvenile court movement, for selecting qualified judges and correctional administrators.

Where the community is uninformed and does not understand the nature of the problem and the remedy, professional leadership may become stagnant and the result is a destructive treadmill of arrests, sentences, and indiscriminate imprisonment.

The Citizen Action plan is basically simple. A national Citizens Council and the central staff of the NCCD have sought to identify states most in need of action, yet having the potential for citizen activity, and have attempted to stimulate leadership in these states and to reinforce their action programs through consultation and help. In the meantime, broad public interpretation has been sought nationally through newspapers, magazines, radio, and television. Staff services are provided in the states from two sources: project personnel and specialist consultants on the NCCD staff.The core of the action program in each state is a state council of approximately fifteen outstanding citizens from industry, business, and the professions. Much of the impressive success of the program in the early years is, in fact, associated with the ability of the project to attract top state leadership from these fields—many of them individuals never previously connected with programs for offenders and to stimulate them to a point where visits, study, and consideration have convinced them of the ultimate economy and effectiveness of increased public investment in these programs and high standards of service. By virtue of their community stature, these councils have been effective in relation to legislation and appropriations. Programs were developed in eight states during the first five years: Michigan, Washington, Montana, Texas, Oklahoma, Ohio, West Virginia, and Indiana. They have in common the following: Each state council works with judges, bar associations, and correctional administrators and technicians, to:

1. examine and evaluate specific ways in which the state deals with the offender from first contact to disposition and treatment;
2. recommend innovations and improvements, assigning each recommendation a priority according to its urgency;
3. inform the public in every way it can, so that deficiencies are considereal openly, widely, and realistically;
4. act to get public and private individuals and groups to work for the recommended improvements.

The actions, legislation, reforms, and special projects adopted vary with the state. Some councils have concentrated on the delinquents, others on adult offenders. Some have given more attention to prisons, others to community services. The Michigan council began with a demonstration of what a well-staffed probation department could do in an adult court and then undertook, at the request of a legislative committee, a comprehensive review of children's services in probate courts. One of the first significant actions of the Washington council in 1957 was the passage of constructive prison-industry legislation and of more adequate corrections budgets. The use of probation as a disposition was liberalized. Next, with the help of local citizens committees, the Washington council conducted probation and detention surveys in thirty counties, with resultant local improvements and a state-wide move for state subsidies to local juvenile probation services.

In Montana, the council chose to concentrate, first, on juvenile delinquency, but turned its attention to the state prison after a riot and played a major role in setting the direction of much-needed reform. The council has systematically studied various aspects of the state correctional picture in close cooperation with the bench, the bar, professional groups, civic groups, and official groups, depending on the issue. It has reported frequently to the public and has had wide attention. The Texas council began successfully by "selling the idea" of a state parole system and, then, the sponsorship of a minimum program for young offenders: buildings, rehabilitation services, parole. Oklahoma began with a broad survey of the total correctional system, at the request of the legislature, and employed a group of experts for the task. The final report had widespread attention. Major reform proposals are now before the legislature.

Both Washington and Ohio have conducted impressive citizen information programs and the latter initiated a training institute for juvenile court judges.

The Indiana group has placed particular stress on community services, especially probation, as opposed to the increase of institutional space. The first major action in West Virginia followed a state prison scandal, which allowed opportunity for investigation and sound planning.

On the basis of its 1960 grant from the Ford Foundation, the NCCD is moving its program into a number of additional states and seeking ultimate self-support for it. At the present writing Citizen Action Programs exist in thirteen states. The expansion will undoubtedly involve new patterns of organization and the ultimate creation of state groups which, in combination, could be effective nationally as well.

Clearly, the Citizen Action Program is one which would serve well the situation in many states. It seems able to play a planning role as well as an action role since it may undertake comprehensive surveys, at legislative invitation, and may stimulate local surveys and planning. Its validity is not affected by the type of official structure which exists in the state. On the other hand, unlike some of the official structures described, it is not in a position to make a major contribution to the coordination of ongoing operations or to service integration. Its scope is relatively narrow.

A state plan. What, then, does the examination of state measures suggest? First, the coordination function, when broken down further, is really several functions, each suitable for its own mechanisms. There is need for a structure to coordinate program and policy of operating departments; this is a function of the executive arm of government. On the other hand, citizen leadership opinion should contribute in some way to policy formulation both in the executive branch and in operating departments. An appropriate advisory body with a clear charge might be constituted by either the chief executive or a legislative body. There is also a forum function whereby people in all parts of a state may communicate needs and views both to government and to the citizen policy advisory arms. Planning and research may be related to each of these in a variety of ways.

It would thus seem that official and unofficial bodies are needed and that there should be clarity about their differences. Too many of the existing arrangements blur such differences and leave gaps either in coordination, planning, or citizen action.

Second, the distinctions between direct service and operational coordination are significant and one should not ignore the consensus that high level coordination is most effective when carried out as a function of an agency of the executive branch which is not at the same time responsible for direct services and thus not adequately "neutral" about issues which arise. In fact, all direct service operations as well as state aid to localities for special services (except perhaps demonstrations, experiments, and local coordination and planning) should be assigned to operating departments, not to the coordinating machinery. Third, there is no disagreement that even if it is found desirable to focus certain services and even some coordination of services primarily on delinquency, *other coordination machinery and planning machinery must relate the delinquency program to children's programs, more broadly defined.*Fourth, coordination and planning require research and evaluation of both the short-term spot kind and the more basic kind. Competent professional staffing is essential for this purpose, as it is for the administrative, community organization, and social action phases of the work.If a state were beginning *de novo* and sought to provide all necessary elements, one would be tempted to suggest the following-with full recognition that the total "package" has been tried nowhere and that the evaluations of the pieces are far from comprehensive:

a. A coordinating device within the executive branch of state government and involving the active participation of the commissioners or their committee of alternates sitting as the equivalent of a "family and children's cabinet."
b. A youth commission or its equivalent, made up of citizens, not of public officials, with an advisory and investigatory charge. It would stress policy and long-range planning recommendations and would channel reports to the executive or to the legislative branch and to the public at large.
c. A planning, coordination, research, and evaluation staff to service these two bodies and to ensure liaison between them.
d. A citizen forum structure on a state-wide basis, which might also sponsor local conferences and forums from time to time with a view to locating problems, defining priorities, and assembling citizen proposals. Reports might channel to the youth commission although opinions on legislative and executive issues should also be routed to governor and legislature.

Since few states begin with a blank slate, it is assumed that there will be many variations on this pattern and experimentation with other approaches to the definition and allocation of functions. Differences in the size and complexity of states will also call for modifications and other approaches. Comparative study in the future would be instructive and helpful.

A slightly more detailed but nonetheless brief look at New York State's planning and coordination machinery may serve as a way of illustrating the possibilities and implications in more detail.

Planning and Coordination in New York State

New York State abolished its Youth Commission, transferred major functions to a newly constituted Youth

Division in the governor's office, and assigned operational responsibilities to it. The Youth Commission had been a "temporary body" from 1945 to 1956 when it was reorganized and made "permanent" by statute. It had been created initially as a response of the legislature to the wartime delinquency rise and was charged, in rather broad terms, with the task of stimulating localities, guiding them, and helping financially in the development of programs for coping with delinquency. Under the original plan, the commission was composed of both lay members and the heads of all state departments involved in youth programs. The 1956 legislation created a "commission within the executive department which shall consist of the chairman and eight other members who are not holders of public office." The chairman was to be a paid, full-time official. A separate inter departmental committee of the Youth Commission was created at the same time and was given a quite broad assignment to initiate policies relative to youth, to advise on matters brought to it by the commission chairman, and, generally, to advise the commission and help achieve its objectives.

The statute's statement of the New York State Youth Commission role allowed a variety of emphases and directions:

> *. . . to recommend and put into effect those measures most suitable to supplement and aid in coordinating the work of existing religious and social institutions for the prevention of delinquency and youth crime, and the advancement of the moral, physical, mental and social well-being of the youth of this state, and to encourage the municipalities of this state to undertake increased activities in this field by assistance and financial aid as provided in this article.*

The spirit of the program was reflected in the following excerpt from the 1957 report of the chairman, Mark A. McCloskey:

> *The Commission's small staff goes unendingly from county to county through the State bringing the technical skills and knowledge of the State's formula of financial aid. The staff strives to build sound public attitudes; helps with the improvement of existing services; helps build new services as the communities recognize their need; helps communities to realize that coordinated effort multiplies the strength of their work, and helps them to*

> *understand that isolated effort in a job of his kind is never so effective as combined operations. Success in our effort will only come from the closest working cooperation of State and municipal, public and private undertakings.*

The financial aid provision, a unique pioneering feature in a state program, represented the Youth Commission's major leverage and set much of the direction for its program. It was continued when the commission gave way to the Youth Division. While the details of the financial formula are not immediately relevant, it may be helpful to note that the state reimburses localities for expenditures for recreation programs, youth services, and youth bureaus which meet statutory requirements, at a level equal to half of the local expenditure within certain limits defined by the size of the locality and its youth population. The subsidy system includes special incentives for the creation of what is judged to be a "coordinated program for youth guidance in an area or areas with a high delinquency rate." Under the provision, the state aid appropriation totals $3,500,000 at this writing. This is apart from funds for the "rehabilitation" and "opportunity" centers. New York City has tended to receive slightly more than half of the state grant over the years. The system of state financial aid has achieved its purpose of stimulating local expenditures as well as giving state aid to major programs. The matching feature has tended to result in responsible planning and modest proposals.

In analyzing its charge, the Youth Commission listed four major functions: to encourage coordination at the local level, to carry on educational activities, to conduct basic research in the causation of delinquency and the effectiveness of programs, to encourage municipalities to develop youth programs through technical aid and financial help. The commission was staffed by a small headquarters group of administrative personnel and specialists, two area directors, and nine field representatives, and also had authority to grant funds in support of local programs. Given access to such resources, most of the communities in the state sought technical and financial help in the development of local youth programs. The coordination, education, and research tasks were by no means ignored by the commission, but they were secondary to its concentration on the development of subsidized youth bureaus, youth service projects, and recreation projects. A number of these programs, in turn, developed coordination, research, and education on the local level.

Brief definitions of the latter terms will suggest the scope and nature of the program. A youth bureau is, in a sense, a local equivalent of the parent state body. A full youth bureau program would include: early case finding and treatment; expansion of services (ranging from recreation to psychotherapy); public education to stimulate citizen action and support; administrative research related to identifying areas needing service and the service needed, as well as evaluating results; encouraging coordination and service integration, involving both public and voluntary services. The New York City Youth Board, which is a youth bureau, is described later in this chapter. As of the present writing, there are ten others. The bureaus have undertaken the activities listed with varied degrees of emphasis and "with varying degrees of success." Youth bureaus received approximately 5 percent of the total state grant in 1961.

Youth bureaus organize a variety of programs within the scope of their charge and tend to do broad local planning. Youth service projects may be organized in a community whether or not a bureau exists; they are defined as "any experimental plan or organized activity, other than a youth bureau or a recreation project." To illustrate: Onondaga County reorganized the Juvenile Aid Bureau under this provision and added two deputies, partially paid for by the Youth Commission grant. Another project permits employment in the county of a supervisor and field workers to work with youth groups who "are potential delinquents but who cannot nor will not associate with established community agencies or programs."

Syracuse, too, reorganized its Juvenile Aid Bureau under the Youth Service Projects provision, while Madison County created a psychological service in its schools and Poughkeepsie organized a community center in a housing project, with the participation of Vassar College which used the center for student training. Fallsburgh and Woodbridge organized a remedial reading project. Until the creation of the New York State Community Mental Health Program, many localities received financial help toward the development of child guidance services through Youth Service Projects. Such projects accounted for about 43 percent of the total state grant in 1961 (66 percent of the grant to New York City and 15 percent of the grant upstate, local expenditures not included). The presence of a youth board or its equivalent has proven necessary in the past to generate the kinds of self-examination and planning which result in youth service projects. Youth Commission field staff have undertaken the function more actively in recent years.

While until quite recently it asked for help for only a limited number of youth service projects, the upstate area has eagerly sought state help in expanding recreation, an area of service readily grasped, widely appreciated, clearly visible, and not requiring unavailable staff. Municipalities representing well over 90 percent of the state's population conduct state-aided recreation programs. The Youth Commission stated its own perspective: "Although recreation cannot, by itself, be considered a delinquency prevention program, it is one of many services essential for creating a healthy community environment in which youth can grow and mature." The commission developed an elaborate program of grants-in-aid, technical consultation, publication of helpful guides, distribution of educational films, development of training opportunities, and cooperation in establishment of standards of performance and leadership. Programs are operated by recreation committees, municipal boards, recreation commissions, school systems, and other agencies. Recreation projects accounted for over half of the total state grants-in-aid in 1961 (over 30 percent of the total grant to New York City and close to four fifths of the upstate grant, local expenditures not included).

Beyond the program of local support, the Youth Commission prepared displays and exhibitions for fairs and conferences, undertook education through publication of pamphlets and a free film loan service, made use of radio and television to interpret its philosophy and program, encouraged town meetings on youth and numerous informal reviews of needs and services, and sponsored training for law enforcement officers. Its chairman and members were called upon for advice on legislation and other matters by the office of the governor from time to time.

In 1960, for reasons not relevant to issues here under discussion, the Youth Commission was abolished and there was created, in its stead, a Youth Division in the governor's office and a Council on Youth. The director of the Division for Youth became the administrative officer responsible for carrying through all of the original Youth Commission responsibilities and also for developing and operating the system of "opportunity centers" and rehabilitative facilities for youth in the 15-17 age group. Thus, the State Department of Social Welfare continued its training school and aftercare services, the State Department of Correction continued to supervise and to subsidize expansion of local youth probation services, and a new agency also began to operate facilities closely related to each of these and to the Department of Education as well. The new Council on Youth was to become an advisory, study, and review body whose approval was required by the director as he exercised the original Youth Commission grantin-aid powers.

All of these developments, which certainly add to resources and facilities in very significant fashion, do not yet solve the planning and coordination problem.

On the positive side, grants for youth bureaus, recreation projects, and youth service projects have impact on planning and coordination locally, and may have more as the Youth Division sets direction and priorities in the light of broad considerations. The structure also allows for an influential citizen group which may speak to the governor, the legislature, and citizens at large about public policy for youth. The relatively broad Youth Commission interpretation of areas of concern and support, for example, encouraged the notion that decreased delinquency is dependent on improved community and family life and that services for delinquents must be quite extensive and varied, as varied as services for all children. The citizen board has devoted considerable time and effort since its reconstitution in 1957 as a permanent body to becoming acquainted with needs, problems, services; it is in a position to exert far more influence in the direction of policy leadership and innovation than it has in the past. In effect, it is constituted so as to permit it some of the initiative and range of the NCCD Citizen Action Program, despite its official character and responsibility for grants-in-aid as a Council on Youth.

The Youth Commission (and now the Youth Division) has undertaken several brief surveys and studies, including a useful survey of experience with the use of curfews. It has prepared and circulated a manual on Police Juvenile Aid programs and a guide for school personnel in early detection and treatment of maladjusted children. From time to time it has assembled useful statistical data about delinquency rates and institutionalization. It has not, however, carried out any basic research which might shed light on policy but is currently planning rigorous studies of its opportunity-rehabilitation centers. Nor has it attempted the kinds of administrative studies relevant to long-range planning that is, projections as to the amount of institutional space to be needed in the coming decade.

Of some concern too is the fact that the plan does not meet one of the other state needs, the need for operational coordination. In fact, creation of the Youth Division further fragmented operations. There is no definite operational coordination charge or structure. An Interdepartmental Health Resources Board demonstrated some years ago how effective such a body can be, but its scope was subsequently limited.

What, then, of the forum function? In 1956 a "temporary commission," which superseded the Youth Commission during a delinquency "crisis," held well-attended regional meetings while its staff carried out studies. The process was capped by a state-wide conference. The Youth Commission itself gave leadership to a similar process in preparation for the 1960 White House Conference on Children and Youth. The Youth Division is now charged with follow-up on that conference. In addition, many of the youth bureaus conduct local conferences, meetings, and forums. The previous chapter described the New York City Youth Board's community program.

The New York State program thus provides for many of the coordination and planning functions listed in the previous section but would seem to need to undertake some sorting out and redefinition. Although the opportunity-rehabilitation services are essential innovations, they should obviously be joined with the Social Welfare Department facilities when the pioneering, innovation, testing phase has passed. Until this occurs they inevitably must continue to divert the Youth Division somewhat from its basic coordination and planning task. Located as it is in the governor's office, the Youth Division is ideally situated for such a role, but will have to reorient its staff services for it. Consultation to localities is valuable and important, but there is also need for administrative research which projects trends and needs, evaluates programs, tests effectiveness—all oriented to posing policy issues and to making long-term plans.

Given movement in this direction, the Youth Council's role will gain new importance. It will be ideally constituted in an advisory role to help develop policies and plans, to react to division reports and studies, to respond to new community needs. Currently the statute makes it an advisory body to the director; it should probably have a more direct channel to governor or legislature.

The Youth Division has a variety of channels to local citizens through its youth bureau programs. The Council on Youth should perhaps establish some systematic way of tapping local opinion. It is already planning to conduct regional hearings and state-wide meetings as White House Conference follow-up.

Finally, to cover all dimensions, the state will have to implement a regular plan of interdepartmental coordination. As the Youth Division gives up direct services, it should be in a position to staff a vital interdepartmental committee which should be convened by the governor at a cabinet level and might operate routinely as a committee of deputies. There are beginnings in this direction.

City-Wide Planning and Coordination

It is possible to support the generalization that six of every ten cities have some sort of coordinating structure for the control and treatment of delinquency but only if one stretches the definition. Larger cities have substantially greater rates of coverage, according to a survey by the American Municipal Association; but the count includes both welfare and community councils, official direct-service programs, advisory bodies, and a program as elaborate as that of the New York City Youth Board. There is no one pattern, and there should not be.

For lack of nationwide, systematic, comparable data, it is impossible to say much about the variety of coordination patterns. The one available survey merely illustrates several types. Mention has already been made of parts of several municipal programs in connection with neighborhood organization and accountability. The New Jersey Youth Study Commission reports a variety of devices in use in New Jersey communities: (*a*) children's and special service bureaus, such as the bureaus in Jersey City and Passaic which are school-administered services to coordinate school efforts with police case finding and treatment; (*b*) municipal youth guidance councils; (*c*) case conference committees; (*d*) councils of social agencies. One interesting pattern is represented by Detroit's Mayor's Committee on Children and Youth, which functions as a community "sounding board," as an advisory board, and as a group which contributes, on one level, to planning. This committee of fifty has twenty-three members appointed by public and voluntary organizations and twenty-seven by the mayor. An administrative committee (board) is appointed by the mayor and may, in turn, set up working committees which draw upon qualified citizens from the city at large. An executive secretary, who is a city employee, heads a small technical staff. The quarterly meetings of the total committee consider both matters on which advisory action is needed and proposals requiring mutual action and support by the organizations represented in the committee membership. The committee reviews studies and reports which provide the background for action.

In 1954 the mayor of New Haven, Connecticut, appointed a Commission on Juvenile Delinquency which began with a period of orientation and study, divided itself into nine subcommittees for more intensive study and formulation of specific recommendations, transmitted the recommendations and a general report, and then, convinced that continued citizen involvement was essential, sounded the call for a Citizens' Action Committee.

San Diego, California, has placed a comprehensive, city-wide effort in its Social Service Department. The program includes a variety of case finding efforts to locate deviant children, parent discussion groups, group guidance with teen-agers which is directed at street clubs and neighborhood groups, short-term family counseling in the neighborhood, and general public education about delinquency.

Lincoln, Nebraska, had a relatively inactive community council when a local foundation created the Lincoln Youth Project. In addition to assisting in the establishment of a needed youth employment service, organizing a youth council, and surveying recreational programs and facilities, the project set up a research-demonstration program in "reaching out casework" which sought to promote a new kind of service and increase service integration. The experiences of this program and subsequent supplementary research and data analysis provided the basis for a series of reports published between 1957 and 1959, evaluating existing services, outlining needed services, and urging adequate standards. Particular emphasis was placed in these reports on a coordinated community program; case finding, adequate police, court, and clinic services; child protective services.

Action to implement the various proposals is under way and a Lincoln Citizens' Committee for Children has been created as an action coordination-fact-finding group. St. Louis has an active, staffed Metropolitan Youth Commission which initiates citizen action, studies, planning, and coordination. A U.S. Children's Bureau listing also calls attention to the following specialized, large-city agencies for delinquency control: the Los Angeles County Department of Community Agencies; the St. Petersburg, Florida, Juvenile Welfare Board of Pinellas County; the recently created Chicago Commission on Youth Welfare; the Cincinnati, Ohio, Citizens' Committee on Youth; and the Commissioner's Youth Council in Washington, D.C.

From 1954 to 1957 the Philadelphia Youth Services Board had an advisory and coordination function, but the need for direct services led to expansion in the form of a Youth Services Division in the Welfare Department, guided by a Youth Conservation Commission.

There are at least fourteen municipal youth commissions or their equivalent. They tend to concentrate on the improvement of public services to delinquents and the development of demonstrations and projects. They have emphasized work with gangs, "reaching out" to multi problem families, case conference machinery, special employment programs for youth. Some have initiated coordination.

Community welfare councils, traditionally, "have continued to provide a channel for operating agencies and interested organizations to share ideas, coordinate programs, raise professional standards and interpret services and problems to the community at large." Despite impressive records of accomplishment in the coordination realm in specific instances, they are more effective with voluntary agencies than with the public programs which provide the bulk of services. They are best at specific projects, rather than at long-range operational coordination which may infringe on agency prerogatives. Many would now change the emphasis "to include research and planning on the larger social welfare issues." But it is not certain that they have the needed standing, resources, or access to power. Of interest is the fact that several quite strong welfare councils have sought to initiate youth commissions because of the advantages of official status and ability to combine lay and professional leadership.

It seems reasonable to conclude this section with the notation that municipal coordination must be approached pragmatically. A few obvious principles may serve as a point of departure. Examination in some depth of one ambitious effort (the New York City Youth Board) does permit a few additional suggestions.

New York City Youth Board

New York City's size and resources are matched only by the scale and scope of its task. If it would plan and coordinate, it must suit its machinery to its unique circumstances. Since the New York City Youth Board has set the pace nationally in a variety of areas, its development and program deserve relatively full treatment. The detached worker program and borough and neighborhood organization programs have already been discussed in proper context. The Youth Board's contribution to planning and coordination, as well as its limitations in these fields, demands examination here. As will be seen, the agency must make certain choices between direct service and coordination. The city has begun to face the issue of adequately relating Youth Board program planning and coordination activities to the planning and coordination of all services for children and youth in New York City.

The New York City Youth Board was created as an agency in the office of the mayor by a local resolution in July, 1947. It was set up to qualify as a youth bureau under the *State Youth Commission Act of 1945*. As was true of the state agency, the Youth Board's status was uncertain as long as the state program was a temporary one. Steps toward fuller incorporation into city government, including civil service status for staff, followed the legislation making the state program permanent. The resolution conferred five powers and duties upon the Youth Board:

a. To coordinate the activities of public, private and religious agencies devoted in whole or in part to the welfare and protection of youth;

b. To make studies and analyses of the problems of youth guidance and the prevention of juvenile delinquency;

c. To seek to remove the causes of juvenile delinquency through the means available to City Departments and private agencies;

d. To collect, correlate and disseminate information, statistics and data on the subject of juvenile delinquency and the methods of removing the causes of juvenile delinquency;

e. To approve applications of City agencies for the maintenance of youth projects under the State law.

An Executive Order issued by the mayor in September, 1957, added to this general authority of the Youth Board a specific grant of coordinating responsibility to the board's Executive Director.

The New York City Youth Board consisted initially of thirteen members, six representing city departments and seven appointed by the mayor, who was also empowered to designate one member as chairman. The membership was subsequently increased to twenty eight, of whom eighteen are private citizens appointed by the mayor on a staggered membership plan. The other ten are the heads of city departments having important youth services or special responsibilities in the field of delinquency.

The Youth Board has qualified for maximum state reimbursement by developing what the state law describes as a "coordinated program for youth guidance in an area or areas with a high delinquency rate." Its budget is over five million dollars, with the state contributing almost 45 percent (the city having exceeded, in its own expenditures, the maximum for state matching). One of the unique features of the Youth Board program has been its authorization to expend the bulk of its funds through contracts with public and voluntary agencies. Contracts permit expansion of existing programs and creation of new services all designed to meet the needs uncovered in Referral Unit efforts to obtain needed treatment or services and in the fact finding of the Youth Board staff and advisory committees.

Thus the creation of the Youth Board began an era of stepped-up public subsidization of voluntary agency programs in new fields in New York City: recreation, group work, child guidance, vocational guidance, family casework.The nature of the state's reimbursement pattern has significantly affected the scope and emphasis of the New York City Youth Board's program. Although the Board of Estimate resolution did not focus the Youth Board's efforts upon the neighborhoods with high delinquency rates to the exclusion of others, the board in defining its own program very early limited its operations to these areas (now twenty-two in number). This concentration has been explained as a means of securing the greatest impact upon delinquency with limited funds; it also enabled the city to obtain the maximum state contribution to the board's work. Besides this geographic focus, recently relaxed somewhat in connection with neighborhood organization, the board decided early in its life to confine its program to services to children living in the community in theft own homes, to give preference to projects serving youth directly rather than indirectly, and to work as far as possible through existing agencies and facilities rather than through the creation of new ones.

The scope of the program. The Youth Board program began in the summer of 1948. Although its basic character has been set for over a decade, there has been subsequent modification involving a gradual shift in the Referral Unit function; considerable expansion of the work with gangs; much increased emphasis on coordination, planning, neighborhood organization; transfer of mental health programs to the subsequently created Mental Health Board; transfer of one program to the Welfare Department. Prior to analysis of the planning and coordination program of the Youth Board, it may be helpful to outline the service and contract programs, which draw the bulk of the resources.

a. Recreation projects conducted by the Board of Education and the Police Athletic League, on a contract basis, account for over one quarter of the annual Youth Board budget. The bulk of the program is assigned to the afternoon, evening, weekend, and summer recreation centers in the schools and to the community centers in housing projects which, in turn, are operated either by voluntary agencies or the school system; but several PAL centers have been expanded and improved and its summer play street program expanded. The premise is that mass recreation facilities belong in a delinquency prevention program.

b. Over 10 percent of the budget is devoted to group work contracts with voluntary settlements and centers which then accept referrals of Referral Unit cases and seek to "reach out" to groups which do not ordinarily make use of their programs. Group work involves considerably more individualization and higher staff standards than mass recreation.

c. The program of detached workers, the street club project of the Council of Social and Athletic Clubs, is a direct Youth Board operation. As the community has become increasingly concerned with gang conflict in recent years, the program has risen in importance. Its budget is close to one and one-half million dollars annually, constitutes over a quarter of the whole, and is second in size only to the recreation program.

d. Referral Units established by the Youth Board for case finding, brief service, referral, and identification of resources in short supply in "high delinquency" areas were school-based for over ten years. They are now Youth Board operated and in transition. Referral Units account for almost 10 percent of Youth Board appropriations.

e. Prior to the establishment of the Community Mental Health Board, approximately 13 percent of the budget was expended through contracts with voluntary agencies for casework and child guidance treatment upon Referral Unit request. "Youth Board" caseloads were created and new staff employed. More recently the contracts have emphasized family service to multiproblem families. Family agencies hold contracts either on a fee-per-interview basis or an annual caseload basis, accounting for almost 11 percent of the budget.

f. A casework treatment program for multiproblem families, Services for Families and Children, which pioneered in "reaching out" methodology, was originally a cooperative Youth Board-Welfare Department enterprise, but was fully transferred to the Welfare Department late in 1957 and was then absorbed by a revised program.

g. The recently developed and expanding program of borough planning offices and assistance to neighborhood councils now receives almost 15 percent of Youth Board funds but is in transition.

h. Research, administration, in-service training, and the planning and coordination operations described below account for about 12 percent of the budget.

i. At various times the Youth Board has included in its program subsidization for expansion of court diagnostic and treatment clinics (taken over by the Community Mental Health Board), group therapy contracts (taken over by the Community Mental Health Board), contracts for vocational guidance programs which emphasize "reaching out" techniques (continuing), the Three-Schools demonstration of school-based clinical services (completed), a central registration project for accurate study of delinquency statistics (converted into a more modest index), free summertime transportation for children to beaches, etc. (continuing).

In general, contracts account for over half the annual budget, direct services for close to 30 percent, administration for over 10 percent, and city-wide planning, coordination, and related services for another 10 percent.

This summary of program would hardly be complete without mention of the substantial impact of the Youth Board program and philosophy on agencies and professional persons in New York City and throughout the country. There is of course no way to separate those general trends of which the Youth Board is a part from the developments which would not have taken place without the Youth Board's stimulation and support. One can only cite the substantial demands made on staff for conference papers, panel participation, workshop leadership, consultation. The board's publications are in demand throughout the world. Even its terminology has been influential. Certainly, all who are involved in helping delinquents and their families are aware, in a way seldom articulated before 1947, of the agency's responsibility vis-a-vis clients not immediately prepared to fit into a traditional pattern of taking service. The emphasis on the consideration of social dimensions in diagnosis and treatment has been given urgency and clear purpose. Experimentation with unorthodox patterns of service and professional role-definitions has been encouraged, particularly in the Street Club programs and the "reaching out" casework efforts. In addition, the Youth Board program has emphasized early case finding, has clarified the technical problems of successful case referral, and has contributed to the needed expansion of programs and to the increased volume of services.

Moreover, it seems reasonable to add, in a period of considerable public outrage at delinquents and their conduct, that the very existence of the Youth Board and its wide range of programs provided an outlet for constructive community action where there might otherwise have been only emotionalism and punitive policy. While one may differ with specific policies and actions, a total appraisal would describe Youth Board services and influence as constructive, valuable, and effective. For purposes of the present chapter, the specific planning and coordination role demands more intensive examination.

Planning and coordination. Under the charge "to coordinate the activities of public, private and religious agencies devoted in whole or in part to the welfare and protection of youth," the board gave the following restricted interpretation to its responsibilities until 1955: "The agency would perform coordinating functions through its relationships with its contract agencies, through its advisory committees and through Board activities, but would not enter actively into over-all coordination of community activities, except through representation by staff and Board members on committees under auspices of other agencies and professional organizations." The resulting activities were significant if limited in scope. In fact, criticism of the Youth Board's program has often centered upon the sizable proportion of its energies devoted to direct operations that continue long past the demonstration stage and the consequent underemphasis of the planning, coordinating, and standard setting through which some believe it could make its greatest contribution. However, in the Youth Board's view, the major portion of its program, including direct operations, has been aimed at actual coordination. For example, the Referral Units provided the machinery for helping school personnel identify maladjusted youngsters and potential delinquents and for follow-through on referral to appropriate treatment resources. Contract arrangements were made to permit expansion of voluntary services specifically geared to accept these refferrals. The Council of Social and Athletic Clubs, now a major direct operation, was created in an effort to provide essential coordination in the approach to working with street gangs found to be necessary after unsuccessful earlier experience in contracting for this type of service with voluntary agencies.

1. Increased interest in planning: Several reviews urged that the Youth Board undertake *community-wide planning*, whereas its previous planning had been limited to its own programs. In an official evaluation, the then deputy mayor said:

> *In addition to a broadened research perspective, I therefore believe the Youth Board needs a small unit of full-time experts who can bring various special skills to the problems of coordination and long-range planning. This team would be responsible for smoothing working relationships with other agencies and for the development of over-all operations plans with the Youth Board members and Executive Director. It would be well to involve in planning the chiefs of the Board's operating divisions, and perhaps private agency representatives as well. But the pressing need is for additional personnel who can look beyond day to day problems and have no direct responsibility for operations, no commitment to a particular aspect of today's problem.*

In the several years which followed, a considerably increased budget was used in part to develop the borough and neighborhood organization machinery. Planning and coordination operations developed slowly and became the province of the Youth Board director and his top staff, while the Youth Board as board continued to devote itself to direct services and to contracts. Advisory committees, composed of lay and professional members, were appointed in the areas of child welfare and family services, jobs, group work and recreation, work with volunteer organizations, problems of changing neighborhoods, problems of protective and correctional services, religious groups, and work camps.

A series of crises demonstrated that there was not yet adequate provision for planning and coordination: large numbers of children were suspended by the schools without joint planning with the many agencies affected; detention and institution space proved wholly insufficient; needed diagnostic facilities were not available and the ramifications affected many services; and so on.

Nor was the expanded program of borough committees and neighborhood organizations pointed to the requirements of a planning structure. The concept was that a borough committee would offer advice to the borough office but could initiate projects through citywide "channels." It was unrelated, in any formal sense, to ongoing borough administration or to area meetings and neighborhood council programs. Thus, while the borough structure gave substantial support to neighborhood community organization and gave the Youth Board "listening posts" in major localities, it was not a long range planning body. (Changes are now being made.)Then, as a result of the community concern over particularly violent outbreaks of juvenile delinquency during the summer of 1957, the Youth Board was given clear authorization (although its statutory charge has always been broad) to assume through its Executive Director a larger role in the coordination of the community's delinquency-control efforts. An Executive Order made the board's Executive Director the "coordinator" of the city's anti delinquency program. He was charged with uniting the efforts of public and voluntary agencies for the more adequate provision of social services in "potentially hazardous areas."

All municipal agencies were directed to cooperate with him, thus conferring upon him a measure of the mayor's authority over the other municipal departments concerned. The Youth Board also received additional state and city funds to strengthen its own programs. To strengthen the director's role and to place him on a par with department heads, he was named Commissioner of Youth Services and Executive Vice President of the Youth Board in December, 1058.

2. Evolution of the Role: A more detailed review of developments from the fall of 1957 is already available. Relevant to long-range issues are the following:

a. The Youth Board intensified the activities of city-wide advisory committees and created a standing committee of citywide voluntary coordinating agencies and fund-raising bodies.

b. Borough and neighborhood activity was stepped up and local "town meetings" held.

c. Social services, employment programs, and gang programs were expanded in high-hazard areas (and, again, in subsequent "crises").

d. The Youth Board reached an agreement with the Community Council specifying that the latter was responsible for the over-advice to the borough office but could initiate projects through citywide "channels." It was unrelated, in any formal sense, to ongoing borough administration or to area meetings and neighborhood council programs. Thus, while the borough structure gave substantial support to neighborhood community organization and gave the Youth Board "listening posts" in major localities, it was not a longrange planning body. (Changes are now being made.)Then, as a result of the community concern over particularly violent outbreaks of juvenile delinquency during the summer of 1957, the Youth Board was given clear authorization (although its statutory charge has always been broad) to assume through its Executive Director a larger role in the coordination of the community's delinquency-control efforts. An Executive Order made the board's Executive

Director the "coordinator" of the city's antidelinquency program. He was charged with uniting the efforts of public and voluntary agencies for the more adequate provision of social services in "potentially hazardous areas." All municipal agencies were directed to cooperate with him, thus conferring upon him a measure of the mayor's authority over the other municipal departments concerned. The Youth Board also received additional state and city funds to strengthen its own programs. The latter definitions were soon dropped. The general weakening of the Community Council, for reasons not here relevant, resulted in a vacuum which the Youth Board filled to a degree through a variety of *ad hoc* project committees involving religious leaders, mass media, employer and labor groups, educators, and so on.

The Youth Board director, in his capacity of commissioner, moved into City Hall to advise the mayor. His new role there had elements of two types of role: use of a City Hall base to lead an antidelinquency campaign; coordination of the entire social welfare effort on behalf of children. Thus he developed plans to screen and serve suspended pupils. At the same time, a program of maximum summer coverage of services ("summer vigilance") was evolved, to meet the expected delinquency increase, and has been repeated annually. Finally, the director undertook a series of tasks as trouble shooter and representative of the mayor in regard to a wide range of social welfare situations and budgetary demands on the city. Meetings which might lead to new programs or to coordination of efforts were also begun.

Between 1959 and 1962, when he retired and was replaced in his Youth Board executive role, but not as commissioner, the Commissioner of Youth Services undertook a large trouble-shooting role in the youth services field, particularly in relation to delinquency, aided by the Youth Board Central Planning Unit and research staffs i.e., the Youth Board coordination machinery. He initiated some operational coordination through the device of commissioner cabinet meetings, called with the authority of the mayor. The degree of cooperation and participation varied with the urgency of the matter and the degree of the mayor's concern and backing. At the same time, the Youth Board per se continued its major concern with direct services, contracts, and borough programs. Direct services were decentralized through the borough offices. Coordination and research were central office functions. In his role as Executive Vice President of the Youth Board, the Commissioner of Youth Services directed that program. As commissioner, he reported to the mayor, not to the Youth Board, in relation to planning and coordination.This "case history" of the Youth Board coordination and planning effort would seem to hold certain general lessons:

a. An agency which grants funds for services and which conducts a case finding and referral program is in a strategic position to coordinate operations related to its own area of service and to promote service integration. Thus, the present case conference program and the as-yet-undeveloped use of the multiproblem family register for accountability purposes are appropriate functions for an agency such as the Youth Board.

b. When a long-range planning effort bases itself on the initiative of advisory committees composed of personnel whose primary ties are to other programs, it tends to generate useful, vital, but unrelated projects. Basic long-range planning requires a technical planning staff with considerable initiative and a citizen-based policy board. The Youth Board itself might have played the latter role but, as indicated, its commissioner members are oriented to their program needs and its citizen members are not personally related to enough of the program. Moreover, it is burdened with the statutory responsibility of administering grants to agencies through "contracts."

c. As soon as a delinquency program which is community-based turns to problems of prevention and long-range planning, it must deal with public welfare services, family agency services, education, recreation, health—and many aspects of child welfare. Local neighborhood self-help activity becomes important. It is questionable, as a matter of community policy, to seek to encompass so wide a range of services under a delinquency program "umbrella" for purposes of planning and coordination, even though financing may be facilitated thereby.

d. It is exceedingly doubtful that the selfsame person should seek to function successfully as director of a series of direct-service programs related to delinquency, a program of grants-in-aid and contracts to public and voluntary agencies, a series of mechanisms for service integration and accountability—and at the same time coordinate all child care services in the role of commissioner, in the mayor's office. One role or the other will be played down; the role conflicts will probably decrease the effectiveness of all roles.

Other cities considering their own patterns will find interesting the Los Angeles appraisal which recorded the program and method contributions of the Youth Board but which argued against duplicating the Youth Board plan. Stating that each locality must develop its own structure, Los Angeles noted that its organization is on a county, not city, basis and lacks the strong private and sectarian agency development which characterizes New York. It favored creation of a Youth Commission to coordinate planning and operations as well as a citizen policy advisory body. No direct services except for research would be assigned to this machinery.

Search for a Planning and Coordination Structure

The analysis would seem to suggest a well-defined, if narrower, role for the Youth Board or its equivalent. As a planning, coordination, and accountability instrument of community policy relative to *delinquency*, it might continue to implement a program of contracts. Its board requires both sound staff work and full policy discussions of its own in order to relate the system of allocations to broader community strategy, new needs, coordinated operations. At the same time, the Youth Board's direct operations should probably concentrate on case finding, service integration, and accountability (Referral Units, case register, case conferences). Direct service operations of other kinds should be for purposes of demonstration and training so as not to interfere with the coordination-accountability role. Thus, the Street Club Project should ultimately be housed elsewhere if an appropriate base can be found. The Youth Board's research program should involve administrative studies vital to its functions and evaluative studies of its demonstration experiments.

The borough and neighborhood efforts would be most appropriate as devices for tapping citizen opinion and sentiment, channeling local project suggestions, and promoting education. Members of the Youth Board itself should participate in or have ties to the borough committees, to make the latter effective. In turn, Youth Board borough and neighborhood efforts should be related to and even be incorporated into a broader program of neighborhood organization, preferably under voluntary auspices. If public funds are required for staff services, it would seem wiser to expend them through a Community Council than through a public network of neighborhood councils and borough offices. By definition, neighborhood organization, in a democracy, should be free to direct its pressures to city government, as needed; staffing by public employees complicates the process. Separate auspices for neighborhood organization and case conferences would not preclude experimental ties between the two. Although this kind of refocus is not proclaimed as the Youth Board direction, it would seem to be implied in the city's decision late in 1961 to define the Youth Board's coordination role as lying in the delinquency sphere while the office of administration develops machinery for public planning and coordination of family and children's services in general. The latter designation follows a long period of analysis, discussion, and experimentation in New York City, in the course of which claims for the role were advanced in various forms by the Youth Board, the Commission on the Foster Care of Children, the Community Mental Health Board, and the Community Council. Analysis of the total New York experience of the past two decades would seem to suggest the following:

a. City-wide planning and coordination of services to families and children requires a cabinet committee or its equivalent, directly responsible to the chief executive. It should be presided over by the chief executive or his deputy—i.e., by an official who outranks a departmental commissioner. It requires a research staff and other staff to implement its role of study, planning, and operational coordination. Only interdepartmental coordination based on the commissioner level will truly permit significant operational coordination. Only a staff based in the city administration can undertake significant planning.

b. While coordination bodies may be needed in a variety of fields (delinquency, recreation), the over-all body should have a broad charge in the family and children's field.

c. There is also need for a citizens' planning commission, an advisory group concerned with policy and planning priorities. It should have close liaison to the cabinet-level body and be served by the planning-coordination staff. It should report periodically to the chief executive and the public in addition to expressing itself on ongoing policy and planning priorities and issues. It should be in a position to initiate and receive the reports of evaluation and research.

This proposal is based on the assumption that it is appropriate for department heads, sitting as a "cabinet" under a top municipal official, to deal with major policies and to use committees of alternates or deputies for handling details of implementation or program development. This approach has been successful in many places.

The question then arises, why would such a body not be able to do the *whole* job; why an additional body, a commission?

Response with reference both to city and state levels would be similar. The coordination through cabinet, staff, and top-official chairman has an inevitably serious handicap which derives from the necessary concern and orientation of each commissioner toward his own program, his problems in meeting his department's budget, and his healthy reluctance to raise questions about the services of other departments. Somebody not responsible for execution of any one part should see the whole, be free to ask questions about any of the parts, note the gaps and weak spots, and be able to make objective and disinterested recommendations.

In addition, it is necessary to face the fact that department heads are members of the "administration," politically speaking, and are under administration discipline in many areas. They are often not free to air differences about policy or practice. They are certainly not in a position to report vital issues and recommendations to the public unless a mayor or governor chooses that they do so. However, the function of reporting to the public on crucial matters so that sound policy direction may crystallize, *even if contrary to current administration policy*, is an important part of the job to be done. Thus, although a cabinet is strongly recommended for the things it will be able to do best, there is need, too, for the planning commission.

From this perspective New York City would appear to have gone part way. The city's administrator has the function temporarily, and his office may convene the commissioners and deputies. A study to develop over-all structure is under way. The Youth Board role, if logically developed, would now seem much clearer. Unclear, as yet, is how and where the citizen advisory function in the form of a planning commission will be discharged. It would seem possible to assign this through a change in role and status of one of several existing advisory bodies (Foster Care, Mental Health, Youth Board, Welfare, etc.), each of which would require a broadening of concern, separation from any operational department, and assignment of membership in individual, not representative, capacities. Another possibility is the creation of a new over-all citizen body while existing ones continue with their tasks in specific spheres.

The limitations of the New York City Community Council do not make a third alternative realistic for New York, but there are some communities in which the planning council function is well discharged by a welfare planning council. A precondition is that the council be a *community* body neither public nor voluntary be much more than an instrument of social agencies, and have broad citizen support. Given such a situation, the council might then also serve to coordinate public and voluntary agency operations and planning as well. The existence of such a body does not, however, obviate the need for the public cabinet and interdepartmental structure. The scale, scope, costs, and ramifications of public operations are such that no outside body could conceivably discharge the task.

A final note about planning: Much of this chapter would seem to stress planning *for*, while our political philosophies and social ethic give priority to planning *with*. Consumers of all services, agency clients, and youth all have their contributions to make. In part, this is the case for a public planning structure: in a representative government, a public body reports and is ultimately accountable to the supporters and consumers of service, who are one, for what is done. In part, too, this is the case for neighborhood organization, local self-help agencies, youth councils, and community planning bodies. These too are channels for all the people and make it possible for them to react, challenge, initiate, and support services.

6

Group Work Method for Social Work

Introduction

Some are elaborately devised and others informal and even accidentally engendered. There have been instances of probation officers trying to develop group methods in an effort to save time, or to offset large caseloads by the labor-saving device of seeing several probationers together instead of one by one. Usually this does not have the desired effect on the officer's schedule, for although there has been some experience that shows a saving of work in the sense of more accomplished, the general experience is that group work may be even more demanding of time than casework with individual clients and it may easily be more demanding of the emotional energy of the worker.

Actually, group work introduces certain chores for the worker not involved in a casework approach. Clients must be selected for the group and must be assembled with regard to the personality types that will work together successfully in a group. Much preparation of clients is needed for the group experience. A meeting place must be found and not just any old place will do. A time each week must be found when the group members can all come; and sometimes even transportation has to be arranged. With all these logistical problems, it is still a uniquely rewarding experience, for it can give the worker a sense of action, of case movement, that at times can be quite exhilarating. If it is less time consuming than casework it is so only in the sense that, if all goes well, group work can, for some cases, accomplish greater or more rapid progress than casework would for an equal amount of time and effort. In the group work process there is not the time lapse while a relationship builds up as is usual in casework.

There is no more magic in group work than in casework, but we are finding that the supplementing of one technique by the other is more richly effective in treatment than either technique by itself.

In Minnesota the Department of Corrections conducted a research project with its group work among parolees, seeking to test several hypotheses. The findings are interesting and significant:

Hypothesis 1: The group method of supervision reduces recidivism. When viewed in terms of months-per-man completed on parole without revocation, the Experimental Group had a significantly higher "success ratio" than did either of the control groups.

Hypothesis 2: The group method permits more intensive and extensive parole supervision and the smallest investment of money and time. Each member of the Experimental Group received three hours of supervision per month; the parolee supervised under "normal" practice received approximately two hours. The group leader was able to supervise ten men in four hours per month (including travel time); to supervise ten men on a one-to-one basis usually requires approximately thirty hours. Transportation costs were reduced substantially because the parole agent had to travel to only one location rather than make ten separate visits. The extensive number of topics discussed in group sessions and the opportunity for all members to express their own viewpoints freely created a dimension of individual involvement not usually experienced in the traditional agent-parolee dialogue.

Hypothesis 3: Permitting controlled associations among parolees has no inherent negative effects. Waiving the rule prohibiting association among parolees, for purposes of this experiment, produced no difficulty whatsoever.

Administrative Arrangements

Group work is met with resistance nearly everywhere when it is first introduced. It is typical that the probation or parole officer will be skeptical of it and unenthusiastic about becoming involved in it. A California parole officer who later became sold on the value of the group technique wrote about his initial reaction: "When, by administrative decision, the writer was directed to establish a group from his own caseload, he had serious misgivings about doing so. He saw himself primarily (in view of his previous experience in the honor camps) as a non-directive counselor. He was blocked by the apparent incongruity between the two roles he was expected to play: the first, authoritarian, and the second, permissive. Actually, it must be confessed that the formation of the group was delayed for several weeks while he attempted to resolve his own conflict regarding these seemingly opposing roles he must play. With the interest and advice of two members of the administrative staff he was able to work out a rationale for combining the roles, and thereafter proceeded to develop the group."

Often the casework staff will look at the proposed group work as a frill, as frosting on the cake. The comment will be made that, after all, casework is the function of the agency and casework cannot be sacrificed in order to experiment with frills. Even so, a few agencies are realizing that a probation or parole agency's staple function should be couched in more basic terms to help people and protect the community and any process that furthers this intent is a proper one whether it is casework, group work, community organization, or even just surveillance and enforcement. The first prerequisite for bringing a resistive staff to a happy use of this broad social work approach is the genuine, active support of the agency administrator. Without such support from the top no such new concept or technique has a chance.

There is no easy way to bring group work practice into a correctional casework agency, but some good experience is accumulating. The most usual approach is to encourage certain of the regular probation or parole officers to select a few individuals from their caseloads and start meeting with them in groups while still carrying the bulk of the caseload in the conventional manner. Another approach is to let the regular casework staff carry their cases as usual while a trained group worker is added to the staff to specialize in group work by forming groups from cases referred to him from the regular caseloads. The first method has the advantage of not requiring cases to be transferred from one worker to another, and it provides for a more general infusion of the method through the total agency caseload. It has the disadvantage of requiring a considerable effort in persuading caseworkers to try this technique, and it requires a substantial amount of training for those staff members who do decide to use it. As with many such issues, the best choice in the long run is likely to be a combination of the two. The specialized group worker will, finally, serve most usefully to entice the caseworkers into experimenting with the group process and then will be available to give them consultation if he personally and professionally has their confidence.

This is important because group work can be an unsettling idea to the uninitiated, and the person who must advocate and teach it needs to be comfortably acceptable in the face of the caseworkers' anxieties. The typical worker who has a B.A. degree and no graduate-level specialized training gets accustomed fairly quickly and easily to the handling of cases on a one-by-one basis. The dynamics of interaction between him and the client can be kept relatively uncomplicated, or at least not too threatening. With his mantle of authority he can ordinarily deal with his manipulative and hostile clients when they present themselves just one at a time. And when he becomes experienced, and has had good supervision, he can learn, too, how to handle the hostile client with skill and understanding, rather than just by pulling his rank and issuing peremptory orders. But when a group of such clients is confronting the worker they gain courage in each other's presence to let their hostility show more freely, and the worker may find it crackling about his head like lightning. The feelings that he could handle in the one-to-one situation may suddenly seem to overwhelm him in the group situation and leave him shaken to his roots. If he has been accustomed to being treated with the outward signs of respect, and sees this as being important in his relationships with the client, he will be deeply repelled by a group work philosophy that allows clients in a group to lash at his agency with profane expressions of cynical resentment. Sooner or later he has to discover that if the group experience is going to be effective it will have to permit the expression of anger so that the source of that anger can be examined and treated. But this will be a jarring experience for many people who may not have the inner serenity and sense of security to permit such hostile expression. Or perhaps, instead, the worker has picked several clients who are not articulate, who do not strike sparks with each other, and so he goes home afterward with deep discouragement because he could get no real discussion going, could engender no useful interchange and no sense of group feeling among the several individuals.

These are the sorts of reasons why the average worker needs some close, supportive supervision when he tries the group work technique. The administrator who encourages his casework staff to try working with groups without giving them some specific training will find that they move into the group work process with reluctance and that they either discontinue it after experimentation, or else continue it with uncertainty, aimlessness, and lack of satisfaction.

Staff Training

If the casework staff is composed of persons with graduate training in social work they will be able to move fairly confidently toward the group work process, but will still need supportive supervision in it if their training was in casework rather than group work. Persons with the master's degree in social group work are increasingly looking toward opportunities to conduct for agency staffs intensive indoctrination programs in group work that deals with emotional disturbances, and their training is highly appropriate to this type of professional supervisory program. In some agencies consultative and supervisory service is furnished by a psychologist and this is satisfactory if his training has included an emphasis in group work. Either a social group worker or a psychologist may be good in giving supportive supervision and either may be poor, according to the individual's personal qualities and the emphasis in his training.

For persons without specialized training there are various ways that this extra help can be given. It is useful, of course, to allow the worker to attend an institute, conference, or summer course on the subject. This is a splendid start but is not enough by itself. The learning process must continue on an intensive basis when the worker later begins to handle groups. He runs into situations that are surprising and challenging and offer magnificent opportunities for learning if he has access to a supervisor who can help him analyze the event and consider the ways that it should have been handled. So it is well for the administration of an agency to find some way that a group work specialist can be made available for continuing consultation if there is to be assurance that the group work program will thrive.

In one probation office (the county court of Philadelphia) use, after surprisingly thorough training, of the regular juvenile court probation officers for supplementary group work has been tried. These officers are expected to become a part of a discussion group themselves first, and under the direction of the psychologist who is responsible for the training they pursue the same sort of personal examination that they are later to handle with clients. It is a remarkable effort at training in depth, for the worker not only must enter wholly into the sharing of feelings in a group with his colleagues, but must continue this training for six months to two years before he is considered ready to direct groups himself. This training is given, of course, while he is occupied full time with a caseload, so the group work training is just an hour and one-half a week. Up to ten probation officers will be in the training discussion group at the start but there is a considerable reduction in its size as time goes on, for many of these probation officers find it difficult to tolerate this kind of shared personal examination with their colleagues and they drop out.

In view of the experience of other offices it would seem that this training plan requires staff time and effort that are out of proportion to the realistic requirements of the situation. Admittedly, two years of training is desirable for this demanding kind of leadership, but it should be a well-rounded training with supportive studies in related subjects. Furthermore, no matter how thorough an experience is gained with a group of one's colleagues, the trainee may be left without even his first sight of a group process involving clients. For most people, effective training should include actual supervised experience in handling groups. For this reason a better plan seems to be one used in Sacramento where it was, again, the staff psychologist who was responsible for instructing the probation officers in group work methods. In this case, however, the officers were given preliminary orientation to the group process in class sessions held for two hours per day through ten consecutive workdays. After that the officers proceeded to select cases and start their groups. Once the groups were meeting regularly a system of individual consultation was arranged for the staff. Each officer spent an hour with the psychologist for each hour spent in leading a group. This permitted intensive analysis of what happened in the meeting and how the officer handled it, which was considered the really effective part of the training. With both the group work and the continuing training under way, this office, too, turned to the use of group discussions for the staff. Once a week the psychologist conducted a small staff group discussion, but contrary to the Philadelphia training process, this staff group followed the rule that the discussions could cover any subjects except the administration of the department and intimate personal matters that were not voluntarily brought up by the person concerned. To all appearances the staff group discussion works better as an experience that comes *after* the members have actually gotten into the task of leading groups and their interest in the process has become more solidly based.

Another device for staff training is the use of a co-leader. A group that has been meeting long enough to develop a group feeling can easily tolerate a trainee who sits in to observe the experienced leader. In fact, much experience has shown the value of having co-leaders for a group as the standard procedure. This presents a splendid opportunity for a training situation in which the experienced leader carries the responsibility for the group process while the trainee is present and participating as much as possible as a co-leader, with the two then holding an evaluative discussion together after the meeting.

Continued training when the new leader is conducting group sessions by himself is effectively accomplished by means of tape recordings of the meetings. These can be useful even when the supervisor has been present in the meeting, for the trainee, in listening later to his handling of the group, is sometimes surprised to hear himself saying certain things, or saying them in a way he had not been aware of at the time. This can contribute much to his self-understanding in areas that affect his rapport with the group.

In Los Angeles the state parole agents have a cooperative group practice and training arrangement that is unique in some respects. The plan is a joint arrangement between the several parole officers who work as one unit under a common supervisor. Each of the officers has eight to a dozen men from his caseload whom he sees as a group once a week. All the officers in the unit meet with their groups on the same evening, in the same building. On that evening there are four distinct stages of the process.

The first starts about suppertime and is referred to as "sensitivity training." The several officers, their supervisor, and a psychologist adviser meet together shortly after the close of regular office hours. They bring their sandwiches and coffee and spend about an hour and a half in discussion of group techniques. It may be a general discussion concerned with sharpening their talents as group leaders or it may be discussion of specific matters that will be handled in the groups that evening. One parole agent, for instance, may mention what he intends to do with his group or a certain parolee in the group. The staff unit then discusses the ways to handle the proposed discussion most effectively, with the psychologist giving technical advice. By seven o'clock the parolees arrive and the officers go off to assemble with them for an hour and a half in small group discussions in various assigned rooms in the building. The next step is an unusual one. After these small group discussions the parolees and staff convene in one large room for a one-hour group discussion that involves all fifty or sixty parolees, the five officers, the supervisor, and the psychologist. The discussion in this large group is ordinarily a continuation of one of the small group discussions. When the large group discussion is over and the parolees have gone home the staff unit again sits down for another hour of discussion to analyze, while it is fresh in their minds, the success or the errors in their evening's work.

Altogether it makes a long day. The large discussion period is a feature that is characteristic of California agencies where correctional leaders have been impressed with the therapeutic community concepts of Maxwell Jones. Most group work devotees have been convinced that the small cohesive group is best, since it gives more opportunity for participation by every group member and, in fact, forces the involvement of each one. Jones agrees with this but advocates the use at the same time of large groups which he considers to have a value of their own. "The whole atmosphere tends to be more emotionally charged than in the small therapeutic groups, where there is much greater cohesiveness and a better opportunity to work through a situation with gain in insight. The large discussion group is more permissive in the sense that, as one of a large crowd of patients, the individual is in less direct contact with the doctor, and is more ready to reproduce his own particular emotional patterns."

Whether or not the large group is included in the evening's sequence, the format is a useful one. By having all meetings on the same evening an ideal opportunity is presented for sharpening staff skills and giving mutual support through the pre-meeting and post-meeting discussions.

Group Discussion

A group discussion, like a casework interview, can be held with any of several purposes in mind. It may be set up with a specific purpose of considering a problem of one group member and coming to an action regarding it. Or it may be an open, undirected talk-fest with no more immediate purpose than giving the group members a needed socializing experience. It may be focused on an educational topic for the simple increase of knowledge in some particular sphere. Or it may be a sharing of intimate feelings, a discussion in depth which aims at basic changes in attitudes through the client's increased understanding of himself.

These widely varying forms of the group process call for varying degrees of professional skill, and we consequently see a range of practice, from groups conducted by untrained lay citizen volunteers to groups under the leadership of such professionals as specially trained psychiatrists. However, these two extremes account for the smaller part of total group work efforts; quite properly, most group work in corrections is being done by the professional probation or parole worker with a B.A. degree plus a graduate degree or some in-service training.

Though the novice may approach the task of group leadership with the uneasy assumption that group work skill is something elusive and profound, actually the essence of it is found in the attributes of simplicity and honesty, and the device of constantly requiring that answers be reached through discussion by the group rather than through pronouncements by the leader. But still it usually requires training, experience, and courage to pursue a simple and honest course in dealing with groups. It is too easy to assume that skill is something that has a devious quality about it, that it is an artfully esoteric way of handling people. This may also include the assumption that the delinquent group would almost categorically resist a direct, forthright approach from the authoritative person, so they must be reached by indirect (skilful) means.

Not So

It is true enough that neither in casework nor in group work can we address a hostile or skeptical person or group and just flatly say, "Now remember, if you are going to avoid trouble in the future you must do so and so." Our words would be wasted on cynical ears. But suppose instead we sit down with a group of delinquent boys and start out by saying, "All of you guys have been arrested two or more times in the last year; as a result you're all on probation which you'd rather not be. What we're going to discuss is the question of how to keep from getting arrested any more." What could be more simple, direct, and honest than that? And that is the skilled approach. It does not bluntly set one cultural concept against another. Instead it starts with what is common concern in both cultures. The boys as well as the leader can agree on the desirability of avoiding arrest. And yet it does not compromise or dissemble regarding the intention of the leader or his value base.

Along with the concepts of simplicity and honesty the group worker must also keep in mind the principle that his goal is for decisions or conclusions to be enunciated by the group not by the leader. The element that is unique about group work is that client is listening to client; client is interacting with client; client is being influenced by client. This is totally different from the idea that you get a group together just so more people can listen at one time to the advice of the leader. The probation or parole officer using group work must recognize that delinquents, young or old, are predisposed to listen more receptively to fellow delinquents than to the authoritative person, and that with some guidance they have a capacity to find their own path to improvement. So by pointing the boys in the direction of finding ways to avoid arrest the leader has set in motion the process of having them find their own answers. It will take them hours to find the answers that he could formulate for them in a minute, but the answer they find for themselves will stick, whereas the answer pronounced by the leader would hardly even be heard.

A common problem the group leader in corrections faces is the expression of hostility. This is particularly true when he has a group of men or women who have been recently paroled or who are preparing for parole. The hostility they feel will show itself in the group process in a predictable pattern of development. The members of the newly formed group start out cautiously, saying little, or talking on neutral, bland topics. As they become more secure with the leader, they test him with expressions of hostility that at first are safely directed at remote objects such as the parole board, the governor, the system, or other persons or offices that are fairly well out of range. The group next will shift its attack to more immediate objects, and then the parole officer, as group leader, may find himself being bitterly criticized. Also attacked are other staff members, the rules of parole, employers, etc.

It appears that these stages have to be worked through in the typical group before the members come into the more mature final stage of looking at themselves. Overlying these steps in the process will also be a tendency of the group members to indulge in a superficial discussion of group and personal problems in an effort to satisfy the leader and more quickly gain whatever favors they hope for him to give. Probationers or parolees are adept at sensing the kind of answers and expressed attitudes that authoritative personnel like to hear. They will almost instinctively mouth the phrases that the group leader is encouraging them to use, so that the discussion may have a fine sound to it, though actually it is quite spurious. A sign of group maturation is the giving up of these empty recitations in favor of a more genuine probing for underlying feelings.

The difficult stage for the leader to endure is, of course, the second one, which subjects the leader to criticism that can be downright vituperative at times. The officer who has been accustomed to expecting the forms of respect from his clients will at least be uncomfortable with this development, and may at that point abruptly reject the technique altogether. Actually it is not necessary for the officer to endure meekly, like a sitting duck, any purely splenetic goading that might be aimed at him. The skilled leader can maintain the kind of demeanor that says that such attacks are out of order. If he is competent in this the group itself will do its own policing, for while these are people with hostility, they are also anxious people who do not want to see things get out of hand. At the same time the leader's skill must enable him to recognize and tolerate the more therapeutic hostile expressions. A profane speech of bitter complaint and personal criticism might actually be an honest attempt to express a problem and ask for a solution — expressed in the vernacular which is altogether natural to the voicing of intense feelings in this client's cultural setting.

At this point in the group process the leader's job is to help the group to an increased or new sense of comfort with, and confidence in him, the parole officer. This will be accomplished if the barbs of the group are met with a cool, unruffled, and objective reaction on the leader's part. If the group is criticizing him for making a mistake, and if they really can make a case for its having been a mistake, the officer will gain, not lose, by freely admitting the error.

If the group is complaining about any of the many problems of being on probation or parole the nuisance of being checked on; the nuisance of reporting; the injustices of discrimination against the man with a record; the unreasonableness of the rules the officer is losing no status with them in letting the complaints flow. He will, instead, gain status by letting them talk and by turning their questions back to them. If he does pronounce some decision it is desirable although not necessary that the clients be able to see the rightness of the leader's stand. But it is important that they see that he himself is convinced of its rightness in terms of an honest concern for them and subject to a willingness on his part to hear and consider their views. Forthrightly he must avoid being shaken by their attacks and must constantly insist that they find most of their own answers. His attitude should seem to say, "Sure it's tough; but what's the practical, sensible thing you're going to do about it?"

With such a stance the officer avoids being their punching bag and instead is another human being joined with them in a practical search for the answers to their problems. The officer, as group discussion leader, has to remind himself that to a large extent a critical and rebellious quality in a group may be a necessary ingredient in the effectiveness of the technique. Consider, for instance, how it would be if a new group of parolees were told by the parole officer in some detail how the group is expected to conduct itself. Suppose he designates himself as chairman and then not only describes what topics will be discussed but also enunciates the rules: speak only on being recognized by the chair, use no profanity, limit each comment to only two minutes, to name a few possibilities. With such an approach the officer may have a fairly comfortable, well-behaved, but bored group. These men are accustomed to rules. They know all about how to adapt to them in their own ways and they can relax on finding themselves on this kind of familiar ground. But not much that is therapeutic will be happening. On the other hand, an open, unstructured situation will be anxiety-provoking for them. Invite them to a group discussion and present them with no chairman, no rules, no discussion topic. In such a situation they no longer have the familiar touchstones or crystal-clear criteria of behavior to conform or to circumvent. They are forced to their own resources in finding rules of conduct and relationships in the group. It is this condition and not the former one that has potential for promoting growth.

But growth is an uncomfortable experience and it comes at an uneven rate. Group members groping with the no-rules freedom of such a method will go too far at times, will become intemperate and abusive as they experiment with letting their feelings go. But this is true of any experiential learning process and if the officer remains consistent in his handling, and keeps the group facing its own responsibility for finding answers, the group members will gradually learn how to control themselves through controlling the more difficult ones among them. The uncertain or insecure leader will want to insist on controlled and respectful talk, but the skilled leader will know that the free flow even of bitterly rebellious talk from some group member presents the group with immediate problems of how to get along with that person, and in solving such problems therapy is begun.

The leader will also have to resist the temptation to indulge in preachments. This is one of the harder lessons to learn, for the average leader will want to give earnest cautionary advice when he finds his group members continuing their delinquent plans and practices. He is not expected to ignore such things as planning of projected new offenses that he may overhear, but neither should he plunge into a direct assault on all the practices that seem to be characteristic of his delinquent group. If improvements can be made by the group itself in its own time such progress will be far more real. In one discussion group of older teen-age probationers the leader was well aware that most of the boys carried switchblade knives. He made no effort either to suggest or to insist on any change in this practice. It was not long before the boys themselves found a way to bring up the subject in a discussion where they watched warily to see what the leader's reaction would be. The leader pushed the question back to them and helped them discuss the issue as objectively as possible. No final conclusions were reached and no instructions given. The effect of this sort of handling is subtle and may be discovered later, if at all, in unexpected little ways. In this case it was a few weeks later when someone brought the boys a watermelon during their regular discussion meeting that the leader learned how effective his work had been. He was amused and pleased to discover that they had no way to cut the melon. Nobody had a knife.

A welcome and highly useful by-product of the discussions is the improved relationship the clients seem to develop with the leader, notwithstanding any harsh words that fly about in the group discussions. Officers find that probationers or parolees who are members of a discussion group more quickly develop a good working rapport with the officer, making the casework contacts more effective. The group setting exposes the officer to the clients in a social setting and gives them a chance to see him as a normal, human sort of person, rather than just as an authoritative controller of the clients' destinies.

The Minnesota research cited earlier also pointed up this aspect of the value of group work. A fifth hypothesis in this study was that "subjecting the parole agent's activities to the collective scrutiny of his clients reduces the social distance between the agent and the parolee." The researchers report: "Tape recordings of group sessions clearly show the decreasing reticence of group members to question the group leader's decisions and the agent-parolee relationship. Social distance was reduced as members and leader came to know each other better and developed feelings of mutual respect, understanding, and concern. Interaction between agent and group helped the agent develop clearer insights into the needs of the parolee."

The Co-leader

The leader who is moving with uncertainty and difficulty in handling a hostile group may find it helpful to use a co-leader. In fact, as indicated above, the practice of regularly conducting groups with two leaders seems to have special usefulness, particularly in women's or children's groups. Experience with this in California correctional settings, the Minneapolis juvenile court, and the New Orleans juvenile court indicates that a man and a woman working together as co-leaders provide an extra stimulus to discussion and arouse a new kind of interest on the part of group members. The two leaders give more of a family quality to the setting and tend to provoke areas of discussion that are less likely with one leader. Questions about sex may be elicited by the presence of male and female leaders, but at the same time their presence tends to be a healthy influence on keeping the conversation at a more seemly level than might be true if people of only one sex were present.

The more certain advantage, however, is the practical one that two people accomplish more than a single leader does. During the meeting certain subtle asides or covert reactions might not be caught by the leader who is involved in the discussion at the moment, while the other leader will see and note these significant items. Also, during the meeting the two leaders may disagree about some issue the group has raised and may have to discuss it briefly between the two of them. For many clients it is a fresh and useful experience to observe how these two adults handle their difference of opinion with friendly but objective discussion; and also to see the evidence of the leaders' maturity in the way they relate to each other just as person to person at the same time that they relate appropriately as male and female.

After the meeting the two leaders have the advantage of being able to discuss the dynamics of the discussion just completed by comparing their separate observations and their separate diagnostic impressions. This post-meeting analysis affords an opportunity for introducing one more device that involves and helps the clients: to admit the clients themselves to the "debriefing" session. This helps to solve the problem of the gulf existing between the intention of the social worker and the client's skeptical view of that intention. The client has all too often been schooled in a cynical view of authoritative people and automatically discounts a heavy percentage of what they say. It is not unlike the average person's discounting of the slickly presented television commercial. He knows that everything about it is selfishly and commercially inspired, and so he may put very little faith in it. But he would be encouraged to have much more faith in the same product if it should happen to make a straight news report. If a reporter with no bias has reason to present a news story involving the success of the product, the reader is far more impressed. This same sort of psychology is at work when group members are allowed to listen to an analysis of their meeting, conducted just as if they were not present.

At the California Institution for Men at Chino this technique is used in connection with some of the large daily group meetings at which several staff members are present. After the meeting the staff members return to their offices for a discussion of what happened within the group. Nothing is said about group members coming to this post-meeting discussion but it is tacitly understood that they are free to come if they want to. What happens is that the two or three members who were most hotly involved in the discussion will have some anxiety about the staff view of the action and will want to hear the staff's analysis. With no invitation given or requested and with no attention being paid to them, they go along to the staff conference room and sit outside the small staff circle, against the wall, while the staff discusses the session just completed without taking any apparent notice of the men.

In Minneapolis, group workers with the juvenile court have been trying a variation of the same device. The two co-leaders of a girls' group were using a room for their group discussions that happened to have an adjoining observation room with one-way glass between the two rooms. The girls knew that the two leaders stayed awhile after each meeting to discuss what had happened. After the girls became rather mature in their group experience, the leaders invited them to go behind the window and observe and listen to the post-meeting discussion between the co-leaders. In this way, though no one was fooling anyone, the girls were given the illusion of listening in on persons who were unaware of their presence. The theory was that some of the comments made by the leaders would have more impact in this context, but that whether or not this would be so, the girls would be presented with a reinforced image of the probation officer as a person whose discussion of them showed an impressive specialized knowledge and skill and who was genuinely interested in them far beyond the attention that the officer's salary could be expected to buy. This technique gives every indication of being highly successful in cementing the relationships between the leaders and the girls.

In this kind of process, though the discussion should be no less genuine than if the girls were not there, good judgment must be used by the leaders in the way that diagnostic material is discussed. It is not a matter of withholding diagnostic material but rather of using care in word choice. Some diagnostic words can be quite frightening, or at least confusing, to uninitiated persons. Just as bad as words that confuse would be words that conceal because of their strangeness. Use of some unfamiliar words may have an ominous sound to a group member who imagines the worst about a word that is unfamiliar to him. Clinical discussion in front of the group should be kept within the limits of a simple and common vocabulary.

Group Organization

In organizing a discussion group the agency is presented with the question of whether to operate it as an open-end group or a closed group. In the former the group is kept going permanently, with new members added as other members drop out. With the closed group the group members are kept together until the group's purpose is accomplished, then discontinued completely. The most highly developed use of the open-end group is in the Highfields programs and in some of the halfway houses. In these settings the participants are meeting almost daily and developing a group culture that needs to be preserved by the unbroken continuation of the group. The frequency of the meetings also means that a new member is quickly assimilated and does not present the problem that he does in a group that meets only weekly.

In probation and parole settings the closed group is the most common. Such groups, meeting usually just once a week, have to make the most of the limited time they have. A new member being introduced to such a group is a "foreign object" at first; he may be an annoyance to the other members and may alter the pattern of group interaction. The delaying effect this can have on the progress the group is making is a principal reason why probation and parole officers usually prefer the closed group.

One variation on the pattern is sometimes tried when the agency has several staff members working with groups at the same time. In Minneapolis, for instance, the Department of Court Services had several adult groups in which the members were talking about their adjustment to the many problems of being divorced. As the groups approached a natural point of termination a new group was formed by one or two people from each of the original groups. This was by invitation to those who were interested in moving on to a group experience in which they would study their own personal adjustments in greater depth. By this point they had become experienced and comfortable in the group process and even though they suddenly moved into a new group they could do so with a minimum of lost motion.

The novice group leader may be apprehensive about how to introduce suitable topics for discussion. The answer is simply to let the group introduce its own. In a corrections setting the group members would not be there if they did not have problems, and ordinarily these problems are close enough to the surface to be verbalized with a minimum of prodding. It should not be assumed that the discussion has to involve only issues of deep and profound import. Discussion of deep-lying feelings will occur only in a mature group that first has practiced and gained comfort in many, many discussions of simple, practical everyday kinds of problems.

An example of the simplicity of these discussions comes from a group of six girls. They were seventeen and eighteen years old and in the group was one girl who had recently been married. During one meeting a girl asked the leader (who was the probation officer for the whole group) if she would be allowed to move out from home and live by herself. She had got a job just a week before as a clerk in a variety store, and now her father was saying that she should pay rent at home. She had immediately decided that if she had to pay rent she would rather move out and have a furnished room of her own.

In this case the probation officer had ample reason to refuse the request but instead of answering and arguing her point of view she tossed the question right back to the group. The married girl tended to discourage the idea with comments about how expensive it is to move out on your own. The other girls, though, were all bending in the other direction and saying that Sally should be allowed to try it if she wanted to. The leader directed their concern to the practical financial aspects of the question and on the blackboard she listed the expenses that the group members suggested. Sally's monthly pay was set down and then the group struggled to compute probable expenses. They argued with Sally about her low estimate on what a furnished room would cost. They thought of all the things she would have to buy food, bus fare, laundry, dry cleaning, soap, shampoo, hairspray, toilet paper, cosmetics, toothpaste, etc., etc. Sally argued for low estimates on all the items because of her eagerness to win her point. When the total was figured for a month's expenses there was a margin of reserve income, but the other girls were sobered by the unconvincing estimates that made this possible. It was obvious that it would have to be a spartan life. Sally's figure of sixteen cents daily for lunch, for instance, had them worried. They were seeing the bleakness of her idea of just a hot dog and a grape soda for lunch every day.

When they went on to list what Sally's expenses and margin of reserve would be if instead she remained at home, the contrast between the two plans was enough to make the girls shake their heads over Sally's proposal. Their initial, instinctive support of her request changed into remarks about the obvious advantages of staying at home awhile yet. It would not be accurate to say that Sally was convinced, but she was impressed, and she accepted the unanimous view of her peers to the extent of dropping the issue.

As the situation originally arose the leader might well have been tempted to answer Sally's question directly, explaining to her why she could not be permitted to leave home right now. If she had done so she would probably have left Sally unconvinced of the fairness of the decision and Sally would have had all but one of the other girls on her side and supporting her feelings of injustice. However, by turning the question to the group and suggesting their line of inquiry, the right decision was found and Sally was influenced more effectively.

It is of great importance, however, that the leader not allow this technique to trap him because of some less than honest element in his approach to the issue in question. The leader for this girls' group could not have turned the question over to the girls with the spoken assurance that the decision would wholly be up to them. This can be done only when the leader is prepared to take the risk of some quite unexpected outcome. Also, the responsibility for making a recommendation can be given to a group only when the group can also be given all the facts pertinent to the issue. If the question had been affected by highly private facts about Sally's home situation that could not be shared with the girls the leader would have been dealing dishonestly with the girls if she had invited them to recommend action on the basis of incomplete information.

The leader who commits himself to the principle of having the group members make their own decisions within the limits of their capability has to learn to remember this when it comes to some of the smaller decisions that may seem unimportant. He may say to his group, "This room is a little small for us so next time we'll meet in room A down the hall." He might be entirely sensible in this decision but he will be a better group leader if he will say instead, "Room A down the hall is available now and it's a larger room. Do you think you'd like to change to it for meetings after this? We can go and look at it if you want to."

Or some professional colleague may want to sit in on a group meeting some time and the leader may feel that the group process would not be hampered by the observer and that it would be quite all right. But his reply should be that he will take it up with the group. So at the next meeting he tells the group about his colleague who wants to visit; tells who he is and the nature of his interest, and gives the group full freedom to say whether they want to invite him or not.

This would seem to be the most picayune of issues but the real test of a leader's sincerity is seen in these little things. He may be trying to build the group's sense of responsibility and of self-worth by having the members make their own decisions, and this will not be at all hard to remember in respect to the more weighty matters. But if he forgets and ignores the principle when the issue is seemingly trivial the group feels the denial of the leader's stated purpose. In the same way, when the leader leaves it to the group to decide whether the room shall be changed or a visitor invited, the group feels it as a very concrete reaffirmation of the honesty of the leader's announced principles.

Honesty as a Technique

Utter honesty in dealing with the group includes a willingness on the part of the leader to let the group find its own decisions, rather than the expectation of manipulating them into finding and backing the decision the leader has already made in his own mind. It is legitimate, and even expected, that he will give subtle guidance to the direction of their discussion, but it must be guidance without subterfuge and must not promise more decision-making authority to the group than the leader is prepared to sustain.

An illustration of the consequences of well-intended dishonesty may be seen in a group discussion of parolees in which the parole officer was attempting to accomplish group censure of one member. This parolee, whom we might call Carlo, had been out of prison only a few weeks, was living with his wife and working steadily. However, the job did not pay much and Carlo and his wife had different ideas of what money was for. A day or two before this group meeting the parole officer had talked with Carlo's wife and had heard a fulsome account of Carlo's irresponsible use of the house money. The wife had been highly effective in convincing the parole officer of her view of the problem, the main item of which was that Carlo had just bought a car without first clearing this with the officer. The wife was complaining that it was needed and that after car payments were made there simply would not be enough money left for household expenses. The officer did not have a chance to see Carlo after that but, full of the wife's convincing complaint, he decided to bring it up at the meeting and let the group discipline Carlo. His goal was to accomplish a decision that Carlo would have to sell the car immediately.

The trap that this group leader set for himself and then walked right into was that he arranged a session that could be successful for him only if it led to one particular outcome; he was lulled into an overconfident expectation of that outcome by the view of it in his own mind, not realizing that the group would be getting a different view.

As the group convened, the parole officer brought up the subject of Carlo's new acquisition and its extravagance in relation to the family finances. But this was the first time he had confronted Carlo on the subject and he had underestimated the parolee's capacity for self-defense. Carlo's wife was not present to tell her side of the story and the officer could not relay it to the group with her effectiveness. Carlo produced a spirited and convincing defense, bringing up arguments in his favor that were unexpected and, hence, not easily countered by the parole officer. Furthermore, his audience was stacked in his favor. Every member of the group was a man on parole with the same problems and desires as Carlo had. No woman was in the group to give the wife's view. So the officer's effort to get group censure of Carlo backfired as the men gave Carlo complete support and went so far as to make strong comments about how unreasonable his wife obviously was, even suggesting that it was high time he should leave her.

This is the sort of situation that calls for flexibility on the part of the parole officer. The problem he was faced with here might be met by inviting the wife to come to the meeting too. Why not? Or an occasional meeting with all the wives present could be tried. And a bit of refreshment at the end of the meeting would be just the thing.

In another such instance a parole officer was trying to break up an association between parolee A and parolee B. The former had been on parole for a long time, had become very well stabilized, was financially successful, and was developing a satisfying home life. B was a long-time friend of A, and although he was making a satisfactory adjustment he was not capable of the degree of success that A enjoyed. The two men started out associating together very closely as personal friends and B had continued the association with frequent long visits to A's home, attempting to share all his spare-time activities with A. But as A grew more successful, his interests turned more to his own family, and he was increasingly oppressed by B's parasitical friendship.

When eventually A earnestly implored the parole officer to get B "off my back," at the same time stipulating, "But whatever you do, don't tell him I said anything about it," the parole officer decided to bring it to the group of which B was a member. He was trying to say to the group that for various reasons the association between the two men was not good for B and the group should support the parole officer in requesting B to stop seeing A. But though the officer tried to give some reasons why the association should break up, he could not tell the real precipitating reason for bringing up the issue, and the stated reasons sounded as unconvincing to the men as they deserved to sound. Under the circumstances, it was understandable that the group did not support the officer. They were puzzled by the suggestion that the two parolees break up; they saw no sense in it and they wondered quite bluntly how the parole officer "could be so goddam dumb."

Experiences like this give meaning to Gisela Konopka's view that "A helping relationship must be built on trust.

The group worker therefore cannot 'manipulate' a group in the sense of working toward his or the agency's goal, even if well-meant, without letting the members know about this and working it through with them. Not every step of his method must be consciously shared with them or explained, but the intent must be made known."

Authoritative Quality of the Group Process

Probation and parole officers who have tried working with groups have been accumulating experience that teaches us much about adapting the group work technique to the authoritative setting. To many officers it still seems preposterous to ask the advice or help of a group of parolees. The traditional approach would simply be for the officer to order Carlo to sell his car right now; to order parolee B to stop seeing parolee A. Whether or not the blunt orders are appropriate, it is obvious that some matters do have to be handled directly by the officer himself and not entrusted to a group. There is just no substitute for good judgment on the part of the officer in making intelligent selections of situations and techniques.

But just as a parole officer should avoid asking for group decisions in certain situations, there are many case problems that the group can solve more effectively than the officer can by himself. A good example of this occurred in a parole group where one parolee was helped to take a realistic view of his vocational plans. Fred had enough experience around machine shops to have convinced himself that he was a machinist, but he was being completely unsuccessful in getting and holding a job as such. Because he would not retreat from his own view of himself as a machinist this meant that he was remaining unemployed. The parolee who already feels some hostility toward his parole officer is not ready to accept from him any advice that might have an ego-deflating effect. So the officer encouraged the bringing up of the topic in the group sessions.

Over a period of several weeks the group dealt with Fred's vocational aspirations. They even watched for job openings and referred him to them. Eventually, they all saw what the real problem was. Fred simply wasn't qualified as a machinist but could not face that fact and was giving all sorts of excuses about why he couldn't get work. He blamed union shops, automated machines, unfair prejudice toward his prison record, etc., etc. Finally the group gave one full discussion period to the problem and beat down Fred's excuses one by one. There was endless discussion of minutiae about machine shops as the men argued over every tiny point. They pointed out the ads in the paper Fred had not answered; job tips that they had given him but he had not followed; discrepancies between his claimed qualifications and their knowledge of his background. Without the necessity of intervention by the parole officer they relentlessly made Fred see that he was deceiving himself and that it would be no disgrace to admit his limitations and take the sort of work that he really could do. The technique was effective and Fred, with this group support, accepted a revised view of himself and settled down to steady work operating a floor scrubber.

Generally the group process can be very effective for this broad type of problem solving. Given enough time to consider the problem thoroughly, the group will come up with dependably sound attitudes. But the group leader is on dangerous ground when he tries to get a highly specific kind of action and when he cannot fully share with the group all the premises upon which a decision must be based.

Just as honesty regarding the specific issue is important, we must also be honest about the general purpose of the group. A group discussion took place in a halfway house for parolees where the staff sincerely wanted the group to exercise a responsible decision-making function in regard to release plans for members of the group. The group on this occasion was speaking back hotly at the staff because group recommendations for a member's release had not been followed. In sharply profane language they were wondering what sense there was in their being asked for decisions when their decisions were ignored. Somehow the staff had managed to convey the idea that "It's up to the group to make the release decision." This was not a promise that the staff could actually carry through in the face of irresponsible decisions made by an immature group. The staff would have been all right if instead they had said the completely honest thing: "We make the decisions about release, but we do want the recommendations of the group and will follow those recommendations if they are not too much of a compromise with what we see as responsible action."

Ice Breaking

Certain conditions of awkwardness are likely to be felt as a group first begins its meeting and the group members cautiously take each other's measure. The leader may feel the need of some artificial stimulant to get the discussion going and focused on a fruitful topic. Generally this will be less true with an adult group where the process will be relatively simple and straightforward. It should be sufficient for the leader to explain the general purpose of the group in very brief terms and then leave it to the group to start conversation in whatever direction they wish. If they really seem to need help the leader might begin with an impersonal discussion of a type of problem that belongs to no one individual in the group but is more or less common to all. After getting started on this relatively safe ground the group will ordinarily move along to the more personal discussion content that will meet their real needs.

A bolder opening move with a new group is to make no opening gesture at all. It takes a little more nerve for a leader to invite a group of probationers or parolees to a group session and then sit down with them without saying anything. What will happen is that someone soon asks, "Well, what are we supposed to do?" Or, "What are we here for?" So the leader sets the pattern of the process immediately by turning their very first question back to them. "Well, why did you come?"

It's a method that at least surprises and arouses curiosity. It may cause annoyance. But it does get some talk going and immediately puts the group to work to find a purpose and areas of discussion content.

This technique has had a greater use in the general field of training in human relations. Juvenile court judges have experienced it in training institutes for judges where the "T-Groups" have been used. In these situations the leader surprises and disturbs the group by giving it no structure, no guidelines. "What makes the T-Group unique is that the trainer (instructor) does not prescribe what the trainees are to talk about or to do, lead the discussion, or even lay down procedural rules for the group e.g., how one gets the floor. All these things are, instead, done by the group itself."

It cannot be said that any one technique is the right one. It will depend largely on the leader himself. Unorthodox and even bizarre approaches will sometimes be acceptable and effective because of the particular talent or personality of the leader.

Generally with younger age groups there may be more need for discussion stimulants. Teen-age girls in a newly formed group are likely to be slow and reluctant in getting into meaningful discussion if they are just put together in a circle of chairs and told to talk, especially if the subject is to deal with highly personal family matters or sex information. In fact, this would be hard for most people. Despite the sex experience of most delinquent girls they lack the sophistication that would enable them to talk about it with comfort in a group, and so the attempted conversation is dissipated in embarrassed giggling. It has been found helpful for such groups to use an activity such as making fudge or popcorn. There can be a substantial reduction of discomfort if some busy and enjoyable manual activity is going on at the same time as discussion.

As a further development of this idea one probation officer and coleader starting a new group of girls held a brief, get-acquainted meeting and set up their next meeting for dinner together. A settlement house had an unused apartment in its building and this was borrowed for the evening. The girls met there, bringing the food items as prearranged and the six girls and the male and female co-leaders got to work in a completely casual way, like a family, making hamburger patties, peeling onions, and brewing coffee. They all sat down to dinner together and later found themselves in the kitchen together washing dishes. They were still talking as they sat around the kitchen table some time later.

The leaders had not said a word about group discussion, but as an utterly natural outcome of the dinner table conversation the talk turned to the "problem" of parents, just the topic the leaders would have picked. It was only the second time that any of the girls had met each other, but in this easy situation they were quickly comfortable and before the evening was over they were, in fact, a discussion group without any formal word or gesture having been used to institute them as such.

With boys' groups the more likely stimulus, when such is needed, is an activity that has an element of adventure. With either boys' or girls' groups that are reluctant to move into discussions of intimate material there are ways to get the discussion going first on a non threatening, impersonal basis. It should not be done by selecting "topics" to discuss. The leader who just arbitrarily announces that "At the meeting next week we will talk about dating" is being too artificial and if his planned discussion next week turns out to be a good one it will be only for accidental reasons. For the best success the discussion should grow out of real, natural, and immediate situations. The chances are that if this group really does need to talk about dating there is something in the current experience of one or several of them that can be used as a natural springboard for the discussion. If not, a springboard can be supplied. One leader has found that it sometimes works just to take the youngsters to a movie, a movie that may have some content that is akin to a subject the group might discuss. At the next meeting it is no problem to begin a quite natural discussion of some social problem that was presented in the movie. After discussing how the characters in the story handled or mishandled their problem it will not be long before the group finds its way to discussion of similar problems that are closer to home. In a somewhat contrived sense, then, this is still a discussion that arises out of a natural situation.

Phonograph records have been used similarly. There are records available with talks on dating, personal hygiene, marriage, etc., and sometimes these can be useful to get a group started in areas which interest them at the same time that they find it difficult to relax and talk about them.

Another variation of these approaches is the idea of presenting a problem situation by acting out episodes with puppets, a device that is used at the Philadelphia Youth Study Center.

With adult groups some leaders may find it useful to use a "transplant." After a group has met regularly for a long time and has come to its natural cessation it is likely that one or more persons in it are so enthusiastic about the process that they are willing to help get another group started. Such persons can sometimes be used to join a newly formed group and help to give its members reassurance at the same time that they supply stimulation for the discussions. This method has also been used with delinquent girls' groups.

Role Playing

From time to time a group may be wrestling with the problem of understanding why people acted as they did in some provocative situation and it may be that a bit of role playing would clarify some of the questions more quickly than straight discussions. Acting out parts in the course of communicating with others opens up a wide range of possibilities. The most structured use of the technique would be the play or skit, written and acted almost formally to demonstrate and teach better attitudes or ways of problem solving. Or there is the more extemporaneous psychodrama that a psychiatrist will use with a group of patients as he has them impulsively assume certain roles and act out their feelings toward other people.

The least structured and least conscious role playing is the simple quoting of other people in everyday conversation. As we might see it in a group discussion, one person is describing an incident or perhaps a conversation with his mother. He quotes his mother's purported exact words and in doing so mimics her facial expression, bodily posture, and tone of voice, usually with exaggeration of those qualities that led him to feel as he does about her or the situation at the moment. This is a type of communication that in varying forms occurs in almost any conversation; and, at a simple level, it is role playing.

It is a fairly easy step for a group leader to carry the device a little further and have two or more persons work together to re-create conversation, complete with feelings and perhaps some action. It is constantly astonishing how easily and fully people can immerse themselves in the feelings of the parts they play and capture the essence of the other person's viewpoints and attitudes. This can be a highly useful device to lift people out of their own concerns and help them appreciate the forces that affect their protagonists.

In a group of girls on probation such a situation arose when they were apprehensively discussing an immediate problem concerning one of their number who was absent that evening because she had just run away from home with a boy who had escaped the day before from a state training school. The girls wondered what would, and what should, happen when the two were caught. The group had co-leaders, Corinne, their probation officer, and Will, her supervisor.

Will suggested that they act out the situation according to what they presumed to be happening. The girls immediately picked up the suggestion and cast Corinne and Will in the parts of the two runaways. Many times the role playing is done while the actors walk about and physically carry out the parts, but in this case they all kept their seats. The girls eagerly started the action by describing the characters. Their ideas popped out thick and fast as they constructed personalities for the two. Corinne, now "the girl," was seen as a sharp dresser, but unhappy and having problems at home. She loved the boy and hated her parents. Her father was always drinking and was never home at nights. Her mother hated the father and took it out on the daughter.

Will, now "the boy," was cool, reckless; said he loved the girl, though actually he did not.

Four of the girls quickly lined up in other parts, the probation officer (reflection of Corinne), the girl's mother, the policewoman, and the judge. As quickly as the girls cast the parts they poured out directions for the action. The girl was to receive a phone call. Obediently Corinne simulated the phone conversation.

The call is from boy mother is present and listening talk has to be careful. Girl tells mother it's a girl friend asking her to go to the drugstore with her. Mother argues but then reluctantly agrees mother stirs the action by yelling at girl to get off the phone.

Corinne began to get caught up in the part as she yelled back at the girl who played her mother and told her to get off her back. She verbally left the house with her mother still yelling at her. The action continued, made up of constant, excited directions from the group and with responding dialogue between the two adults who were now well established in their parts as girl and boy.

Girl meets boy at the corner they talk about going to a party girl knows where to get some liquor. They go ("Now we're at the party"), and there is lots of drinking girl gets sick throws up. Boy has a borrowed car they leave and he suggests they go to a motel in next county. Girl has misgivings wants to go yet doesn't want to go. Boy accuses her of dating other boys she denies it says she just spread that around to fool her mother says she really loves him. Boy gets smart and demanding says girl should show him that she loves him ("But he doesn't show any kindness or tenderness"). They go to the motel. The next morning they leave the motel girl in tears girl scared wants to go home.

The policewoman now entered the act. The group decided to have her stop the car to question the pair.

Boy says girl is his sister policewoman says brother and sister don't sit that close together in a car she also notices that girl has been crying she takes them to headquarters. Questioning gets intense girl is questioned first. Who is she where has she been? Girl lies. Where did she meet boy? She can't remember. Why did she run away? Because she loves boy. Have they been drinking? No. "Then what's that on your blouse?" Girl says she spilled mustard from a hot dog. Policewoman doesn't believe it. Where did they stay last night? In the car. Policewoman says she has talked with girl's mother and knows that she took money from home is also sure that they stayed in a motel. She asks what they did at the motel. Girl says they just slept. Policewoman drops the subject. [The girls knew it was out of character for the policewoman not to pursue this question, but the girl playing the policewoman was herself in character in showing reluctance to demand actual talk of sexual activity.] She asks girl about home. Girl says she hates it and doesn't want to go back. Policewoman questions boy he looks at the ceiling is uncooperative lies won't answer questions.

At this point the girl who was trying to play the policewoman, with flushed, angry face, gave up in complete frustration and, dropping her character, glanced at Corinne and asked with exasperation, "Are all the kids this uncooperative with the police?" The girls reset the stage and instantly the boy and girl were delivered to the juvenile detention. Now the "probation officer" entered the action, visiting and questioning the girl in detention.

Probation officer asks girl why she ran away girl says because she wanted to and she loves boy. Had they planned it? No, he just called and they went. Where did they meet? On a street corner. What corner? Didn't remember. Probation officer pursues the matter must know all the details which corner?

At this point Corinne became truly exasperated herself and snapped back angrily that she didn't mark the corner and didn't see what difference it made anyway. After more of the aimless, provocative questioning for such details by the probation officer, another instant scene shift was decreed and next they were in court.

Girl's mother is present and she and girl are hostile to each other. Girl accuses mother of not caring about her mother denies it and insists she cares, but girl is skeptical and says she wants a foster home. The "judge" asks girl how a foster home would help her. Girl says people would care about her and be nicer to her. Judge says girl would have to make changes too and asks what changes she would make. Girl says she would mind people better if they cared about her. Mother cuts in to say she does care. Girl and mother break into loud argument. Judge asks probation officer for recommendation. Probation officer recommends foster home. Why? Says she thinks girl needs it and would stay out of trouble better. Judge asks mother for her opinion. Mother says she wants girl at home. Judge continues the case for a week and orders girl held in detention.

The illusion of action in this episode became very real even though there was no moving about. The feelings became so intense that anger did arise at appropriate times and the group went considerably overtime without realizing it. It could hardly be said that they answered the questions that prompted the role playing, but there were some very apparent values in the experience. For one thing, from the action of Corinne and Will the girls got a new realization that probation officers know a lot about what goes on among delinquents. This had been apparent from the natural way the boy and girl carried off conversation about getting liquor, deceiving parents, going to the motel, explaining the soiled blouse. The girls also saw clearly that Corinne, their probation officer, understood how they felt about their mothers' yelling at them and how it felt to be questioned endlessly on petty details. The anger in Corinne's reaction to the questioning had been unmistakably genuine. In addition the girls got a taste of what it's like to be a policewoman, a probation officer, or a judge, and to have to deal with stubborn, deceptive delinquents and make decisions affecting families.

It is perhaps too easy to assume that all the value of this type of experience is for the clients, the members of the group. While the process is more than justified on the basis of gains made by the group members, a bonus often received is the value it has for the leader too. In this episode, for instance, the impact of the experience on Corinne was perhaps even more profound than it was for the girls. As her probationers in the parts of policewoman and probation officer questioned her she knew that they were playing the roles in exact imitation of the usual questioning process, and for the first time she had a taste of how it felt from the girls' viewpoint. Corinne came out of the experience with an amazed awareness of the stupidity of much of the grilling that goes on in such situations, and with a new and helpful perspective of herself in relation to her probationers.

Usually role-playing episodes like this should be followed by general group discussion about the experience. Just as group discussion will naturally lead to opportunities for role playing, the role playing will in turn lead to an enriched period of discussion as the group reviews and pursues the meanings of all the feelings evoked by the acted episode. While each group member may have received some value from the experience it is also possible that each member felt a different kind of impact from it, and there can be additional value for them in sharing these reactions.

It must also be assumed that any role-playing episode that cuts at all deeply into people's feelings has an element of risk. A young person who has been deeply affected in some sensitive area by the experience should not have to leave the meeting that evening with his emotional hurt untended, or even unnoticed. The doctor who administers a healing treatment watches for signs of unwanted or dangerous toxic reactions, and in the same way we must be aware of these possibilities in our work. A discussion of the episode just played, even though very brief, will give the perceptive leader a clue to how the experience has affected each group member and whether there is any reaction that needs special attention.

Of course, the mere fact that someone is upset and tearful is not in itself any cause for alarm. In a girls' group in which the members were discussing what makes a "good" meeting of their group, one girl commented, and the others agreed, that in one sense a good meeting is one in which everyone has a good time; but then she added that not so much is accomplished at that kind of meeting. She thought that in a truly good meeting she might be upset and unhappy, but it would be a good meeting because that would mean that they were really getting at her problems.

Generally, the role-playing technique should not be hastily tried with a new group. It needs participants who are sufficiently comfortable with each other to let themselves go in acting parts without being too self conscious. Persons who are new to each other will not so readily enter into the acting in a productive way. By the same token, those persons who have become an experienced and well-knit group can assume parts and feel the appropriate emotional intensity with surprising ease.

The role-playing episode described above was useful in enlarging understanding of other people's viewpoints. At other times the issue may be a more practical, problem-solving one, but this, too, can lead to attitudinal improvement. In a group of adult parolees, for instance, one member has lost his job following an argument with his foreman. The problem now being considered is the way in which this man should have handled his dispute with the boss. So in the group he is invited to act out what happened while another member of the group performs as the foreman. It is ostensibly a simple issue of how a man should handle himself so as to keep his job; but as the group members study and participate by turn in the action, there can be much exploration of motivation, attitudes, and subconscious feelings.

Even such a simple episode can get all group members thoroughly involved. For one thing, the action need not be limited to just the main protagonist and one other. It may start out that way but then it can be done over and over again with different concepts of how the action should have been handled. In fact, the man who started the whole thing with his argument with the boss may get the greatest help by seeing several of his colleagues portray their impression of him. It is not uncommon in these experiences for the member to be amazed at how stupid he obviously was as he sees himself depicted.

One of the most common variations of role playing is the reversal of roles. After the parolee has acted himself in an argument with another group member in the role of foreman, the leader may ask that they trade roles and go through it again. This parolee who has been carrying a sharp resentment toward the foreman is thus beguiled into the task of acting that foreman's part. If the group is a strong one they will not let him get away with a less than honest representation of the foreman's approach to the issue, and so there is a good chance that the parolee will pick up from the experience a new awareness of the other man's position.

Sometimes it can be said that one good role-playing experience demands another. In this case, for instance, the affected parolee may have acquired some new bit of insight into the reasons why he reacted as he did to his foreman. He may be able to see that it was a reaction pattern he uses all too often in various kinds of situations. So the role playing which helped open his eyes to his basic problem should be followed by other role playing to give him some simulated practice in applying his new-found insight.

Role playing, like the group work method generally, is a highly fluid method which is subject to endless innovative variations. While there are certain important general principles, a skilled leader may use great freedom in adapting the technique to the group and to the situation at the moment.

One interesting variation is the use of an alter ego. This would be used in a fairly sophisticated group with members who are accustomed to recognizing underlying motivations as contrasted with ostensible ones. After some group members are assigned their parts to play in the episode, one or more others are assigned as alter egos. Or it may be that just one principal character has an alter ego assigned to him. As the action begins, the alter ego sits immediately behind his assigned character and whenever he reads his character's motives or feelings differently from their surface appearance he speaks up as if voicing the more secret thoughts and true motives of the other person.

Member: I don't think we would get very far with that suggestion.

Other self: What is Jones trying to do, promote himself into the chairmanship? I'll have to block that. If I do not I stand to lose status.

Techniques like this require a fairly experienced group and also should be tried only by a leader who is trained and experienced enough to be quite sure of what he is doing.

Selection for Groups

There are two aspects to selection of persons for groups. There is the problem of choosing those among a large caseload of probationers or parolees who would be suitable for the group process, and there is the other problem of selecting from among these qualified ones the particular persons who would fit together as one group.

The first problem is less of an issue today than it was a few years ago, as more and more the casework and group work methods are being considered universally appropriate. It now seems apparent that nearly all our clients can benefit from group work and that usually they will profit most from a combination of the two methods. Exceptions remain, of course, but a probation or parole office will usually find that if it has any client who is not assignable to a group it will not be so much because of personality characteristics as because of mechanical problems such as his hours of work or his residence location or similar reasons that make it impracticable for him to get to group meetings.

The more important and interesting question is how to pick those several individuals who will successfully coalesce into a group with therapeutic potential. One basis for grouping may be the particular purpose of the group. In one situation it may be a grouping of persons from a neighborhood who will be discussing their problems or behavior in the context of that environment. Another group may be adult parolees who are facing a common problem of adjusting to the first weeks of community living after release on parole. A group might be formed of persons who had all been arrested for the same kind of offense, such as narcotics use or forgery of checks.

It is not essential that each group have such an expressly identified common denominator, but the leader should at least see in his own mind a common goal for them to reach by a common path, and be able to state the goal for the group if they are uncertain of it themselves. It needs to be stated in terms that are superbly simple and practical — no empty moralizing is suitable here.

If a group is formed to explore a problem that is external to them it is not so necessary to be concerned with selection of personality types among them. For instance, if it is a group from a certain neighborhood and the purpose is some aspect of neighborhood improvement the group can function even though there is a wide age range in it and some imbalance in personality types. However, in probation or parole work we are usually more concerned with a helping process aimed at the group members themselves in a very personal way, so in our selection of them we must be concerned with a combination of types that will function together productively in a process that depends upon highly personal interaction.

It would be fine if we could point to some exact rules for grouping, but this is an inexact skill and even if we do have definite principles in mind concerning personality types we will often have to compromise with certain practical exigencies that control the availability of individuals. In selecting adults, the group will sometimes almost select itself. It may, for instance, be as simple as taking into one group all the men on one officer's caseload who live in a certain housing project and who are not working on night shifts. And this may work out quite all right. Probably the worst that could happen would be that the officer has to ask some member to drop out if he presents too much of a hindrance to the group's effectiveness. Generally adult probation and parole groups will be selected less on the basis of individual personality characteristics and more on the basis of the caseload, the residence location, the work schedule, and the client's degree of motivation or interest in using the group experience.

Group therapy with children has produced a more refined body of experience regarding grouping, and some of the principles developed there may have applicability to some extent with adults also. In working with children's groups the most general principle is that a variety of personality types should be assembled, producing a balanced group. Of course, this is desirable with the adult group too since it brings to the group the stimulation of different viewpoints, a variety of social experiences, and the opportunity for group members to profit by comparisons between contrasting approaches to life situations.

Another general principle is that we should not introduce into a group a youngster who is a natural type for group rejection by that group. A boy who has a distinctive physical appearance that makes him the instant subject of a belittling nickname will not have a helpful experience in a group that promptly sets him aside in this way. He must be accepted truly as a group member if the experience is going to help him mature; but if he is ridiculed, even subtly, he is outside the effective group dynamics and is forced to find some protective device for handling his rejection. He may, for instance, become the group's clown or mascot. This way he salvages an illusion of group acceptance and defends himself from the harsher kind of rejection; but he still is not, in this condition, able to use what a group has to offer.

A person who is a natural whipping boy can actually be helped greatly by a group experience if he is put in the right group. It needs to be a placement where, because of his age or some other superior quality, he can slightly more than hold his own with the others until he gains a more secure self-image. S. R. Slavson states that a group "must consist of children who potentially have therapeutic value to one another. Obviously, a beaten down and rejected child would only be more traumatized if he were to be assigned to a group where he would be beaten and persecuted. A frightened, withdrawn, and sensitive child becomes only more frightened and withdrawn in a tumultuous and aggressive environment they must have an environment in which their particular difficulties are counteracted and their needs are met."

In balancing the personality types there should be wide differences in degrees of aggressiveness. A juvenile group can contain at least one dominating, aggressive member, but too many of this type would destroy the group's potential, for the leadership effort would be dissipated in a constant problem of control. One aggressive member can be controlled by the group itself and in that case the process of control will itself be part of the therapy. The best group will have a balance of aggressive, withdrawn, seductive, passive, hostile, dependent, or other types that serve both to counteract and to stimulate each other.

With adults, a grouping on the basis of age is not as important as most other factors will be. With juveniles it must be remembered that a difference of even a year in age can sometimes make for a substantial social gulf, so the range in a teen-agers' group should preferably be no more than two years.

Though use is being made, particularly in institutions, of large groups of fifty or more, these have a purpose that is not identical with the purpose of the discussion groups that are intended to involve fully and affect strongly each group member. In the large group the dynamics are substantially different since there cannot be active involvement of every member. It is not possible for more than a few of the more verbal persons to talk. This means that the situation becomes, in effect, a small group discussion with a large number of observers.

To have a small group discussion that has maximum impact on each member it is necessary that lines of relationship connect each member of the group to each other member. As any member of the group talks, his feelings reach the other members along these lines of relationship and his words and feelings are given a particular character and impact according to the nature of that particular relationship. After all, we are seldom deeply affected by expressions from someone who means nothing to us. If the group is too large these lines of rapport are weak it is not possible to maintain acquaintance with and a "caring" sort of feeling for everyone in a room full of people. If a group gets much larger than six or eight persons, consequently, its capacity for investment in the process and its ability to dig deeply are noticeably impaired.

Group Work with Parents

For many years there have been attempts here and there to work with groups of parents of delinquents. T[illegible] early efforts were often disappointing in their failure t[illegible] achieve sustained interest or to develop any convincing impact. Probably the most common reason for a [illegible] [illegible]f success was the usual lecture format for the mee[illegible]ngs. Even when group discussion was used it was often a prescribed and formal discussion of the mater[illegible]al presented. More recently the technique of natural, free discussion, such as has already been described for use with client groups, has been extended to parents' groups, with distinctly greater success. The difference in basic philosophical approach can be seen in such a simple thing as seating people in a circle around a table instead of in rows, facing a speaker or chairman.

The increased use of group discussions for parents accompanies the increased awareness of the vital importance of working with the total family situation in each case. One author comments: "The hypothesis is now made that where there is a disturbed child there is a disturbed family." Certainly one of the most significant developments in the social work field is that we have begun to see the futility of working only with a single patient when he is a symbol of a total family problem.

The use of parents' groups is a splendid device whether their children are in groups themselves or are being worked with individually on the probation caseload. But parents' groups tend to develop more often when the children are in groups too, for the involvement of a juvenile in a group tends to produce more parental involvement and leads more surely and naturally to the provision of a group for the parents. The group for the juveniles creates constant issues for the parents to face or chores for them to help with. The group occasionally wants to go somewhere, to do something. Parental permission must be gained, and parents may be importuned to help with transportation.

In one probation office the use of groups raised the problem of permission for smoking. Though the probation officers had always in their casework contacts discouraged smoking by the juveniles, it was apparent that it was a meaningless effort, for any youngster could abstain from smoking during the short period of a casework interview, and the probation officer seldom really had to confront the problem. But when group work came with its one and one-half hour meetings and its occasional outings the staff was brought face to face with the issue. It was decided to put the question to the parents, and since it needed to be answered by them in concert if possible, the value of their having their own group discussions is obvious.

The much more basic reason for a parental group is that we cannot work with a young person in isolation. The problems that have brought that juvenile to court are problems that have certainly made themselves felt in the home. We would like to think that if we are able to ameliorate the child's adjustment we will hear sounds of gratitude from the home as the improvement is felt there. This may happen, but not necessarily. We may even get complaints instead of thanks. A family finds ways to adjust to problem behavior of a member so that life can go on in tolerable ways. Sometimes the alleviation of a long-standing problem at home will upset the compensatory adjustment that other family members have made and they will react with pain and protest to improvement which they do not recognize as such. Caseworkers and group workers are both aware of the need sometimes to give help to a parent or wife because the client is beginning to improve and in doing so has upset the adjustment mechanisms in the home.

A marital relationship may be considerably affected. Father and mother may have developed an unspoken and delicately balanced equilibrium in handling their adjustment to each other at the same time that they contend with a difficult child. If the child's conduct begins to change it can threaten the parental armistice and cause a sharp reaction from either spouse who might fear loss of the marital stability. When this happens, the threatened parent is likely to be on the phone to the group leader protesting the group process and attempting to withdraw the child from it.

If the parents are meeting regularly in their own group the resentments, anxieties, or other painful reactions to their children's changed behavior can be expressed and dealt with as they arise. The parents are not left with a sense of mystery about the experience their children are having. In their own group, under the same leader their children have, they have a feel of what it is that the children are doing. In the presence of other parents they feel less inclined to take unilateral action about withdrawing a child, for they see other parents also expressing anxieties, yet sticking with the process. And gradually there can come a great sense of relief in finding that other people, too, have problems and worries in the parental role, and that comfort can be found in talking about it.

The leader must be acutely aware of the parents' feeling of failure and the need to alleviate this rather than adding to it. It starts with the invitation to meet with a group. It is so very easy for the parent to feel that in being asked to join a group of parents he is being labeled as the cause of his child's delinquency. In formulating his invitation the probation officer must try to base it on practical, non threatening reasons, but without deviating from reasons that are entirely honest. He would not be honest if he asked them to get together because they need to arrange transportation and other services for the children's group; but he would be smart to use his contacts with them about transportation problems to suggest that there might be other interests in common that they could talk about in a group of their own once a week.

Actually, this can be accomplished in a more authoritative way too. The juvenile court judge may need to set the process in motion in the courtroom at the time of the disposition hearing. Parents who would never be able to respond to an "invitation" to join a parents' group may need to be prodded into it by the judge at the time he has their anxious attention in court. There is still no need to do it callously or punitively. The judge can make it clear that he considers the parents' involvement in the treatment plan essential and that he must insist that they attend at least a specified number of the parents' group sessions. He need not suggest in any way that this is because they are at fault and must be corrected, but may assure them that while the probation officer can help the child he needs to have the parents' cooperation.

This procedure is usually effective in getting the parents involved, but the kind of handling they get when they arrive at the meeting will determine whether they stay with it and derive value from it. A coffee pot helps, especially if the women can help in the brewing instead of having everything already done for them. The probation officer's approach needs to be a disarming one. These are often people who have been blamed, or feel as though they are being blamed, for failure in raising their children. They are afraid that here again they will be blamed and lectured about how they should do better. So the approach must be a low-pressure one, essentially an invitation to talk about whatever is on their minds.

Parents will be puzzled about how they can get help from just undirected talking and may have a vague feeling of being cheated. This is the leader's chance to gain in his rapport with the group as he shows understanding of their feelings in freely admitting that it seems peculiar just to talk. But he can assure them that it does indeed help and if he says so with self-confidence he will have gained greatly with them when they begin later to see that he was right.

Parents will want specific answers. They will want to know how to handle a certain situation at home. A son or daughter may be showing some improvement and the parent will want to know what is being done with him in the other group; "Tell us so we can try it too." They may ask for diagnostic explanations. Again the best response is to bend the questions back toward the group, giving the members constant practice in discussion, in sharing each other's views. A therapist who works mainly with disturbed children and their parents comments, "On the whole it is better not to explain the child's psychodynamics to them, even in terms they would understand, for they often interpret it as criticism of themselves or infer that the therapist is more understanding of the child and takes his part. As a result they may become resistant to treatment or resentful toward the child and so defeat the purpose of therapy. For that reason the therapist does not answer this question but listens instead for the emotional undertone in their discussion and points it out in such a way that they will feel understood and accepted rather than criticized."

Questions will inevitably arise in both the juvenile group and the parents' group about what is going on in the other. The leader needs to take the firm stand that each group is the privileged guardian of its own privacy. The members of either group must be serenely confident that the leader will reveal absolutely no content from one group to the other without permission from the members. A boy may go home and tell his parents what his group discussed, and the parents likewise are free to discuss their group with their children. Generally, however, there is not an appreciable amount of such information exchanged between the two groups, but one of the most noticeable results of the parallel groups is the improvement in the relationships between the parents and children. And after all this is probably the most basic factor there is in the prevention and control of delinquency.

Stressing this principle of keeping the content of parents' meetings and the children's meetings confidential from each other is not meant to suggest that a family problem should not be discussed with parents and child together. When there are separate groups it is only a matter of basic integrity to give each group its own privilege of sharing or keeping to itself its discussion content. But it is also very true that the various members of a family can be assembled as a group and under skilled leadership they can be led to discuss the problems of their relationships with candor. Sometimes it is as hard for the social worker to face this prospect as it is for the family members, so concerned is he with the right of the individual to privacy of his feelings.

But much is being learned about dealing with families openly as a unit, with no secrets retained. It is being recognized that family problems, which invariably involve impediments to communication, cannot be fully resolved by a helping process which reinforces the barriers to communication. As one psychiatrist comments, "What is the propriety of a therapist's dealing openly with intimate matters when more than one member of the family is involved? Can confidential material be so handled? Under what conditions must an individual's privacy be completely safeguarded? Under what conditions may his personal secrets be exposed to family scrutiny for legitimate therapeutic purposes? With great frequency I have found that these intimate matters, these so called secrets, turn out not to be real secrets at all. Far more often they are common family knowledge, surrounded by a tacit conspiracy of silence. What is involved here is not so much a true secret but rather a barrier to emotional communication, a barrier to the free sharing of certain experiences. Some forms of privacy are needed and healthy. Others are pathogenic. When a therapist supports a sick need for privacy, he affirms guilt and fear; he reinforces the patient's isolation."

Parents are not the only family members who should be offered this kind of service. In adult work there is no reason why wives of probationers or parolees could not also be worked with in groups. The staff that has the time and energy to do it would find great potential effectiveness in working with a discussion group of parolees while a parallel group of their wives also meets weekly, with the two groups having a joint meeting at periodic intervals.

In San Francisco the Federal Probation Office has made good use of the discussion process for relatives of prospective parolees. The staff was interested in preparing the homes of parolees to receive them constructively. To start the process the staff first talked to the future parolees instead of the families. Staff members visited the reformatory and met with the inmates (youthful offenders) who would be returning to the San Francisco area and told them of the plan. They encouraged the men to write to their families and ask them to participate. Then notices were sent to the families by the probation office. Responses came from nearly all the invited families and the group soon was started with wives, parents and one fiancee.

One problem the situation presented was that the process started out, properly enough, as an informational one; movies were shown of the institution, and in other ways the two probation officer leaders tried to answer the families' questions. The group members, in turn, tried to use the leaders as question answerers instead of discussion leaders, and attempted to manipulate them according to their individual interests. The degree of anxiety in such a group runs high. The staff was surprised to find that the members actually feared that their participation in the group could work against them. They worried that if they made a bad impression on the group the probation officers would report this to the parole board and there would be less likelihood of a favorable parole decision. This is another convincing reason why the group leader must be non threatening in his approach; and it is also additional evidence of how much need there is for this kind of work to involve the total family.

As we see the many fascinating attempts to develop socially therapeutic programs using groups of clients it is apparent that here, as in so many areas of treatment philosophy, we have moved from one strongly held position to its opposite. And we shall see this phenomenon reflected in other chapters of this book. Parole officers who earlier in their own careers were enforcing the nearly universal rule that parolees could not associate with each other are now instead bringing them together for their mutual help—and with a sense of satisfaction that enforcing conformity under the more repressive rule in the past could never match.

7

Contribution of Criminals for Social Work

Introduction

In its newer form it is a recognition that the prisoner, the probationer, or the parolee may have a skill to offer that can be used to great advantage in helping others, and that by calling on him for his unique contribution to the helping process we contribute substantially at the same time to his own rehabilitation. The skill that he has to offer is an extra capacity for rapport with his fellow offenders, an ability to talk their language with special effect because he has been a part of their same culture. Consequently, he is not easily conned, and he can cut through defenses that would be baffling to the conventional corrections worker. He meets his assigned client with the immense advantage of little or no cultural distance between them, while the professional is handicapped by having to bridge the cultural gap before he can be effective with the client.

As one writer has expressed it, "The nonprofessional has no need to validate his presence in the community, which gives him a considerable advantage over the professional from the outset. Communication can be short-cut and friction eliminated because much is taken for granted as a result of the common background. The nonprofessional has a sense of life's meaning to the client out of their shared experience."

Such reasons are in themselves sufficient to make the use of indigenous workers more and more attractive in recent years, but there is the additional advantage that the helper himself is helped. The client who is tapped for work in helping others may sense that the assignment to guide others to improvement suggests that he himself is improved. More important is the inference that he is seen as having a skill, a competence, a basis for social status; and any device that enhances his self esteem like this is a material contribution to his improved adjustment. Inherent also is the principle that a person is never more effectively converted to a belief than by the process of having to convert someone else.

Our clients tend to be people who have had little reason to feel that their lives are purposeful, for they are usually on the receiving end of help and so are seldom able to enjoy the ego-building effect of being important to someone else. Alcoholics Anonymous and Synanon have exploited this need with great effectiveness, for in either organization the member finds that one of the most basic expectations is that he will be ready at any time to help another person with his drinking or addiction problem.

Although the client who is being invited to be a helper to other clients is not given responsibility for counseling in depth, it is nevertheless desirable that human contact, and personal rapport on some sustained basis, be involved. This suggests the defect in the idea of the juvenile juries that have recurring popularity with some juvenile courts. Service on such a jury puts the young middle-class person in a pseudo-authoritative role in which he must recommend corrective action for another young person who may or may not be his cultural peer. He only sits in judgment, making decisions on the basis of superficial knowledge of the problem, and does not have a chance to give of himself personally to the other young people who come before him.

A plan with more promise of being helpful to both the helper and the helped is a program that was experimented with in Champaign, Illinois. In that program the same sort of young people who might elsewhere be used on juvenile juries were recruited to work with younger children who were in special need of a helpful relationship with an older young person. High school seniors were trained to work in a "pal" or "big brother" type of relationship with children who were in need of such friendship because of personal or family inadequacies. As contrasted with service on a juvenile jury, this kind of experience gave the high school student a chance to have actual training in social work concepts, to have the experience of understanding a youngster's problem instead of acting peremptorily on the basis of the surface aspects in the episode of the moment. The student was given opportunity for growth through a sustained relationship with a youngster whose problems could become understood in some depth and whose need for the helping person would be very evident.

Former Delinquent as a Model

Although the program in Champaign is not concerned with delinquents it involves a principle which is applicable for our purposes and which is being experimented with increasingly in correctional social work practice. Now that workers are getting over their instinctive objection to letting probationers or parolees associate with each other, and now that group work practice has actually brought clients together as a part of the treatment effort, the way has been opened to the next step of deliberately using clients as active agents in the treatment processes for other offenders.

That step has been taken in some instances as part of a structured program which recruits, trains, and employs suitable clients as assistants in regular helping processes. In others, there are highly informal adaptations of a treatment plan to the availability of some suitable client-helper of the moment. An example of the technique developing from this kind of serendipity is the case of Jerry Riley, a probationer in St. Paul, Minnesota. The probation office had been disconcerted to learn that Jerry, an inveterate petty offender, was being placed on probation after a stay in the workhouse. Jerry's Irish temper had kept him in trouble constantly until no one in the city was better known to the police. He was a good worker at his trade of painting, but he drank too much and his hefty physique made him a terror when anyone irritated him. He piled up a long record of convictions for disorderly conduct, assault, drunk driving, leaving the scene of an accident, resisting arrest.

He was just thirty-two years old when one wild episode brought him into court with a series of charges that earned him a total sentence of 240 days. After about 120 days were served the judge decided to suspend the rest and try Jerry on probation.

To the mild surprise of the probation office Jerry had been sufficiently sobered by his workhouse stay so that he actually managed to avoid more trouble for several weeks. When he had been on probation for about a month someone in the probation office who was working with a teen-age boy got to wondering if Jerry could be helpful. The boy was difficult to reach and seemed to be developing the same kind of behavior pattern that had been Jerry's problem. The officer was brash enough to try the idea and called up Jerry to ask him if he would be willing to help give probation supervision to the boy. Jerry was understandably startled by the suggestion that he could help someone else keep out of trouble and replied that he would have to think it over. But on thinking it over he decided to try it, and he did, in fact, essentially take over the probation supervision entirely.

After several months of progress the probation office felt that the boy's case was handled with more success than they might have expected without Jerry's help, and they made their appreciation clear to him by asking his help with other individually selected cases. Jerry became caught up in the work and took an aggressive interest in keeping his charges straight. When any boy assigned to him had a court appearance Jerry was right there with him and was probably at his best in the courtroom. He had the advantage of firsthand experience in courtrooms and did not in the least stand in awe of court processes. His experience had also given him an appreciation of the feelings of the young defendant in the courtroom and he could consequently gain tremendously in his rapport with his "probationer" when he stood by him and spoke for him in court. Jerry had an unabashed way of going to the bench and talking turkey with the judge, and had the personality to get away with it.

In due time Jerry was discharged from probation with no new offenses having occurred and with much tangible evidence of improvement. He had become active in Alcoholics Anonymous and had shown on several occasions a remarkable new restraint of temper in provocative situations. He still carries one or two cases at a time for the juvenile division of the probation office.

Generally the cases referred to Jerry are boys who are older teenagers and the more sophisticated and hostile of delinquents. In the assigning of cases it is necessary that the parents be able to tolerate the plan. This is not always easy, for Jerry's name and record are well known and parents have a natural aversion to the implications of their son's being assigned to such a character. However, Jerry's utter dedication to any case he works with, particularly his practical helpfulness in difficult situations, invariably wins the support of parents. The support of the police has been harder to accomplish, although they have relaxed from their initial shock since they have seen the vast improvement that has been accomplished in Jerry himself when he came to feel a sense of usefulness to others. Newspaper publicity briefly jeopardized the arrangement, and social workers in other agencies were highly critical of it, but the fact that Jerry could ride out these episodes of turmoil and not betray either himself or his assigned cases is still more testimony to the potential that this technique may have.

The experience with this client as an aide to the probation office is similar to the experience of agencies in

New York City that have used indigenous workers as homemakers to train overburdened clients in better home management. Jerry had a breezy, informal directness with his boys and their families. It contrasted sharply with the more self consciously professional demeanor of the probation officers, but it quickly won the loyalty of his "clients." In a similar way the homemakers recruited from the same social strata as their clients were also refreshingly direct and practical. They won the good feeling and cooperation of their clients quickly by their direct attack on ostensible external problems and in this way proved a valuable supplement to the professional workers, who guided the management of the case with concern for the more basic problems involved.

The use of the former client in these ways is an asset not only because of his ability to communicate with clients from similar backgrounds but also because of what he represents in his personal self. He is proof to other clients of the reality of upward social mobility. In hiring staff the administrators of character-building organizations and correctional agencies have typically kept in mind the desirability of finding men and women who would serve as good examples for young people to emulate. While the value of this has not been proved it would have to be said that with our belief in the usefulness of relationship as a major rehabilitative tool, we would have to believe too in the value of the therapist's presenting a good image. Where strong relationship exists there is likely to be imitation.

However, like so many aspects of correctional efforts, this measure may work best for the person who is in little or no need of the treatment. The boy from a good middle-class home who goes to camp and finds his hero of the moment in his camp counselor is easily capable of having this experience contribute further to his normal social growth if the counselor is a fine example of masculine virtues. But for a deprived, hostile, and delinquent boy the presence in his life of this role model, no matter how excellent, is not likely to have as much impact. The normal boy could look at his handsome, athletic, likable camp counselor and aspire to be like him some day, for there is not a substantial difference between what this adult is and what this boy can reasonably hope to be. The deprived and delinquent boy, looking at the same model, and instinctively aware of the social distance between them, assumes without even thinking about it that his world is a different one from the world of this adult and that he not only cannot reach it, but is not at all sure he wants to. Accordingly, in his case there is need for an additional ingredient in his relationship with the role model. He needs a model who demonstrates the actuality of progress from a disadvantaged condition to a better one. A program that has attempted to exploit this concept is the SCORE program which has been used in Cambridge, Massachusetts, New York City, and Syracuse. Charles W. Slack, who developed it, comments, "Notice that it is not sufficient to bring the delinquent in contact with an individual who can demonstrate the *desired behavior*. We must bring him into contact with an individual who can demonstrate the desired *behavior change*."

There are many variations possible in applying this principle and each community would need to find its own adaptation according to the diverse kinds of neighborhood problems and kinds of resources available. In the SCORE projects three types of persons are involved. There are, of course, the delinquents who are the objects of the program. A second type of participant is a former delinquent or an ex-convict who has matured and stabilized to the extent of now serving as a model of behavior change. The third is a more conventional behavior model, a young man of the typical, conventional middle class, a well-adjusted and successful young businessman. Usually in the SCORE projects this role is played by members of the Jaycees, and the Jaycee organization carries much responsibility for support of the program.

The SCORE program uses a technique which is known as "operant conditioning," a theory of which is that random behavior is observed until some specific desirable bit of behavior occurs and the subject is then promptly rewarded. By consistent and persistent repetition of this the person's pattern of behavior can be modified.

This treatment approach also includes the concept that the confirmed delinquent who is well identified with a delinquent street culture will not respond to a therapist-patient relationship but will accept an employer-employee relationship. The "employment" can be any of a variety of activities concerned with learning about delinquency or learning how to control delinquency or crime. The SCORE program utilizes a number of the principles already mentioned in this or preceding chapters: boys are paid for the work they do, i.e., coming to meetings to discuss the problem of delinquency; boys are rewarded unexpectedly for extra performance; boys are exposed to the behavior model (Jaycee) and the behavior change model (ex-convict); boys are treated as much as possible as equals by all persons involved in the program; boys are paid promptly in cash each time when the work is done; the functioning of the project centers on some type of delinquency research that is likely to be frequently revised to avoid loss of interest by the boys; and when a goal is established for the group it is limited, achievable, and realistic.

In addition to the three types of people mentioned it is necessary to have one staff or professional person. In fact, the continuation of the program depends on this person who coordinates the efforts and furnishes the project's motive power by devising the research or whatever other activity it is that forms the basis of effort and interaction by the component members. But the other persons also serve highly important purposes. The lay members are needed for their help in financing the program but are needed equally for their presence in the meetings. They join in the discussions in an unpatronizing, elbow-rubbing way with the delinquents, participating honestly with them in exploring the subject of the moment. For the delinquents this makes their first opportunity to mix with the remote, law-abiding business world on a manto-man basis. Any such experience can help to give them a little better image of themselves. The former delinquent, or ex-convict, serves as a link between the laymen and the delinquents, for he is a model to both, an interpreter of either to the other, and, especially, a person who can help the delinquents to articulàte their feelings.

When we talk about the SCORE projects in connection with using the client as staff we may be talking about either the former delinquent who enters the project as the behavior change model or the delinquents themselves. For even the delinquents who are the focus of the helping process are received into the project as employees and are, in effect, paid to find their own means of improvement. A typical goal for the project to attack would be a simple reduction in arrests or negative police contacts. The boys may start out with discussions of why they seem to be having their particular brand of trouble car thefts, fights, or whatever. The discussion has an extra quality of seriousness about it which derives from the fact that they have all been paid to come to the meeting as expert consultants to help the staff person do his research on why boys are delinquent. From this discussion they may go on to explore ideas on how arrests could be reduced. This in turn leads to experimentation with the ideas suggested, and involves keeping score for arrests during an experimental period which can be compared with a former period.

The persons who plan, organize, finance, and direct such a project focus their efforts ostensibly only on the accomplishment of external change. Not the least suggestion is made to the boys that they are being "treated" or "helped" If any change is proposed it is only in respect to statistics, such as the simple reduction in the number of police contacts per month. But experience has shown that outward change does not occur on a sustained basis without some degree of inner and more basic change being likely. Even if nothing does change except the outward behavior this would seem to be a very worthy accomplishment in view of the resulting reduction of offenses. In an appraisal of the New York City SCORE program it was found that "During the first month there were nearly one hundred police contacts, i.e., on the average each of the boys had either three police contacts that month or spent three days in jail. In the month of April there were less than ten negative police contacts and during July when New York City was extremely hot and unpleasant, there were no police incidents or incarcerations of these thirty-four 'worst' boys."

This kind of program is not found within the administration of a probation or parole service. A principle reason is that the funds involved are spent in unconventional ways that would be painful to the auditors who must police the spending in governmental agencies. Money is paid directly to the delinquents themselves and furthermore is paid out on a highly flexible basis with the treatment needs of the moment being more important than penny-by-penny accounting processes. However, it should not be impossible for correctional field services to adapt such techniques, and some probation and parole offices have made moves in this direction. Until the day when governmental agencies can be more flexible with their expenditures, it should be possible to combine public agency staff and private financing for program expenses. If there is an organization or a foundation to pay the direct program expenses, and if the agency does not balk at having some non-probationers in the program, then there should be no serious impediment to the operation of such a program by a correctional agency. St. Paul's Jerry Riley is the obvious type to function as the former delinquent, and probably any large probation office would have Jerry's counterpart who could be persuaded to help with such an endeavor and in doing so would find his own means to improvement.

Adaptability as a Program Asset

The SCORE idea, obviously, is meant to be extremely fluid. Unlike a more conventional community program which remains fairly fixed while the clients come and go according to their fleeting interests, SCORE attempts to adapt continually to the clients in order to keep them involved and have the maximum possible impact on them. A somewhat more fixed type of program that still tries to adapt to and hold the persons in it was tried in Washington, D.C. A program was developed in 1964 which attempted to utilize disadvantaged young people as leaders in social services with families like their own. The persons involved were not primarily offenders, although arrest records were a part of the evidence of their disadvantaged condition and a reduction of such trouble was part of the evidence of their improvement. The Community Apprentice Program, operated by the Center for Youth and Community Studies of Howard University, simply advertised that jobs were available for young people from sixteen to twenty-one years old who were out of school and who did not at the moment have any pending arrest or sentence.

After extensive interviews and physical examinations ten boys and girls were selected, most of whom had records of delinquency and backgrounds of family breakdown. Employment for them was planned in areas of child care, recreation, and social research, preceded by twelve weeks of training. The training consisted of almost daily group discussions plus meetings with experts who talked with them on various social problem topics. "Starting from their own experiences, the members of the core group were encouraged to examine the process of adolescence, and the problems of living in a poor area of the city. As the group progressed, it drew upon experts to discuss and examine with them areas of knowledge of human services common to all."

This program, supported in part by federal grants, demonstrated some of the problems in developing clients as staff, as well as some of the dividends. Here, the apprentice applicants were brought into an already structured program, and since it was not something that had been engendered by these young people themselves they did not feel a sense of commitment to it. This points up the value of the SCORE approach in which the delinquents have a fairly free-wheeling opportunity to let their own group discussions determine the shape and direction of their endeavors, and so they give themselves more genuinely to the activity. In the Community Apprentice Program it was noticed that the group members were able to avoid responsibility for the outcome of the program and could even feel content with any signs of its failure because that would just reinforce their alien feeling toward the middle-class world.

The Community Apprentice Program nevertheless achieved a satisfying measure of success which perhaps is all the more impressive in view of its initial built-in handicaps. All ten of the apprentices stayed through the training and remained with the subsequent employment satisfactorily. They performed adequately in their work and made notable progress in their own socialization. The improvement was partly in specific skills: "Although the procedures used were not rigorous or stringent, it was clear that the youths' ability to use language had increased prodigiously. On entering the program, the youth had found it difficult to perform reading and writing assignments. As they gained more experience in the program, however, they became increasingly competent and confident in their ability to handle these assignments. Since very little specific remedial instruction was included in the program, the increased skill might be attributed to a change in self-esteem. That is, through continued reinforcements of various kinds, the youth had been convinced prior to the program that they could not perform reading and writing assignments. However, through engaging in successful non threatening and rewarding experiences, their underlying skills may have become manifest." There was also improvement in general social functioning. "The 'therapeutic process' essentially focuses around ego issues involving identity, the relationship of the individual and group to meaningful work, a stake in the social system, and that other hallmark of adolescence 'action.'"

Therapists on Parole

In the probation setting, or in the general community, it is obvious that the use of clients as staff can be attempted in many different ways, and that a high order of flexible ingenuity is called for in seducing the clients into the program and holding them in it. The fact that probationers can be ordered into an activity has no application here, for this type of endeavor must be clearly voluntary if it is to have the slightest effectiveness.

But in regard to parole there is a slightly different condition. Voluntariness is important there too, but we are presented with the fact that before a man becomes a parolee he is involuntarily incarcerated for a period of time that permits us to expose him to a substantial amount of training in the guise, perhaps, of group therapy, whether or not he feels inclined to involve himself in it. If such treatment in the institution proves effective the prisoner may be ready to work in some helping capacity on being paroled and to do so not only voluntarily but with eagerness.

An exciting experiment and certainly one of the most courageous ones has been tried in a unique prison camp near Chapel Hill, North Carolina. As the program started in May 1964, it was a camp for young felons transferred from the state penitentiary, and it was staffed entirely by parolees! This kind of staffing was partly a matter of expediency rather than altogether the original intention, but it produced an experimental program that was a splendid contribution to correctional experience.

The program, known as Chydaru (Chapel Hill Youth Development and Research Unit), was the result of cooperative planning between California and North Carolina corrections officials who wanted to try the use of the therapeutic community with selected first-time offenders. The intent was to operate a small open prison camp with an appropriately experienced professional as superintendent who was to direct the group therapy process. His other staff members would be "culture carriers" former inmates who had gone through the intensive group process themselves in a therapeutic community setting.

The theory was that inmates who are experienced in the kind of group therapy used at the California Institution for Men at Chino sometimes develop the kind of skill needed for initiating others in the process. Some inmates gain considerably in their maturity and stability; they gain an appreciation of the potency of the group therapy method and develop skill in using the events of the day as content for the discussion sessions. The idea that took form in North Carolina was that men of this kind who had been truly helped might be used as particularly effective staff members in bringing the same helping process to other clients. Hardly less important was the recognition that in this situation the therapist may himself be substantially helped.

The North Carolina prison system acquired a small camp a short distance from the university at Chapel Hill. This semi-rural acreage, with a few simple wooden frame buildings and nothing else but woods, became the prison camp with a capacity of twenty. The staff members were selected from among parolees in California who had been on parole without new trouble for six months to a year and who had shown marked progress in their personal maturation and in their skill with the group therapy process. Six of them accepted the jobs offered them in North Carolina and were transferred there under the usual provisions of the interstate compact on parole. Since no professional had been found for the superintendent's position, one of the parolees was designated superintendent while the search for a professional continued.

The enterprise was backed by the governor of North Carolina as well as the prison director, and it was considered a joint venture of the Prison Department and the Institute of Government at the University of North Carolina. The camp superintendent was administratively responsible to the prison director but the whole project received close professional supervision from the Institute of Government. The prisoners selected to be residents of the camp were young adult felons who were serving first sentences. They were selected jointly by the prison administration and by clinicians from the Institute of Government.

The atmosphere at the camp was utterly unlike any conventional prison setting. Reversing the usual pattern of extreme regimentation, the camp had no daily schedule or any planned and imposed work programs. Each day it was left to the residents themselves to decide what work needed to be done around the camp and to organize and do the job. This created an atmosphere of freedom and brightness that was an impressive departure from the usual tense and repressive mood of prisons. A visitor coming on the grounds would be greeted cordially by a friendly group of young men among whom the staff and residents were indistinguishable from each other. They obviously felt under no pressure and yet it was evident from the projects completed that work was getting done. Furthermore, there was pride in the work accomplished. No one who has been acquainted with prison atmosphere could avoid feeling deeply gratified to find a group of prisoners in a setting where obviously there could be so much more healthful preparation for return to normal community living. And, what is more related to the focus of this book, it was equally gratifying for such a visitor to see a group of parolees functioning with a sense of importance and mission, in a fully genuine situation of responsibility, and with a sense of pride in having a peculiar skill and so a peculiar opportunity to be important. For the staff members were not just holding the camp together; they were actively conducting a therapy program. Every night of the week the staff, all of whom were housed on the grounds, would conduct group discussion meetings, teaching their clients the technique they had learned in their own prison experience.

In addition to the nightly group therapy sessions there were other, smaller group meetings in the afternoons for the discussion of work projects and problems or other special matters. There were also daily meetings of staff with clinicians from the Institute of Government for the discussion of any kind of administrative or treatment issues.

But, of course, the program was not all cheerfulness and promise. Something so radical and so loaded with men with problems is certain to have its daily frictions and potential dangers. One problem with new residents was the convincing they required that the staff members could not be manipulated. There was an understandable assumption on the part of any new resident that the ex-convict staff would naturally be on the side of the inmate in any mischief; so the staff had a constant problem in having to reject firmly the role of fellow convict and to insist strongly on being "staff" in a true sense.

A more persistent problem was the anxiety-provoking nature of so much freedom within the camp. The well-adapted convict has a great appreciation of rules and schedules. This does not mean that he respects them or feels conscientious about abiding by the rules. It does mean that he wants to know exactly what is expected of him and exactly what will occur when he either obeys or disobeys the rules. That way he can decide when it is worth the gamble to defy a rule covertly, and he knows or thinks he knows just what objective criteria will be considered when he meets the parole board. But when he is put in a setting with no rules and not even a daily work schedule, and nevertheless knows he has the parole board to face ultimately, the effect is potentially very provocative. How will the parole board know that he has been obeying the rules if there are no rules to obey? How can he know what to do to present himself in a good light if there are no structured and highly specific norms for what constitutes a good record in this kind of place? Because of fears like this some of the residents became too uncomfortable and requested return to the main prison. This too was a challenge to the parolee staff but presumably they would have a special appreciation of the feeling and unusual ability to handle the residents' anxiety in this area.

Although a professional for the superintendent's job was sought throughout the life of the project, no suitable person was found and so the parolee first designated carried that responsibility during the full thirteen months that the camp operated. It was closed in June 1965 because of failure of the state legislature to appropriate funds for its continuance.

For the most part the use of the parolee staff was highly satisfactory, although the experience showed that the steadying influence and close supervision of a professional superintendent was clearly needed. As the group therapy process begins to take hold in such a situation the intensity of the feelings developed calls for not only skill but very dependable emotional stability on the part of the staff. This was a severe test for the parolee therapists and the frustrations developed in them by the impact of the intensifying experience tended to emerge as some potentially dangerous acting-out behavior, both within the camp and in the community. Fortunately no serious problem behavior occurred and no parolee staff member violated parole. It did become necessary, however, to make some reassignments of duties and three of the parolees returned to other jobs in California.

During the latter months of the Chydaru program graduate students from the university were used as replacements for the parolee staff members who left and this seemed to be satisfactory during the short time that it operated this way. The general feeling was that with strong and close professional supervision on the job the parolee therapists could have been quite successful and that this staffing could have been entirely feasible in a permanent program. It is a tribute, finally, to the value of this technique that the parolee who carried the superintendent's role throughout the experiment was subsequently hired as the assistant superintendent of the Southfields Residential Group Center in Jefferson County, Kentucky.

In Reno, Nevada, the Synanon Foundation assists with a unique prison camp which is like the camp at Chapel Hill, North Carolina, in the sense that it is a small open facility with much of the program being presented by persons who are themselves former inmates. Beyond that, however, there are substantial differences.

Nevada's camp on Peavine Mountain north of Reno is an outgrowth of a Synanon program at the main prison in Carson City. The prison warden had invited Synanon to work with inmates in the prison and had been much impressed with the results. The Peavine camp had been operating as an honor camp under the penitentiary administration but it had not had a distinguished career. Anyone looking at the camp would hardly find this surprising. It was a minimal facility consisting of a quonset hut and three trailers. One trailer housed the kitchen and the other two contained bunks for a total capacity of about twenty. The quonset hut doubled as the eating and indoor recreation room. Around this cluster of drab and cheerless accommodations was an equally drab landscape, devoid of anything but sagebrush.

There was not even a well on the property, so water had to be trucked in from Reno.

The Synanon group, after having shown its effectiveness in the prison, was invited to participate in the program at the camp and also to advise the institutional classification committee in the selection of inmates for transfer to it. At the camp the twenty inmates are assigned daily to work with other state agencies, going without guard to conservation or forestry projects over a wide area. Three times a week the Synanon group visits the camp in the evenings to conduct discussion sessions or to participate in recreation for the men. The Synanon Foundation maintains a house in Reno from which members go both to Peavine and to the main prison at Carson City to carry on their programs for inmates.

It is a deeply satisfying experience to see such high morale as exists in this inmate group, housed in a physical setting so abjectly poor as the one on Peavine Mountain. There has been almost no problem of escapes, fights, or other prison abuses. The camp has no custodial features at all and the one unarmed guard who is posted there takes no part in the program but acts mainly as a custody representative of the prison.

The significant thing about this for the purposes of our discussion here is that essentially all the persons who conduct program activities at the camp are themselves former institution inmates. Most of them have served sentences for narcotics offenses and, most remarkable, one of the Synanon members who goes daily to the prison and is in charge of the Synanon program there is himself a parolee from that same prison. Unlike the North Carolina experiment, these men are not state employees, and the relationship between them and the prison is only cooperative and quite informal. Nevertheless, the project gives every appearance of being highly successful.

The Peavine camp was the first major instance of Synanon's helping offenders generally instead of limiting itself to addicts. As indicated in the preceding chapter the developing belief of Synanon leaders is that addiction is only a symptom and that Synanon can attack the basic immaturity that leads, in one instance, to narcotics use and, in other instances, to quite different kinds of antisocial behavior. Some of the inmates transferred to Peavine are addicts but usually most of them are not.

While Peavine and Chapel Hill are vastly different from each other in character they both have made a significant contribution to the concept of helping offenders by use of people who themselves have been helped. They both are tributes to the courage of prison administrators who were willing to take a chance on a bold and untried scheme. The fact that the two camps have both shown such potential even with their many differences makes it clear that the concept is a potent and adaptable one.

Pre-Parole Training for Social Service

As an example of more deliberate and structured planning for the hiring of parolees there is the New Careers Development Project based at the California Medical Facility, a reformatory at Vacaville, California. This project, financed by a National Institute of Mental Health grant, was set up originally to train selected inmates from various correctional institutions who were transferred to Vacaville for the program. They were to be prepared for eventual work in social service jobs by four months of training while in the institution and a similar period of training on the job after being paroled.

The assumption is that some of the young men in the prison population have had much natural contact with the world of the poor and so have a greater sense of comfort and a greater communicative ability in dealing with poor people. If such inmates have shown improvement under the therapeutic programs offered them in the prison, and if their records do not include alcoholism, use of narcotics, mental illness, or severe offenses against the person, they may be suitable candidates for training as "change and development agents." If they perform satisfactorily through the training period they are paroled to jobs wherein, as employees of the state, they are engaged in social research or other kinds of social service among disadvantaged families.

The training process includes instruction that will give the inmate background information in a wide variety of social problems. Lectures and discussions have included such subjects as the dynamics of current social forces, the effects of automation, the effects of the current population trends, the dynamics of group therapy, mental retardation, cybernetics, the civil rights movement, and the nature of governmental social programs. The men at Vacaville who are in this training program have much more freedom in their institutional schedules than the other inmates. They are much less regimented in their movements about the building and they are free to stay up at night as late as they want. They have class work each day in the form of seminars and discussions for which they are expected to do a substantial amount of reading. They are provided with plenty of sociology texts and they obviously delve into the material with great interest. Much of the learning process is accomplished with techniques that cause the men to raise their own questions and then search for their own answers. Sample projects are devised in which the men must gather and analyze data, write a report, and present the report for class discussion. Frequent group discussions and role-playing sessions are used.

In this program the inmate is trained to work as a member of a team consisting of at least one parolee and one professional, the latter usually being a graduate student, who enters the program in partial fulfillment of his work toward a graduate degree. The students participate in the training on a part-time basis and later, when the inmates are paroled, it is hoped the team that has thus been developed will continue to function.

The team is seen as having particular usefulness because it cannot be expected that either the professional or the parolee will have a facility for all the types of communication involved. The indigenous worker will communicate well with the disadvantaged families being worked with, but he may not be able to deal easily with government officials, community leaders, and others who must be involved in a social service program. But if the team members who work together have close rapport they, collectively, have a very wide range of effective communication at their disposal.

Although the team idea was an important part of the original planning, it is not being adhered to exclusively. The administrators of the program are careful to be adaptive and flexible in order to exploit their growing experience and to take advantage of any new ways that appear for using these parolees. In a number of instances the change and development agents are working in single assignments and more uses for them are appearing. The executive office of the state has urged the use of more and more inmates trained for social service functions, and the State Bureau of Vocational Rehabilitation has asked to be supplied with such personnel in quantity.

But while there is this good response on the part of governmental units generally there has not been similar good response from the correctional agencies. It is not surprising that correctional institution staff members would take a cautious view of such a program. The inmates in training for this program enjoy a special status in the institution and as evidence of the heresy in the whole scheme, the inmates are granted an easy familiarity on a casual first-name basis with the professional staff members who direct the project. Furthermore, the free-wheeling discussions and the introspective processes of the group permit the inmates to analyze institutional staff and staff-inmate relationships. This can be a deeply unsettling specter for correctional institution officials and it helps to explain why the growing demand for these inmate trainees is coming from outside, rather than inside, the correctional bureaucracy.

In New York the State Division for Youth has also been experimenting with hiring former wards for social service work. With the help of a foundation grant the division has created a special aftercare service for boys released from its START centers. In addition to giving the usual intensive counseling services to help the boys make the transition to community living, the project selects and trains a few boys to serve as assistant boys' supervisors. It is hoped that the employment of such boys will help convince the other boys of the genuine regard the state has for them, and of the fact that they actually can aspire to important professional work.

The boys receive training in interviewing techniques, in using community resources, in making observations, and in writing reports. They are paid by the hour and may work part time while attending school. In fact, it is hoped that this kind of employment will give them positive encouragement to pursue further education. As assistant boys' supervisors they are not considered social workers and do not carry responsibility for counseling. Their major contribution is in the process of reciprocal interpretation and data-gathering for research. They are expected to "visit various graduates' neighborhoods, go into their homes, and gather data used in the research study. They talk with the other graduates about employment, school, and community interests. This information, so often guarded and withheld from adults by adolescents, is then shared with the project supervisor. In essence, the two new boy supervisors demonstrate positive models to which other graduates may aspire in their own communities."

In the first year of experimentation with this program the Division for Youth had much reason to feel encouraged. Six boys were trained and hired. The worst that happened in the first year was that two of these left because of their lack of interest. The others were proving to be both useful and interested.

The administrators have been coming to feel that the boys selected for this work should be out of the START center and back in the community for some months of successful living before being chosen and put into this kind of job. A successful period of adjustment makes them a better risk and gives the boy himself the added strength and status that comes from knowing that he really can make the grade as a parolee -just as he must help others to do. This is similar to the situation in the Chydaru camp project, where the employees were parolees who had been out on parole for a few months before being hired to work in the camp. In the Vacaville program, on the other hand, the change and development agents are selected while they are in the institution, and are prepared to start work immediately upon release and without a testing period in the community first. This is an interesting difference. The Vacaville system provokes arguments from those who believe that a parolee should be hired only after he has been out long enough to show some ability to adjust successfully in the community.

The use of clients in sociological research is spreading and is being tried in a number of prisons as well as in field services. Another area in which clients can be used is in teaching, and this has been subject to some experimentation in California with the help of a grant from the Office of Economic Opportunity. In one experiment during the summer of 1965 a number of assistant teachers were recruited from among housewives, high school students, and school dropouts, all from the disadvantaged areas where the schools were. Some were probationers assigned to the project. With four assistants assigned to each classroom, the effectiveness of the teaching was greatly increased. "The assistant teachers were especially adept at enhancing communication with the children, as many of them grew up in the area and knew the ways of the children and their families. They served as translators or 'linkers' between children and families, between teacher and families, and between children and teacher. The teacher could take on a new role. She or he was no longer seen as a disciplinarian and did not have to be overly concerned with control problems in a large, overcrowded room of physically active children. The assistant teachers visited the homes, helped the families to understand the purposes of school and to encourage rather than minimize the child's participation in learning. They brought back to the teacher and to the daily discussion groups significant information from the home and community to help understand each child's unique approach to the classroom."

But while the increased effectiveness of the teaching process was important, we are more concerned here with the effect on the indigenous assistant teachers. "Many of the staff were persons who had worked hard at menial labor most of their lives many looked tired when they began the project. Others detested work or obligations, and had been driven to impulse-seeking activities; four were on probation to the project for the summer. During the course of the project, their physical appearances changed, along with their manner of approach to people and to life situations. Many became excited over learning, more thoughtful, creative, and enthusiastic over relations with children, some after nearly a lifetime of tragic economic and social disadvantage." The experiences in this instance have impressive implications for a vital cooperative effort between correctional programs and school programs.

8

Community Response to Protective Services

Introduction

The church worker found no way to intervene on behalf of the child. The police, the district attorney, and various agencies in the community could not, they felt, intercede where the primary rights of parent or guardian were involved. Long tradition of parental power over children and hesitancy about outside intervention remained dominant, even though the right to intervene had previously been expressed and legally justified.

There had been created in the previous decade, in Manhattan, an American Society for the Prevention of Cruelty to Animals, patterned upon an animal protective society established in England in 1822. The mission worker, in her concern, argued that surely a child was a member of the animal kingdom and merited protection, at least as much as a cat or dog. Thus, on petition of the Society for the Prevention of Cruelty to Animals, the suffering child was brought to court and the foster parents were jailed.

The American public took a new step in affirming the rights of children, as many other humane societies, originally founded for the protection of animals, began to intercede on behalf of children who were abused, mistreated, or cruelly neglected. Legislation was enacted protecting children and authorizing special societies to undertake the task. New protective societies were created to work on behalf of children, while others which had animal programs revised their charters to create children's divisions.

New York County's Society for the Prevention of Cruelty to Children, founded in 1875, was followed almost at once by similar societies in Portsmouth, San Francisco, Philadelphia, Boston, and other cities. The American Humane Association, created in 1877 as a general coordinating body in this field, added a Children's Division in 1887 (and has reactivated it recently).

Early American efforts in the tradition of the English Poor Law had been designed largely to relieve the public of the financial burden of caring for children. Indenture and other forms of apprenticeship were the preferred means, and almshouses took care of the rest. Growing humanitarian concern and recognition that "acts of God" or uncontrolled environmental forces compelled many to seek aid finally laid a basis for enforcement of laws, already on the books, to protect children against cruelty and neglect and to strengthen such laws. Some agencies had sprung up to care for or to place neglected and dependent children, but they did not seek directly to promote or to enforce protective laws. Thus, the new protective societies, the S.P.C.C.'s, filled a gap in community provision.

Mary Ellen had played her dramatic role, but the functions of a protective program had to be developed in the twentieth century, as American social welfare, particularly child care, began to reflect a changing social scene.

The S.P.C.C.'s sponsored many progressive child protective laws and demonstrated in their daily actions that society meant to protect certain minimum rights of children over whom parents, even seriously disturbed or totally incompetent parents, had, until then, been supreme. Later, some S.P.C.C.'s became part of the general child welfare movement, often merging with other child and family agencies to develop social services which grew and changed along with social work as a whole. Others sided with the president of the first society, Elbridge Gerry, whose name became synonymous with S.P.C.C., in the view that "it is better to do one thing well." He held that since "child rescue work is a science," it is wiser not to link it to other aspects of "general scientific charity work," but rather to retain the S.P.C.C. in the form of its initial emphasis on law enforcement and rescue.

In 1910 Roswell C. McCrea, teaching at the New York School of Philanthropy, put it even more strongly:

> *The work has to be done in cold blood, so to speak, with a deaf ear to the pleadings and entreaties of mothers and fathers whose love for their children is never so strong as when they think their children will be taken from them. The best interests of the children, and not the feelings of those closely connected with them, have to be considered, and a trained charity worker is seldom qualified by his or her training to absolutely banish the spirit of "love for fellow-man" from his or her work. The SPCC worker, on the other hand, looks at the matter from a colder (a legal) viewpoint, and therefore the only training he should receive is such that will enable him to detect cruelty and apply the remedy, regardless of how the application affects those who are responsible for the cruelty. In short, SPCC is not, never has been and never will be charitable.*

Another note was struck almost from the beginning by some S.P.C.C. pioneers. Henry R. Jones, President of the Brooklyn S.P.C.C., said the following in his first annual report on October 31, 1881: "We have no wish to sever the sacred bond between parent and child, but rather to strengthen it by kind advice and counsel-and yet prevent cruelty at all hazards." By 1915 the Brooklyn S.P.C.C. had set up three divisions: investigation, law enforcement, family welfare. It sought to exert "more effort to bring about betterment in the home conditions of children and thereby avoid the necessity of breaking up families." In 1917 it stated that "only as a last resort do we remove children or institute adult prosecutions."

The two orientations have often merged, and concern with restoring the family has been deepened over the years.

However, the New York County S.P.C.C. has remained loyal to Gerry's concept. At times, too, the pioneering "child saving" function of 1874 has seemed to take on the character of an end in itself, and a routine of removing children from their homes and prosecuting their parents has left its mark on some agencies and personnel.

Today, to limit functions to investigation and rescue would ignore all that has been learned about why parents do not care for their children properly and about how people are most effectively helped. Child protective workers, generally, have understood this. A few have not, and the consequences may be the substitution of community-sanctioned cruelty for parental neglect and inadequacy.

Neglect—What Is It?

Our communities sometimes intervene in family life because of the allegation that a child is being severely mistreated, is endangered, or is not being given urgently needed medical attention, adequate food, clothing, and care, or educational opportunity. Even early nineteenth-century legal authorities, who had no way to implement their theory, saw this as entirely fitting: the rights of fathers, in fact, "result from their duties."

The *Standard Juvenile Court Act*, which does not favor the use of labels, nonetheless suggests that the children's court have exclusive jurisdiction over any child "who is neglected as to proper or necessary support, or education as required by law, or as to medical or other care necessary for his well-being or who is abandoned." In addition, and unlike most statutes, it includes the child "whose environment is injurious to his welfare, or whose behavior is injurious to his own or others' welfare," and the child "who is beyond the control of his parent." Many states list the latter two as classes of delinquent children but students of the problem are giving serious attention to the Standard Act formulation.

The *Standards for Specialized Courts Dealing with Children* proposes original and exclusive jurisdiction over "children whose parents, guardian, or custodian, have allegedly failed to provide them with the care, education or protection necessary for their well-being as required by law."

The British Children's and Young Persons Act of 1933 describes neglect as "want of reasonable care that is, the omission of such steps as a reasonable parent would take." In New York State a neglected child is a boy under sixteen and a girl under eighteen

- whose parent or other person legally responsible for his care does not adequately supply the child with food, clothing, shelter, education, or medical or surgical care, though financially able or offered financial means to do so; or
- who suffers or is likely to suffer serious harm from the improper guardianship, including lack of moral supervision or guidance, of his parents or other person legally responsible for his care and requires the aid of the court; or
- who has been abandoned or deserted by his parents or other person legally responsible for his care.

The legal borders of neglect, as Judge Gill of Connecticut has noted, are far from clear. The state's right to intervention does, however, seem to stem from the *parens patriae* doctrine, under which the state is the ultimate guardian of every child. Neglect statutes are not penal and are not designed to vent community indignation on allegedly offending parents: "The sole purpose of the court's inquiry into the behavior of the parent is the determination of what harm their behavior has caused, is causing, or if uncorrected can be reasonably anticipated to cause in the future to the child."

Children's courts in this country usually have jurisdiction over neglect, but definitions vary and are sometimes indistinguishable from dependency. In general, neglect is taken to involve acts committed or omitted, while dependency or destitution has to do with inability to provide food and shelter for a child. As noted, however, the *Standard Juvenile Court Act* talks of neglect "as to proper or necessary support." Obviously the line between neglect and dependency becomes thin as one begins to understand pressures to which parents are subject and the motives behind their conduct. As suggested by many sources, in fact, the labeling as delinquency or neglect, i.e., as *child misconduct or parental mistreatment*, is often decided by the chance factor of time or the nature and circumstances of the case finding. One third of the states do not use the labels. Some students of the problem would redefine as neglect all juvenile misbehavior now called delinquency which is not the equivalent of a crime in an adult. Whatever the details of definition, however, it is clearly wise public policy that children be "protected against the harmful effects resulting from the absence, inability, inadequacy or destructive behavior of parents, parent substitutes, or others." The neglected child is one who is in need of such protection because of the impairment or threat of impairment of his health or welfare "as the result of a violation of or noncompliance with law or legal responsibility for the protection of children, their education, employment, health or welfare." Many students of the court would transfer all dependency jurisdiction to welfare departments but all agree that courts must continue to concern themselves with severe neglect. One listing suggests that community concern justifiably begins under the following kinds of circumstances (the categories are obviously not mutually exclusive):

- when children lack essential food, clothing, and shelter;
- when a lack of care causes continuing emotional or physical illness, disability, or retarded physical development;
- when parental emotional disturbance interferes with or prevents proper child care;
- when lack of supervision endangers the child's development;
- when a community condition endangers the child and the parents do not seek to protect him even though remedies are available.

Only Minnesota actually specifies emotional neglect as a reason for intervention ("who is without proper parental care because of the emotional, mental or physical disability, or state of immaturity of his parent, guardian, or other custodian"). Gill holds that general neglect jurisdiction permits action in cases of emotional neglect after adequate clinical evaluation. Many experts would ask to see behavioral evidence of negative consequences of emotional problems.

It is possible to misuse society's right and need to intervene. American and British social welfare history has many examples of zealots who have sought to impose their own standards and rules upon others, and who have used their official status punitively and arrogantly against the weak and the ignorant. Such cases of over enforcement or even abuse of laws to protect children do not, however, justify reneging on a primary social obligation.

Even when there is good will and considerable competence, boundaries are difficult to define. How far is society to oversee child rearing? How much neglect (few parents are perfect) justifies intervention? Is the community to organize itself for intimate knowledge of how all children are reared, in order to protect them? Or, as is generally held, can an efficient system of case location operate within a framework which assumes the general competence of most parents, but acknowledges an obligation not to miss clues that certain children require active help?

A democratic society is defeated if it seeks to control family life for all children. Most parents are not neglectful, and the quality of family life is changed if it must be held up to public view to make sure that it is sound. However, a responsible society will not take this as justification for society to neglect the brutalized, the deprived, the starved children whose parents are incapable, for psychological or social reasons, of providing them with at least the minimum of essential care.

Particularly difficult is the question of how much consideration should be given to local conditions in evaluating a child's milieu. Specifically, does one hold up the objectives of the most recent White House Conference on Children, which are more often aspirations than standards, or should the criteria be the norms of the state as a whole or the acceptable conduct in the geographic locality or social subgroup in which the child is being reared?

Social welfare agencies will certainly strive to raise community standards in the direction of national aspirations. Formal, authoritative public intervention at any moment in a family's life is obviously affected by court policy in adjudicating neglect. Court policy, in turn, usually reflects a broader community backdrop than the social or cultural subgroup, particularly a minority, underprivileged, or deviant subgroup. The court must ask whether the apparent or alleged neglect is, in fact, acceptable practice in another subculture. Given cohesive family life and evidence that other children grow up without harm under such circumstances, the court or agency should not wish to intervene. But intervention becomes necessary when a child is endangered (by the refusal to arrange medical attention, for instance), when the child clearly shows the undesirable consequences of such rearing, and when the parents' own mores have collapsed in the midst of the majority culture so that the family offers no cohesiveness and no framework for socialization.

Trends in Child Protection

Protective services and agencies are plagued by confusions in definition, by major differences of opinion as to appropriate organizational forms, and by historical residues. Standard-setting groups and individual agencies, however, are now making major efforts to give sound direction to future development. Facts are being assembled as to current provision; several national forums have been created in an effort to achieve consensus; experimental efforts have pointed to the potential of new professional approaches.

A national survey, under the auspices of the reactivated Children's Division of the American Humane Association, began by defining "child protective services" as a "specialized *casework service* to neglected, abused, exploited, or rejected children." The premise is that a protective service is preventive, is nonpunitive, and seeks the rehabilitation of the home. Characteristically, the service is "initiated on a complaint or referral from sources outside the family." The readiness to turn to the court when necessary and, perhaps, other factors give the agency a degree of authority in its approach. However, the agency may also render a variety of other child welfare services. Thus, excluding the investigatory activities of police or other departments in relation to neglect, as well as court services in this field, the survey sought to determine, nationally, whether there was adequate coverage provided by public or voluntary casework programs. It was found that there was not.

Private agencies, the backbone of the original child protection development, do not exist in most communities. In fact, "32 states and the District of Columbia have no private agencies with a child protective function as defined by this study." There are 84 such agencies in the nation, but 40 of them are local branches of statewide agencies: 5 offices in Connecticut, 21 in Massachusetts, 5 in Rhode Island, 9 in Maryland. Of the remaining private groups, 14 are found in New York State, 9 in Pennsylvania, 6 in New Jersey, 4 in Illinois, and one each in Indiana, Ohio, Kentucky, and Tennessee. Thus, outside of the Eastern seaboard, few communities have private agencies, and even there such coverage is far from complete.

On the other hand, the study showed that in 35 of 48 states (in 1956) the social welfare law imposes general responsibility upon the state for child welfare services, including the protection and care of the "homeless, dependent, and neglected and children in danger of becoming delinquent." In 22 states this responsibility is discharged by the state through supervisory or consultative services to the local welfare agency. A minority of counties have a specialized child protective program. A sizable minority have no program at all. The programs of many counties are severely limited by the size and qualifications of staff.

In 13 of the 35 states, the legal responsibility for child protective services is discharged through a direct service program (although coverage may be lacking in a few counties). Direct service is also to end their cruelty and to ensure adequate care, food, and sleeping arrangements if they wish to avoid court.

The N.S.P.C.C. takes few cases to court (under 1 percent as compared to 5 to 10 percent in most U.S. programs for which data are available) but uses the threat of court frequently. When cases are brought to court, however, British law and tradition make the jailing and fining of adults for child neglect far more common than it is in the United States. In one of the cases cited in a recent study, for example, a parent had left a child with someone else for care, and the other person did not protect the child. Both the parent and negligent "baby sitter" were sentenced by the judge because he felt that the parent had acted irresponsibly and the "sitter" neglectfully.

Modern psychological and social understanding has led to questions about the British protective program similar to those raised in the United States. One case-by-case study in England, for example, showed the neglectful mothers to be in poor health and without anybody who would help care for their children or relieve them, even briefly. The families were often broken, subject to extreme poverty, residing in poor housing, and suffering from mental defect or illness. Analysis suggested, in fact, that misfortune, rather than neglect, was a more appropriate designation for 50 percent of 234 cases studied intensively. Only 11 percent were considered to represent deliberate cruelty or willful neglect.

The study concluded, as have all recent studies of the kind which make use of modern social welfare knowledge and principles, that neglectful families require social casework services which are reassuring and supportive, and which offer practical services as well as emotional help. In some instances, residential treatment may be required.

The N.S.P.C.C. began to devote more effort to improving conditions in the homes visited and hired women as "visitors" to supplement the work of the inspectors. It sought public funds to expand this phase of its work, only to find that the Home Office (the responsible department) preferred to devote its resources to a come to end their cruelty and to ensure adequate care, food, and sleeping arrangements if they wish to avoid court.

The N.S.P.C.C. takes few cases to court (under 1 percent as compared to 5 to 10 percent in most U.S. programs for which data are available) but uses the threat of court frequently. When cases are brought to court, however, British law and tradition make the jailing and fining of adults for child neglect far more common than it is in the United States. In one of the cases cited in a recent study, for example, a parent had left a child with someone else for care, and the other person did not protect the child. Both the parent and negligent "baby sitter" were sentenced by the judge because he felt that the parent had acted irresponsibly and the "sitter" neglectfully.

Those who approach protective programs in modern social welfare terms continue to face complex professional questions:

- Child neglect is basically a social problem. In what way can it be dealt with through individual casework?
- All are agreed that the protective agency cannot withdraw or discontinue service simply because the parent has refused or is unable to take help. Should the service also be organized so that the client is unable to withdraw, or is the potential court petition adequate authority?
- Some emphasize the specialized skill in protective work, while others stress the individual agency or the community pattern. Which approach will yield the best definition of method and the most organized service? At what point is a child in the purview of a protective program?
- What organizational consequences follow from concern with individual legal rights?
- Should all protective services be located under public auspices, or is a public-private pattern desirable?
- In what sense should non-governmental agencies engage in direct law enforcement?

- Should the protective service be a separate unit or part of a more general child welfare or family casework effort?

Answers may be possible if we consider some of the essential functions and their best location, from the point of view of a total community pattern of services.

Functions within a Protective Program

There is no unified conception of protective programs. To some, protective services are functions divided among a variety of agencies and institutions. Others stress the social casework task of the child welfare agency with a protective specialization. Still others emphasize techniques and essential skills. Any detailed examination of what the community requires seems to point to the first of these views: the protective responsibility is lodged in the whole community. In fact, "protective services to children is a total process involving a constellation of agencies, public, private and legal any one or several of which may function at various times in the interest of the care of the child and help to his parents, to insure such care."

The community as a whole is responsible for the adequate rearing of its children. To suggest that any one agency could undertake the entire protective function would be to move backward at least eighty-five years.

This view does not, of course, preclude assignment of specific functions and responsibilities to specialized agencies. Indeed, such assignment of specialized tasks is a necessity. For example, there is wisdom in the recommendation of the National Agencies Workshop on Protective Services to the effect that each state either provide or ensure provision by some agency of protective casework services and related functions. The casework service, however, does not encompass the entire protective process.

Consideration of all the functions to be provided and staffed in a total protective process suggests that the pattern of organization should vary with size, type, and traditions of a community. No matter what the pattern of organization, however, the essential functions of a protective program are the same.

One premise needs emphasis before specific functions are reviewed. Protective services, which operate most effectively within a circumscribed area, cannot realistically aim at satisfying "all the needs of children" or at ensuring "all their rights." Many social institutions and social welfare agencies have a part in meeting children's needs and protecting their rights, including the family, the church, the school, the welfare department, and the court. The protective service moves into action only when socially defined minimums are not being met, or where children are in "clear and present danger."

Case finding. The first step is to identify those families in which parents or parent-substitutes are not providing or arranging adequate care for their children and those not able to recognize and take action on their problem, thereby causing injury to the children. Members of the community at large are in a position to notice and to alert official agencies to situations involving extreme neglect or mistreatment of children, not yet known to agencies. To do so, however, community members must begin to share growing professional knowledge about the consequences of abuse and deprivation upon children. They require, too, knowledge of resources to which they may turn.

Beyond this, however, all the case finding resources come into play: public health stations, police, welfare department staffs, schools, social agencies, doctors, public health nurses, hospitals and clinics, settlements, recreation centers, and so on. What these agencies must have, each according to its function and staffing, is clear information as to the kind of situation requiring intervention, and knowledge about how the community is organized to deal with neglect complaints.

When the problem goes beyond the internal family difficulties, inadequacies, or relationships, case finding may also involve *situation finding*, the discovery of what has been called "community neglect." Response to a complaint or exercise of an agency's normal functions may uncover the lack of "vital health and social welfare services," or community conditions which deny children the opportunities they should have, or which "affect children adversely." While one would hope that all citizens would report such circumstances to proper authorities and would join in community action to correct undesirable conditions, such reporting and corrective action is clearly an obligation of any social agency. It is not the special province of protective work. This does not, of course, preclude the decision by any agency, including one rendering protective casework services, to devote itself to social action and legislative initiative in these spheres. Historically, voluntary protective societies in fact did much to end extreme child labor abuses.

Case evaluation and emergency removal of children. It is essential that the case finder or complainant about neglect know where in the community he may turn so as to ensure adequate evaluation of the situation. The case evaluation or case study function should, of course, be preceded by some measure of screening, to consider the possibility of hostile motivation or clearly incompetent sources. It is agreed, however, that unless the evidence is overwheming that the allegation is unfounded, the report should reach the agency designated for case evaluation; otherwise, children may be hurt.

Evaluation is a protective casework task. Within the protective casework field, it is called by various names: intake, substantiating the complaint, and so on. It is often a specialized assignment, even in departments which encompass protective casework within a general child welfare service. A national committee under the auspices of the Child Welfare League of America urged that each community have one known place authorized to receive complaints.

It has been alleged that at one time the humane society representative would enter a home, inspect the premises, look at the child, perhaps talk to the parent, and decide, on the spot, to remove the child. Today, it is still agreed by all that the community cannot at any time permit children to remain in "situations of serious or extreme danger." Current concepts of individual rights seem to suggest that if such situations exist, it is the police who should enter, remove the children, and take them to a shelter for protection.

There are still some people in the protective field who would retain in voluntary protective agencies the police power originally assigned by statute or charter when there were no other protectors of children. They consider it the protective agency's duty to intervene and remove a child in danger. This seems increasingly to be an outdated view, however, inconsistent with either the expansion of juvenile aid police programs or the emphasis on protecting the rights of people in difficulty.

There are S.P.C.C. leaders who, although they consider the child's removal as an S.P.C.C. responsibility, nevertheless favor having the agent summon a policeman to participate. No effective argument has been made against the view that parents have the right to the possession of their children until this right has been abrogated by the court. It is a law enforcement function to protect all individuals, including children, from personal harm and danger. In situations of danger to children, when immediate action must be taken to protect the child by removing him from the home, this action is the function of law enforcement officials. A court petition and provision for social study should follow at once. If the rights of a parent or child are to be limited in their own or society's interests, they can be limited only in accordance with due process of law and only to the extent and for the time necessary.

Law enforcement officers need to be called in only occasionally-when a child's life or safety is in immediate danger, a crime is being committed, forcible entry is necessary, or when a child or caseworker needs protection against bodily harm. Protective workers attest that few cases require immediate removal. It is now understood, in fact, that apart from the matter of parental rights, an unnecessary separation of child from parent may contribute to decreased responsibility and make permanent family disintegration more likely. There was far less concern about this in the early days of protective work than there is today, when we know that few substitute arrangements match even marginally acceptable parental care.

Skilled investigation of complaints or case study is thus essential in all protective cases and is a major function in the protective field. This is hardly the place to outline the elements of such study in detail, in the manner of a manual, but some indications of the requirements are relevant as an aid in clarifying what the community must be prepared to staff in a protective casework service.

The protective agency caseworker, as already indicated, is usually conducting the investigation contrary to the wishes of (or certainly without an invitation from) one or both parents. Furthermore, both he and the parents know that the situation may reach the children's court as a result of his findings, or if parental cooperation on some level is not forthcoming. Finally, the caseworker may not withdraw despite extreme parental hostility and resistance; in De Francis's terms, his is "a higher than ordinary degree of responsibility," since he represents an agency assigned a protective role through statute or charter. (It is doubtful that a protective casework service can exist without such formal assignment.)

The case evaluation process should reflect the fact that the protective field has shifted from "rescuing the child from the home," to preserving the home for the child wherever possible. This does not decrease the need to follow up a complaint immediately and thoroughly through several means: social service exchange clearance; clearance with agencies which have known the family; interviews with each parent (including a visit to the home); contacts with such other sources of information as the school, physicians, clergy, relatives; an interview with the children alleged to be neglected. Where possible, of course, there should be a prior interview with the complainant to evaluate motives as well as to obtain information. When complaints are made anonymously, as they often are, case studies must usually be initiated without such interview, especially when initial explorations reveal that the situation cannot be safely ignored.

The evaluation should have the full scope of a professionally competent social study, but may focus, in addition, on areas of parent-child relationship, child-rearing practices, household conditions, or other factors which enter particularly into the expressed concern about the child. Symptoms of physical neglect and mistreatment are noted, but there must be equal attention to the manner of functioning in major areas of life, evidences of normal growth or retardation, and the nature of interpersonal relationships in the family.

The caseworker conducting the study requires particular skill at evaluating parental personality strengths and problems and recognizing evidences of serious pathology. He must be equipped, too, to identify some practices as typical of cultural subgroups in the community and not harmful to normal development, even though different and, perhaps, annoying to some community members, including the complainants. Whether or not efforts will ultimately be made to deal with deep-seated personality and social deviance in neglectful parents, the difficulties must be explored, understood, and evaluated, as the basis for decisions which must be made as to the need for community intervention and the nature of the intervention.

Since the objective is both immediate protection and, if possible, long-range help to restore the family (recognizing that some evaluations will show that there is no neglect in the legal sense) all contacts must be carried out with professional skill and with respect for individual rights and dignity. Parents have the right to know the nature of the complaint and the objectives of the protective agency. They often also need help "to express their shock, fear, anger, resistance or hostility" at the complaint and at community intervention. The full problem, community expectations and concerns, possible sources of help, and what is involved in change, all require discussion in terms which have meaning to the parents during initial interviews and later. Clear expression of respect for parents and regard for them is a prerequisite to strengthening them, if possible, in a sound parental role.

The caseworker from a protective agency is described as equipped with authority, by law or charter, to intervene and evaluate the children's situation. This concept requires some clarification, however. As Wilson McKerrow has pointed out, the protective worker must have "the right to be in the situation" on the basis of law or agency charter. This is not the same as the policeman's role, nor does it eliminate the need for a police role described above.

Collaboration between protective workers and the police dates back to the early S.P.C.C. days.

If there is no acute emergency and danger, and if the parent refuses to participate in an investigation, allegations and limited data are assembled and the court is called upon to authorize more formal intervention. The protective caseworker does not use strong arm devices, since they defeat his goals and are unlawful as well. Thus, the real authority in protective casework is not coercive, except in the sense that there is an announced readiness to appeal to the court and a socially assigned charge to be persistent and responsible. At a later date, the caseworker's judgment that the conditions involved in the neglect have changed will also have great effect.

The essence of the protective caseworker's authority, during case evaluation and in the subsequent period of work with people, is, perhaps, his professional and psychological firmness and consistency, which are based on his charge to take the initiative in the relationship with the parents. Agency policies and procedures and the requirements of the law, as used by skilled caseworkers, are the framework for a process of social reeducation. Study has described the psychological authority which develops in the relationship between worker and client as deriving from the competence and expertness of the caseworker and an ability to help which is demonstrated and available to the client for dealing with his problem.

The literature of the protective field and the standards of all national groups concerned concur in the view that case evaluation can be carried out with greatest competence by staff who are trained in social casework. They must be prepared to be confronted by hostility, resistance, and extremely disturbing situations, psychologically and socially. They must give special attention, in their professional preparation, to the use of legal and psychological authority.

The investigation and case evaluation function has been discharged by voluntary protective societies (the Massachusetts S.P.C.C. or New York S.P.C.C., for example), by voluntary children's agencies which include a protective unit (Buffalo Children's Aid and S.P.C.C.), by county and city public welfare departments, or by child welfare programs conducted directly under state auspices.

Adjudication of status, service planning, and referral. The case evaluation by the protective agency leads, as does any case evaluation, to conclusions, recommendations, and plans. In some instances, brief or extensive exploration supports the view that there is no neglect and no need for any kind of service. Sometimes a service may be called for even though no neglect finding can be made. Such service, usually a referral, should be voluntarily offered and clearly labeled as voluntary. Much more often the difficulties are clear, and a skilled caseworker will be able to make, with the client, a gradual and natural transition from the case study to a casework therapy process. To illustrate at random, referrals for housekeepers, day care, or vocational guidance may be part of the service. The relationship should continue until there is mutual readiness to terminate it; the agency cannot do so unless convinced that the children will bc cared for properly.

Experience reveals that a protective service is severely hampered unless it encompasses within its own department, or has available through referral, facilities for direct casework treatment, homemaker services, day care, foster home care, temporary shelter care, institutional care, adoption, and specialized pediatric, psychological, and psychiatric services.

Sometimes the protective agency or somebody else in the community must turn to the court. A case cannot be dropped, for instance, only because the client refuses to participate in case study. On other occasions, community members or public officials may be convinced that formal court action and perhaps child placement are essential. They may wish to exercise their rights to charge neglect formally and to request a court hearing.

Under still other circumstances, the protective agency case evaluation may conclude that only a formal court finding of neglect and subsequent court supervision or placement of the children will help or protect the family.

Most juvenile court statutes define neglect and permit a variety of court dispositions after a neglect adjudication. There is obvious need to clarify court functions in such cases in addition to adjudicalion, if any.

Major national agencies interested in this field of service agreed to differentiate between acceptance and investigation of complaints, on the one hand, and action on neglect petitions, on the other. They felt that all complaints should be referred to child protective agencies, whether or not originally brought to the court, so that there might be the full, skilled evaluation and the offer of appropriate service described above. Where the investigation leads to a decision to file a petition, or where a formal application is made to invoke the court's judicial authority, the matter should have court attention. The court may adjudicate, decide about separation of parent and child, make determinations about custody, and so on.

This formulation may prove rather difficult in practice. To a considerable extent, the dividing line between a complaint and a request for formal adjudication is in the orientation of the intake worker, whether in court or protective agency. It should be possible, nonetheless, to reach agreements within a given community that court intake will make referrals to the protective casework service of all those situations not absolutely requiring immediate court process. This would not preclude brief service, which any intake renders to cases coming directly to court. Nor would it deprive complainants, or those alleged to be neglectful, of the right to court consideration if they wished it.

Where an agency's experience with a family points to the need for court action, the protective agency must enter as the petitioner, and the case data provided should be adequate to sustain the allegations. Witnesses may be summoned and counterevidence offered. The probation staff may be subsequently called upon for a supplementary social study, not to evaluate the evidence as to neglect, but to assist the judge in his disposition.

Once the court decision is made, the protective agency is one resource for treatment among many available to the court. If the child remains in the home and a period of casework help is considered essential, the court must decide whether to call upon its probation department for supervision and treatment or whether to refer to the protective casework agency or to another source of service. The agency's prior role and the character of its relationship with the client might be the deciding factor, assuming that both staffs are equally available and well qualified. The probation officer's orientation in such cases should certainly be no different from that of the protective agency's caseworker. Specific community resources and the desirability of close court surveillance of the treatment may determine the choice between a protective casework service and probation supervision.

Casework treatment of parents and children. The correction of unsatisfactory parental behavior is not achieved through assumption of parental responsibility by a caseworker, nor through intervention between parents and children within the home, nor through holding the parents to a standard by direct supervision, which includes a concrete list of "musts" and a system of checking up.

The casework treatment in the protective situation makes use of all social work services and methods, but, carried out in the context previously described, is characterized by application of formal and psychological authority. The service turns to the court only under the circumstances described above. Treatment might be undertaken in the specialized protective casework agency, in the probation department assigned supervision following neglect adjudication, or in almost any casework agency aware of the problems of working with highly resistant and disorganized people and willing to undertake the responsibility on court referral or on request of a protective agency.

Severe character disorders and psychoses are often found in the parents in these situations, but the caseworker who seeks to treat the parents so that the family will become a safe place for the child must be prepared for almost every diagnostic type and social complication. One study puts it this way:

Through emotional immaturity, instability or mental illness, an adult is incapable of responding to the demands the child makes on him, and because of his inadequacy, escapes from the situation by neglecting or attacking the child and so performs acts of cruelty. The child may be merely a scapegoat for his warped passions, or the focus and victim of his difficulties.

Internal emotional conflicts as well as tension and violence between the parents may often be part of the picture. One parent is often the complainant in neglect cases.

Effective treatment is frequently based on long periods of simple, helpful, friendly service, with understanding of backsliding and with necessary firmness which is nonpunitive. There are many frustrations, particularly in the earliest phases:

To expect such a client to come to the office for help on any regular basis, especially in the beginning of treatment, is as unrealistic as expecting a person with a broken leg to walk to the orthopedist to have it set.

One would perhaps aspire, in all situations, "to help the parents restore or enhance their capacities as parents to the fullest potential, and to modify situational factors so that their children may have the opportunity to develop into mature adults able to handle parental functions in their turn." The obstacles are so many, however, that more modest attainments are more common: sustaining the child in his own home without damage, correcting specific defects in parental care, correcting and alleviating the effects on the child of prior parental mishandling. Between the optimum goal of fur restoration and enhancement of capacities and the minimum acceptable objective of correcting legally intolerable conditions is the effort to "help the parents resolve those problems and modify those patterns which prevented or inhibited adequate parental functioning." Most protective caseworkers would aspire to this.

This type of service and treatment demands well-qualified personnel. Dr. Irving Kaufman, who has worked intensively with the most disturbed of neglectful parents, and who has studied treatment problems, says that one must begin through use of community authority and that it is essential to "go out" to these people, for, "bewildered by the disruptive forces which have swept over them, many of these parents need the protection and reality framework supplied by the caseworker's firm but consistent hand." The work, he finds, is in two phases: (a) a "supervisory protective role" in which the parent is helped to identify with a more adequate parent figure and (b) a more definitive dealing with basic causes. Techniques include going into the home and reviewing the daily routines of when the family gets up, what they eat, and so on. Help with practical planning is often a good beginning. Unless the caseworker is identified from the start as interested in the entire family's welfare, he may tend to "solidify the pathologic aspects of the parent-child interaction." In work with children in the family, caseworkers will seek chiefly to help both parents and children to understand the intervention on a basis which does not harm the child or the relationship between parent and child. Should removal of children from the home be necessary, through court petition or by voluntary action of the parent, all the child welfare knowledge and skills relative to support and preparation prior to separation from the parents will have to come into play. Referrals will be necessary in many eases for specialized help to repair the physical, intellectual, and emotional consequences of neglect. A number of cities have become interested in the programs developed in Europe whereby "training apartments" in public housing are used as the setting for family reeducation or acculturation in circumstances where the problem is severe but the potential encouraging. The distribution of functions. The total protective process thus requires:

(1) full support of community members, agencies, and institutions in case finding and situation finding;
(2) children's courts for adjudication, disposition planning, and some treatment;
(3) a variety of social, therapeutic, and medical services to accept referrals;
(4) agencies offering protective cases work service for case evaluation, for initiative in court proceedings, and for treatment of parents and children, as necessary;
(5) police readiness to enter for emergency protection and removal of children.

Protective casework is now generally defined either as a specialty within the scope of child welfare services or as part of the general child welfare job. Because of regional differences, it would be inappropriate to specify one organizational pattern. The protective casework agency may be public or voluntary, depending on the local situation. If public, the program may be administered by either the locality or the state. The state's obligation to ensure the provision of service by *some* agency has been widely recognized. Language for incorporation into existing state welfare and juvenile court statutes has recently been proposed in order to specify this obligation and to suggest objectives. In an era of expanding public welfare and few new large-scale voluntary developments, it seems likely that the bulk of the specialized protective casework programs, or child welfare programs which include protective service, will be established by public departments. Most standard-setting groups favor this in principle.

Important federal support for the child protective effort began in fact with the 1935 Social Security Act. States enacted laws to conform with the federal law, and expressed their responsibility for "child welfare services for the protection and care of homeless, dependent and neglected children, and children in danger of becoming delinquent." Programs known as "services to children in their own homes" have been initiated under these provisions and have included protective casework within their scope.

Funds were originally devoted principally to rural areas, but recent amendments to the Social Security Act (1958) permit the expansion of urban child welfare services. Some public assistance funds have also become available. There has, however, been concern at the general lack of social services in Aid to Needy Families with Children and other assistance programs granting funds to families for millions of children. The Congress and the Department of Health, Education, and Welfare launched measures in 1962 to remedy this situation and to ensure greater coordination between child welfare programs and public assistance programs involving children.

Organizing for Child Protection

New York City is in transition from complete reliance on voluntar), S.P.C.C.'s to creation of a public protective service in its Welfare Department which will share responsibility with the voluntary agencies. Review of what is involved in this change may serve to clarify in some additional detail the requirements of a protective program.

The programs today. New York County (Manhattan) houses thc parent society of all voluntary child protective agencies. When created in 1875 by an act of the legislaturc, it was dedicated to "the prevention of cruelty to children and the enforcement of the laws relating to or in any wise affecting children." Similar societies followed in the other New York City counties: Brooklyn and Richmond S.P.C.C.'s in 1880, Bronx S.P.C.C. in 1915, Queens S.P.C.C. in 1920.

It was clear from legislative enactments, reinforced by court opinion, that the intent was to create quasi-public agencies and to vest in them powers ordinarily granted only to public agencies. The societies' agents, although privately hired and not subject to public control, were designated as peace officers, i.e., "A constable or police officer *must*, and an agent or officer of any incorporated society for the prevention of cruelty to children *may*, arrest and bring before a court any persons offending [against children, and] may interfere to prevent the perpetration of any act forbidden. A person who obstructs or interferes with any officer or agent is guilty of a misdemeanor." [Italics added.]

The quasi-official status also derived from other assignments of responsibility. Although not necessarily attorneys, society agents were empowered to present evidence in court. Societies were given the right to investigate and make recommendations with reference to applications for appearances of children as entertainers, prior to action by the mayor on the applications.

Most important, special legal provision gave the societies the right to make complaints before the court about violations affecting children, to aid "in presenting the law and facts to such court, to become guardian of the person of a minor child and to accept court commitments and to receive the aid of all magistrates and peace officers in enforcement of laws relating to children." Subsequent provision in the Domestic Relations Court law specified the societies' rights to accept children in detention.

The S.P.C.C.'s long stressed their law enforcement responsibilities. Their mission was to "receive every child suffering from brutal treatment or living in degrading surroundings," and they did it with enthusiasm and dedication. Some of the societies seemed to lack understanding or concern for the parents, while others stressed the family unit from the beginning. Laws necessary for child protection were formulated and actively championed. The New York S.P.C.C. rejected supervision by the State Board of Charities on the ground that the S.P.C.C. "is not a charitable organization but a prosecuting instrument. It is an auxiliary government agency." This position was upheld by the Court of Appeals in 1900.

Transitions are often slow when there is long, traditional dedication to a way of doing things. However, modern social and psychological understanding began to reach some of the S.P.C.C. personnel. Personnel trained in social work schools entered some of the programs. The emphasis on preservation of the home where possible was proclaimed loudly at the first (1909) White House Conference, implemented in Mothers' Pension Laws, and adopted as a principle by the new U.S. Children's Bureau in 1912. This principle had great influence in all areas of child care. Correction and prevention became the objectives in work with parents, replacing the old assumption that one could protect children by punishing their parents.

In New York City, the Brooklyn S.P.C.C. was one of the first affected by the new, humane concept and by the added knowledge. In 1930 it spoke thus of its past:

> *The Society looked back on its accomplishments both with pride and sorrow. It was proud of the role it had played in furthering necessary protective legislation it was proud that it had awakened a community consciousness for the welfare of its children it was proud of its record of protective service and temporary shelter.*

Its sorrow stemmed not from anything it had wilfully done wrong, but rather from the things it had left undone or done inadequately, in the light of the knowledge it had gained in fifty years. In its early days too much emphasis had been placed on prosecutions and not enough on rehabilitation and prevention and only the most casual inquiry had been made into the causes of individual family breakdown children were too quickly removed from homes that were labeled unfit. They were then placed in institutions or sent to foster homes about which little or nothing was known.

The other New York City societies were not prepared to join Brooklyn in this kind of statement as early as 1930; some may not be yet. Brooklyn itself has lacked the resources and support essential to following all the implications of what it saw thirty years ago and has learned since that time.

The several different and independent S.P.C.C.'s in the New York area have evolved to varied stages of professionalization and skill. The Staten Island society is no longer active and all but Queens have ended their shelter programs. With one possible exception all face problems of limited resources and provide only part of the volume of service required in their counties. Because the sum total of all voluntary protective services in the city could provide only a very small portion of the obviously needed protective casework, New York City began to move in late 1961 toward a measure of public provision. Description of one of the most developed programs, that in Brooklyn, will serve as a point of departure for characterizing the voluntary provision and the manner in which public services may develop.

The Brooklyn S.P.C.C. has "law enforcement" and casework services. The former involves a publicly subsidized service in cases of sex offenses against children: emotional support to parents and children involved; advice to the district attorney relative to prosecutions; medical examinations; arrangements for prenatal care; efforts to speed the cases through court. The service is valued by the district attorney but it need not enter into basic issues of function; in most communities it might be rendered by well-staffed probation departments.

The casework service receives allegations of child neglect and abuse, approximately 1,700 to 2,600 cases annually over the past five years, involving six to seven thousand children. Cases get to the S.P.C.C. through parental referral (often a complaint by a separated parent), individuals in the community, relatives, schools, anonymous sources, and other agencies in the given order of frequency. For lack of resources the Brooklyn S.P.C.C. discourages or rejects many potential cases. It refers to the Welfare Department all situations involving children already on the department rolls and turns over to the police all emergencies and anonymous complaints.

This is a casework service despite difficulties in recruiting and holding an adequate number of qualified caseworkers. The staff uses casework methods in accepting complaints of neglect and in evaluating the extent of parental failure and parental capacity for adequate functioning.

Where appropriate, direct casework help is offered or referrals are made. Even though parental resistance may be strong, the casework staff considers itself under obligation to stay with a situation until certain that the children will not suffer seriously. Where parents are not reached and children are endangered, a neglect petition is flied in court. Court is occasionally turned to when treatment considerations in a case suggest the need, despite overt parental cooperation.

Only a very small proportion of new cases are actually accepted for full study and (where needed) continued service by the casework staff. One third are found, following clearance, to be under the care of other agencies and are not served. Many others are referred immediately by the intake unit to other agencies to which they were not already known. Over one third require information and consultation service and nothing more, and about one percent is improper referrals. The intake unit responsible for this preliminary screening is staffed with the society's most experienced caseworkers. Because of its resource shortages, the Brooklyn society has done everything possible to encourage other voluntary casework agencies to increase their services in neglect eases so that they will refer to S.P.C.C. only cases requiring "more authoritative treatment."

Cases assigned to the casework division beyond intake do not all involve intensive treatment. Following investigation, a good number of additional cases are referred for service to public or private agencies, or to court. Some cases show no basis for action and others are "adjusted" satisfactorily quite rapidly. Some cases are served over a longer period. The staff stresses home visits, work with community sources vital to the family, and a responsible "staying with the case" approach.

All other New York City voluntary S.P.C.C.'s are somewhat less developed in the direction of a casework division, because of problems of resources and staffing or (in the instance of the Manhattan society) because they do not accept the concept. Special attention to the latter aspect will clarify some issues in relation to the planning of services in the future.

The Manhattan society long stressed "law enforcement" and "rescue" work, narrowly defined, but was described in the 1930s as beginning to place more stress on the adjustment of children in their own homes and on the use of court as a last resort. It has nonetheless refused over the years to identify itself as a social agency and has persisted in the view upheld by the court years ago that it is not a "charity" and not subject to supervision by the State Social Welfare Department.

Annual reports do point to a philosophy of helping and rehabilitation and a readiness to do "field work," where other agencies may prefer office interviews. It is not clear how well the society is equipped to carry this out. Three phases of the work are identified: the handling of neglect complaints, prosecution of offenses (usually sexual) against children, and review of applications for child entertainers. Apparently the same staff members do the law enforcement work and handle neglect allegations.

Case totals are large neglect complaints in a recent year involved the welfare of over 5,000 children. Referral sources are not specified in detail, but a little less than half of these cases originated in public agencies, probably Children's Court and the Welfare Department for the most part. A good number are cases in which evidence of neglect is noted in court and the judge merely asks the S.P.C.C. representative to serve as petitioner (on "information and belief") so that the case may be officially placed before the court for neglect. The New York S.P.C.C. took about 15 percent of its neglect cases to Children's Court in 1959.

While others would add to casework resources, the Manhattan S.P.C.C. continues to insist that the S.P.C.C. is and should remain a law enforcement service—not a casework agency:

> *The Society becomes active, generally speaking, when it is alleged that laws enacted to protect children against neglect or penal laws intended to safeguard them are being violated. It investigates complaints of neglect and initiates neglect proceedings before the Children's Court when indicated in*

the child's best interest. Such investigations are not merely routine inquiries. Specialized knowledge of the law and rules of evidence are essential. Where the child requires the protection of the Court, the investigation must develop sufficient admissible evidence to sustain the petition. Failure to fully develop and properly present evidence to the Court could result in dismissal of the proceedings which might be interpreted by the respondents as a license to continue the neglectful conduct and the child's plight would be worse than ever.

Although the facts developed by the investigation may not indicate present need for Children's Court action, the family situation may be such that it cannot be ignored. It may be expected to benefit from casework services. *The Society does not consider providing casework sense to be its function.* It must seek to refer the family to an appropriate agency. Unfortunately, this is not always possible in view of intake requirements. Therefore, because of necessity rather than choice, it sometimes must keep open longer than it would like, cases more appropriately handled by casework agencies.

It would be desirable if the Society could dispose of matters without undue delay by court action or agency referral. It is to be hoped that intake requirements of casework agencies will become more flexible and aggressive casework more available so that, when appropriate, successful referrals can be made in more cases.

Planning for the future. In short, New York City—like many other cities faces a problem of systematic allocation and integration of protective *functions* and the assurance of adequate *protective casework coverage*. Its voluntary S.P.C.C.'s are unable to meet the latter need because of problems of resources and, in at least one instance, concept of role. The serious community vacuum which results may be underscored with one specific illustration. The family doctor or the member of a medical group in a health plan is a potentially crucial case finder. Especially in middle-class homes, he sees evidence of neglect or physical abuse of children which will not come to an agency's attention. He notes which parents do not follow through prescribed medical routines, and he encounters extremely eccentric parental behavior. Today, the doctor who would do anything about these things find the prospect discouraging. He must search out the correct channels and be willing to submit and validate a statement of his concerns. Since he has not undertaken to do a comprehensive study, he is reluctant. If he is a private physician, he may hesitate to lose a patient as well, especially when there is no substitute for whatever service he has been able to give. A community needs, but many do not have, a widely known agency or unit with sufficient staff to explore such situations on referral. Other professionals, like doctors, will begin to carry through their responsibilities only when they are clear about procedures, sure about follow-through, and have evidence of the competence of the protective service. The *New York State Social Welfare Law* (which is typical in this regard) authorizes welfare commissioners and city public welfare officers to carry out relevant services. The applicable sections of the law in Section 398 read as follows:

2. As to neglected or abandoned children:

a. Investigate the alleged neglect or abandonment of a child and, if necessary, bring the case before the court for adjudication and care for the child until the court acts in the matter.

b. Receive and care for any child alleged to be neglected or abandoned who is temporarily placed in his care by a children's court pending adjudication by such court of the alleged neglect or abandonment; and receive and care for any neglected or abandoned child committed or discharged to his care by a children's court.

6. As to all foregoing classes of children:

a. Investigate the family circumstances of each child reported to him as destitute, neglected, delinquent, defective or physically handicapped in order to determine what assistance and care, supervision or treatment, if any, such child requires.

b. Provide for expert mental and physical examination of any child whom he has reason to suspect of mental or physical defect or disease and pay for such examination from public funds, if necessary.

Under these provisions, all counties in the state which do not have S.P.C.C.'s (i.e., all except Erie, Monroe, Westchester, Nassau, and four New York City counties) have assigned full protective casework responsibility to their child welfare departments. Occasionally, some specialized staff handles the work, but it is usually part of the child welfare task. Only Onondaga County has created a special protective unit.

New York City has come to recognize that S.P.C.C.'s cannot perform all functions in a total protective process and that a public welfare department must have a major role in the planning. Relevant, too, is the current concept that police powers are not in the domain of a private organization. New plans are being drawn. Inevitably such planning must consider both distribution of responsibilities and pattern of organization. Equally important, any plan made should ensure sufficient protective service and the necessary related resources, services, and facilities.

Case finding is everybody's obligation, and situation finding is a responsibility of every social agency. The juvenile aid police have particular responsibilities in their patrol assignments for detecting hazardous conditions and taking necessary steps.

When children are in danger of personal harm, the matter should be reported to the Youth Division of the Police Department (or its equivalent). Police are legally equipped to remove a child from his home in such an emergency, and to get him to shelter or court, depending on the hour and the circumstances. They are trained to guard individual rights in the process. They can move rapidly. The police will, themselves, detect some of these situations; others will be reported by community members. Both police and social agencies have turned to S.P.C.C.'s in the past for such action, but it now seems clear that the peace officer role, though appropriate in its time and though still in the statutes, is incongruous in a modern city, equipped with a Police Youth Division or police Juvenile Bureau.

The police and district attorney are responsible, respectively, for decisions about arrest and prosecution in cases of sex offenses against children. If police are equipped with a well-staffed and capably led youth service it is both efficient and appropriate for all arrest situations involving alleged adult offenses against minors to be referred for immediate police exploration, screening, and advice. Police youth staff are, or should be, capable of the sensitive interviewing, emotional support, and clarification of procedures in these difficult and tension-charged cases. If appropriate, such cases might in turn be referred to a protective casework service.

When the case reaches court calendars, similar service should be rendered by the probation department. Cases of this kind belong not in adult courts but in a family and children's court equipped with a probation bureau able to provide necessary consultation to the district attorneys and service to the children and their parents.

The S.P.C.C.'s should thus be asked to give up their peace officer and law enforcement roles. There is no question about their backgrounds and legal rights in these fields, but changing times and the scope of existing needs suggest new arrangements. As responsible social agencies, S.P.C.C.'s will always want to retain the potential for situation finding and for initiating and supporting legislation relating to their concern. The function that remains is protective casework: the intake, ease evaluation, referrals, and casework treatment agreed by all to represent the core of services to safeguard children today.

Although the Child Welfare League calls for a public unit in each community and although most service of this kind is publicly rendered, some authorities hold that once the police task is assigned to the police, there is no absolute requirement that protective case work be lodged in a public agency. The National Agencies Workshop, it will be recalled, urged provision in the state's social welfare law for state responsibility to see to it that the service is lodged *somewhere*. From this viewpoint, local history and agency conditions determine which agency, public or voluntary, actually renders the service. Yet New York City S.P.C.C.'s with one possible exception are unable to render the necessary service without almost full public subsidy. In addition, the New York County society defines its role in terms quite different from the national trend or the need here described. Planning must also be affected by the answer to a key question: Can the right to pursue a complaint and to continue an interest in a family, in which children may be in danger, be lodged anywhere but in a department responsible to the public? Citizens understand legal authority delegated to a public department and also know that provisions exist to protect their rights. Most twentieth-century protective casework programs have developed in public departments for this reason. Also not to be ignored is the practical consideration that a large portion of neglect cases originate in families on public assistance rolls, families known to a public agency and more readily reached by an agency which has previous "leverage." In recent years a significant number of communities have created public-welfare-based protective services. For historical reasons which are understandable but which have had a variety of undesirable effects state and local child welfare programs (the casework and service programs) have tended to be organized separately from and not to be well integrated with public assistance programs. The latter (Aid to Needy Families with Children in particular) contain the bulk of the cases of children living under hazardous situations and in need of urgent services. Efforts are currently under way nationally and in many states to integrate these services, making child welfare casework available to assistance cases or creating well-staffed casework services for assistance cases needing intensive work. Protective programs are being expanded in this context in a variety of administrative patterns.

To illustrate: New York City's welfare program has tended in the past to view public child welfare services as residual provision, filling in gaps which could not be managed by voluntary agencies. The latter have had considerable public subsidy toward their work. In recent decades, however, changes in the volume of programs and the character of need have underscored the unsatisfactory nature of such provision and the extent to which many children remain, as the result, under "temporary" arrangements in shelter for many months and years—and the extent to which families in crisis lack needed casework help, homemakers, day care, and other resources. The city is now moving to remedy this situation by the strengthening of its public child welfare services through creation of an expanded decentralized program.

It is thus natural, as a first step in New York City, that decentralized protective services under public welfare be lodged in child welfare in this first phase. Plans are now under way along these lines. Concurrently provision must be made to strengthen the rolè of public assistance workers in case finding and first-line service-to decrease the need for specialized protective services. Gradually, the city will have available a case finding network in public assistance, specialized decentralized offices able to accept allegations of neglect from all sources and to become involved in intake as appropriate, a system of protective casework, liaison with youth police for emergency purposes, and provision for protective service access to specialized resources which may help to preserve family life where possible: intensive casework, homemakers, medical service, short-range foster care. Given such development, S.P.C.C.'s so qualified by staffing and orientation might continue to offer an intake service to those who choose to call upon them. More important, several might offer ongoing, intensive treatment services to disorganized, neglectful, "multiproblem" families. In addition, they have much to teach the new public service in a transition period about creating centers to which allegations will be channeled and about the early phases of case processing.

These general lines of development would seem to have broader applicability, the ultimate objective being a protective program in an integrated public welfare setup buttressed by police and school services on the one hand and voluntary agencies (including S.P.C.C.'s which are involved in treatment or situation finding and legislative matters) on the other.

Finally, it should be said, there are few general categories of cases more in need of an accountability system than cases of alleged abuse or neglect.